CAMBRIDGE
ILLUSTRATED
ATLAS

WARFARE

Renaissance to
Revolution
1492–1792

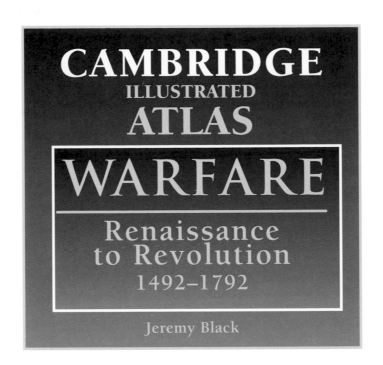

CAMBRIDGE
ILLUSTRATED
ATLAS

WARFARE

Renaissance to Revolution
1492–1792

Jeremy Black

CAMBRIDGE
UNIVERSITY PRESS

To Paul Binski and Gregory O'Brien, two good and old friends.

Published by the Press Syndicate of the University of Cambridge
The Pitt Building, Trumpington Street, Cambridge CB2 1RP
40 West 20th Street, New York, NY 10011-4211, USA
10 Stamford Road, Oakleigh, Melbourne 3166, Australia

First published 1996

This book was designed and produced by
CALMANN & KING LTD
71 Great Russell Street
London WC1B 3BN

Project editor: Liz Wyse
Picture research: Anne-Marie Ehrlich
Layout design: Alastair Wardle
Cartography by European Map Graphics Ltd, Finchampstead, Berkshire
Battle plans by Advanced Illustration, Congleton, Cheshire

Printed in Great Britain at the University Press, Cambridge

A catalogue record for this book is available from the British Library

Library of Congress cataloguing in publication data
Black, Jeremy.
The Cambridge illustrated atlas of warfare : Renaissance to revolution / Jeremy Black.
p.   cm.
Includes bibliographical references and index.
ISBN 0-521-47033-1 (hardcover)
1. Military history, Modern–Maps.
2. Military art and science–History–1492–1792–Maps.
3. Renaissance–Maps.
4. War and society–Maps.
I. Title.
G1035.B4 1995 <G&M>
355'. 009' 03–dc20
95-36852
CIP
MAP

ISBN 0 521 47033 1 hardback

CONTENTS

PREFACE

This has been a very difficult book to write. In seeking to offer a global coverage, an account of warfare, that includes land and sea, and moves away from the customary dominance by western European developments, I have become all too aware of my limitations. In addition, the discipline of writing in accordance with particular guidelines and a tight word-limit has been very demanding, and what has been discarded in endless redrafting could have made several books. I have also been affected by limits on the number and detail of the maps.

Yet this has also been an exciting book to produce. War, its conduct, cost, consequences, and preparations for conflicts, were all central to global history in the early modern period: as European discovery and trade linked hitherto separated regions, so force played a crucial role in these new relationships and in their consequences. Conflict was also crucial to the history of relations between the states in particular regions of the world, as well as to the internal history of individual countries.

I am most grateful to Geoffrey Parker, David Aldridge, Matthew Anderson, Kelly DeVries, Jan Glete, Richard Harding, Michael Hill, Knud Jespersen, and Peter Wilson for commenting on earlier drafts. A number of others have also contributed to the production of the volume, especially Mary Scott and Liz Wyse; the collective nature of the historical enterprise is particularly apparent in the case of historical atlases. Personally, it has been most instructive to create this work. My other current project is a study of historical atlases, and my own effort has reinforced my more general conclusions: of the excitement and value of the genre and of the need to appreciate the great difficulties that their compilation pose.

Jeremy Black, Exeter University

INTRODUCTION

Modern armed forces use weapons which differ little from those of their opponents, and their tactics are similar worldwide. This was not the case at the close of the fifteenth century. The cannon and firearms of the large Ottoman armies were a world away from the wood, bone, or stone weapons of the aboriginal peoples of Australia or Siberia, yet such military systems co-existed and even competed in a world in which military pressures and opportunities differed greatly.

Warfare in 1490 was subject to social and physical conditions very different from those of today. First, the conduct of war in all societies was very much the duty of men: women were closely involved, not only as casualties but also because their agricultural labour was crucial to the economic survival of societies at war; nevertheless their direct involvement in hostilities was exceptional. Second, the relatively low level of technology in even the most developed societies ensured that all warfare remained subject to physical constraints which were common worldwide. The limited nature of industrial activity, low agricultural productivity, and the absence of any real understanding of infectious diseases ensured that population figures were low everywhere and that the potential pool of warriors was restricted. Most labour was exerted by generally malnourished human or animal muscle, and other power sources were natural and fixed: water and wind power and the burning of wood. There were no rapid communications on land or sea. This affected the movement of soldiers, supplies, and messages everywhere in the world.

These constraints affected the scope and conduct of warfare at every turn, but there were major differences between peoples. At the simplest level these distinguished states based on settled agrarian societies, such as those of Europe and China, from nomadic or semi-nomadic peoples, for example those of North America, Siberia, Central Asia, and Australia. The agriculture of the former supported larger populations and thus possessed the resources for substantial armed forces and, thanks to taxation, for developed governmental structures. Relatively defined frontiers were an important aspect of such structures and they led to an emphasis on fortification. The Incas of South America created an effective system of roads and bridges that sped not only trade, but also troops and commands. Nomadic peoples were less populous and their governmental structures less developed. They did not therefore tend to develop comparable military specialization, especially in fortification and its corollary, siegecraft. In war, nomadic peoples often relied on raiding their opponents.

Looking forward from 1490, it is all too easy to take a Eurocentric perspective, not least because of the imminent impact of the Europeans in the New World and the Indian Ocean. But it is important to note that non-European powers were also dynamic. In 1501, Shah Isma'il I and his nomadic Turkmen followers founded Safavid power in Persia when he captured Tabriz. Seven years later Baghdad fell. Meanwhile, further east, the Uzbek tribes from the steppes repeatedly attacked Transoxania, seizing Samarkand and, in 1507, Herat. In 1476 Annam (Dai Viet) annexed Vijaya, the capital of Champa (southern Vietnam). The Songhai empire of the middle Niger pressed hard on the Hausa, extracting tribute from Kano. In South America, Topa Inca (1471–93) extended Inca power far to the south into modern central Chile and northern Argentina. His successor Huyana Capac (1493–1525) extended Inca territory north into modern Ecuador. But the most dynamic of all the powers were the Ottoman Turks.

MAP 1

The most populous states were the most developed and powerful. They were based on regions of settled agriculture, especially plough cultivation in Eurasia and Africa, and hoe cultivation in the New World.

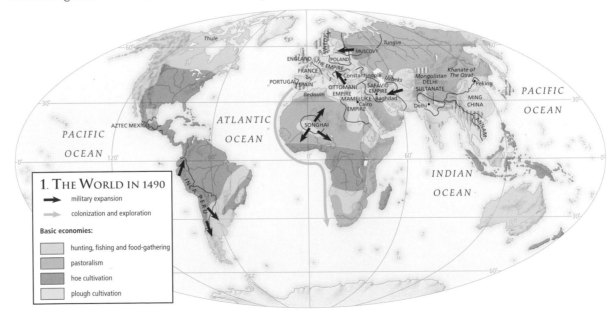

I

WARFARE IN THE WIDER WORLD, 1490-1700

This section examines the non-European world to 1700, and Part Two then goes back to 1490 to look at the Italian wars and other topics in European military history. As with any division of topics this creates some problems. The European powers acted both on a world stage and in Europe. This is also true of the Ottoman Turks; in order to emphasize the global dimension of Ottoman expansion, they are considered in Part One. Firearms and naval power are two important themes in the military history of this period. The long-distance extension of power and influence by sea was scarcely novel: the Vikings had colonized Iceland and Greenland and reached Newfoundland; the Chinese had sent a number of major expeditions into the Indian Ocean in the early fifteenth century. Yet no state had hitherto dispatched and sustained major naval and amphibious forces across the Atlantic or the Pacific, let alone to the other side of the world.

Naval force was also important because it was easier to move men, munitions, and supplies by sea than by land. Such movement came to play a greater role in many struggles. The Turks, for example, learned in the late fifteenth century to move cannon by sea, and then land them for the sieges of coastal fortifications that played such a major role in the military system of their rival, Venice. The conflict in the Horn of Africa between Ethiopia and Ahmad ibn Ibrihim al-Ghazi of Adal (1506–43), known to the Ethiopians as Ahmad Gran (the left-handed), was affected by support received by sea from foreign powers. The war is indeed an instructive instance both of how such struggles could become aspects of wider conflicts and of the transforming role of firearms. Ahmad, a fiery *iman*, conquered Adal in the mid-1520s and then launched a holy war against Ethiopia. He also trained his men in the new tactics and firearms introduced into the Red Sea region by the Ottomans, who conquered Egypt in 1517. Ahmad overran much of Ethiopia in 1527 and, thanks to better leadership and weapons, higher morale, a more effective command structure, greater mobility, and more flexible tactics, he was able to defeat the Ethiopian Emperor Lebna Dengel at Shimbra Kure in 1528. Ahmad then conquered much of Ethiopia, including the wealthy Amhara plateau, though Lebna Dengel continued to resist from the Christian highlands. In 1541, the Portuguese despatched 400 musketeers to the aid of Ethiopia. A joint Ethiopian and Portuguese army defeated Ahmad in 1541. He then turned to the Ottomans for help. They in turn provided him with 900 musketeers and 10 cannon, with which he defeated his opponents in August 1542, killing 200 Portuguese, including their commander Christopher da Gama. The conflict in Ethiopia, hitherto the land of the mythical Prester John for Europeans, had thus been integrated, at least partly, into global military relationships.

WORLD MILITARY POWER, 1500-1600

IN 1492, the major land-based global powers were the Ming Empire, the Lodi Sultanate of Delhi, Persia, the Mameluke and Ottoman Empires, Russia, Poland-Lithuania, France, Spain, the *Aztec and Inca Empires*, Mali, and the Songhai Empire (map 1). The major maritime powers were Portugal and Venice. The sixteenth century was to bring significant change.

EUROPEAN AND NON-EUROPEAN EXPANSION

Soon after 1500, the Portuguese began to establish a maritime empire around the Indian Ocean based on naval power (*pages 15–16*), while from 1519 the Spanish embarked on the conquest of the Aztec Empire of Central America and the Inca Empire of Andean South America (*pages 12–13*). During the course of the century, Portugal and Spain also extended their power in other directions. The Portuguese established themselves on the coasts of Brazil, in Angola, Mozambique, and West Africa, the Spanish in the West Indies, Florida, the Plate valley in South America, and in the Philippines. They thus demonstrated their ability over a wide variety of opponents and in a number of politico-military situations.

It would be misleading, however, to see global military history primarily in terms of a struggle between Europeans and others. Much of the conflict in the sixteenth-century world did not involve Europeans, and there were several dynamic non-European powers. One of the most decisive battles of the century, Panipat (1526), established Mughal power in northern India (*page 22*). Babur, the founder of the dynasty, was descended from Genghis Khan and Timur (Tamberlaine). He inherited the central Asian kingdom of Farghana in 1494, captured Kabul and Ghazni in 1504, thus gaining power in eastern Afghanistan, and in 1526 overthrew the Lodi Sultanate of Delhi. As with the fall of the Aztec and Inca empires, that of the Lodi Sultanate owed much to political weakness and division. Far-reaching campaigns then led to the Mughal conquest of northern India. Toyotomi Hideyoshi reunified Japan by 1590 and the new state launched invasions of Korea in 1592 and 1597–98 (*pages 20–21*). Altan Khan (1550–73) revived Mongol power and attacked Ming China. In Africa, the Islamic Sultan of Adal routed the much larger army of Christian Ethiopia at the Battle of Shimbra Kure (1529); the Songhai Empire destroyed Mali in 1546, and was itself defeated by a Moroccan expeditionary force at Tondibi.

THE IMPORTANCE OF FIREARMS

Although there were important military and political differences between these conflicts, there were also interesting similarities. In general, decisive victory reflected a technological gap in different weapons systems, specifically the advantage that gunpowder afforded infantry over cavalry: missiles over shock. Thus at Panipat (1526), Babur employed both matchlockmen and field artillery against the cavalry of the Lodis, whose armies did not use firearms. The following year, Mughal firepower defeated the cavalrymen and armoured war elephants of a confederacy of Rajput rulers led by Sarga, Rana of Mewar, at Kanua. In Africa, at Tondibi (1591), Moroccan musketry defeated the cavalry of Songhai, and Ahmad Gran, Sultan of Adal, and Idris Aloma of Bornu were similarly successful thanks to their musketeers. At the Battle of Jam (1528), Safavid artillery played an important part in the victory of Tahmasp I of Persia over the Uzbeks.

Although other factors, most obviously the matter of leadership, were important, access to firearms often enabled relatively small forces to destroy far more numerous opponents. This was true of the Spanish in their conquest of the Americas, of the Moroccan defeat of the Songhai cavalry at Tondibi, and also of the Mughals defeat of the Rajput rulers.

The Siege of Chitor by the Mughal Emperor Akbar, 1567, from the *Akbar-Nama*, the annual recounting of events of his reign. Akbar led his troops in a holy war or *jihad* on Chitor, the capital of Mewar, a fortified city rising 656 feet (200m) above the Rajasthan plain. His siege lines surrounded the city and after initial attacks failed, Akbar used artillery and sappers. On the night of 22 February 1568, the Mughals made several breaches and then launched a general attack that succeeded after a day's hand-to-hand fighting in which nearly all of the 5,000 defenders died. Akbar then destroyed the fortress. The illustration shows the Mughal batteries and sappers.

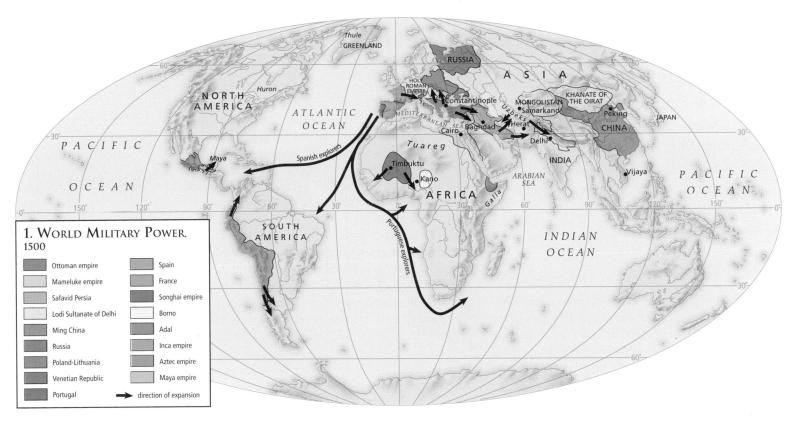

1. WORLD MILITARY POWER, 1500

- Ottoman empire
- Mameluke empire
- Safavid Persia
- Lodi Sultanate of Delhi
- Ming China
- Russia
- Poland-Lithuania
- Venetian Republic
- Portugal
- Spain
- France
- Songhai empire
- Borno
- Adal
- Inca empire
- Aztec empire
- Maya empire
- → direction of expansion

MAP 1

In 1500, a number of dynamic powers were expanding. The conflicts involving Ottoman Turkey, Mameluke Egypt, Safavid Persia, the Mughals, and the Lodis were all important, although with hindsight Portuguese and Spanish naval activity may appear most important. China was less affected than other major Asian states by external challenges.

Babur had only 12,000 men at Panipat and a similar number at Kanua; his Rajput opponents had 80,000 cavalry and 500 war elephants.

The use of firearms also altered the balance of military advantage between areas. Expertise in firearms became the first priority in the struggle for military predominance, but it was an exportable commodity, and in some cases was disseminated very quickly. The Ottoman Turks provided Ahmad Gran of Adal with a corps of musketeers, while the Portuguese sent troops to the assistance of Ethiopia, leading to its eventual victory over Adal. The Portuguese also provided Safavid Persia with artillery that the Uzbeks, who understood its importance, were unable to match. Sultan Idris Aloma of Borno, an Islamic state based in the region of Lake Chad, obtained his musketeers from Tripoli, which after 1551 became part of the Ottoman Empire.

However, not all battles were decided by firepower. In 1573, to crush a rebellion in Gujarat, the Mughal Emperor Akbar's 3,000 troops travelled by camel 500 miles (800km) in just 11 days and then defeated 15,000 rebels in a cavalry engagement. Eight years later, Akbar's massive field army still included only 28 cannon in a force of 50,000 cavalry and 500 war elephants.

In Africa, firearms had most impact along the savanna belt, where European and Islamic 'foreign' influence was strongest, but the overall military situation was more complex. Towards the close of the century, the nomadic pagan Galla advanced from the Ogaden and overran both Ethiopia and Adal. Native fighting methods could be very effective. African coastal vessels, powered by paddles and carrying archers and javelinmen, were able to challenge Portuguese raiders on the West African coast. Although it was difficult

for them to storm the larger, high-sided Portuguese ships, they were nevertheless too fast and too small to present easy targets for the Portuguese cannon. In 1535, the Portuguese were once more repelled when they tried to conquer the Bissagos Islands. On land, the Portuguese cannon proved to have little impact on the African earthwork fortifications.

In Angola, the base of Portuguese operations in the 1570s, the slow rate of fire of their muskets and the openness of the African fighting formations reduced the effectiveness of firearms, and the Portuguese were successful only when supported by local troops. Initially, their position was saved by the intervention of an army from the kingdom of Kongo. The global range of the European maritime powers and the impact of gunpowder must be considered alongside the importance of the non-European users of firearms and the resilience of the peoples who lacked them. Both are themes throughout this period, and remind us of the dangers of adopting a teleological perspective in which the future is read back into the past, made to appear inevitable with the perspective of hindsight.

The fact that the Europeans dramatically increased the percentage of the world's surface that they controlled in the course of the sixteenth and seventeenth centuries, and were to continue doing so in the eighteenth, does not mean that the process of European expansion was inevitable, although it would be foolish to discount its significance and interest. It is, however, important to appreciate also the great complexities of this process, the many imbalances between the military and naval developments of the various regions, and the contrasting trajectories of European success in many different parts of the world.

THE CONQUEST OF THE AMERICAS, 1500-1600

DESPITE the remarkable Spanish overthrow of the Aztec and Inca empires, European penetration of the American continent during the sixteenth century was limited (map 1). Though significant, the European advantage in military technology was far outweighed by their limited numbers and by problems of conflict between the European powers.

THE FALL OF THE AZTEC AND INCA EMPIRES

The Spanish conquest of the two leading American states, the Aztec empire of Mexico and the Inca empire in the Andes, is often presented as the impact of a military new world, Europe, on an old world, for neither the Incas nor the Aztecs had firearms or horses. Slings, wooden clubs and obsidian knives were no match for cannon. The cannon, harquebuses and crossbows of the Spaniards all had a greater range than their rivals' weapons. In hand-to-hand combat, the Spaniards also benefited from armour, made of either steel or cotton; their opponents had none. Technological superiorities are said to explain the victories of tiny European forces: Hernán Cortés (1485–1547) had about 500 Spanish soldiers, 14 small cannon, and 16 horses when he landed at Vera Cruz in 1519 and marched on the Aztec capital of Tenochtitlán on its island on Lake Texcoco (map 2). His initial welcome owed much to the Emperor Montezuma's conviction that Cortés was the god Quetzalcoatl, but in 1520–21 Cortés had to fight to impose his control. Francisco Pizarro (c.1475–1541) had only 168 Europeans, 4 cannon, and 67 horses, yet he overran the Incas in 1531–33, and entered their capital Cuzco in November 1533.

There were, however, other important factors, particularly the weakness of Aztec and Inca leadership and the Spanish ability to find local allies. Montezuma was fascinated by Cortés and unwilling to act decisively against him. After Montezuma was killed in an anti-Spanish rising in 1520, the Aztecs lacked clear leadership. The Inca Empire had been dynamic in the fifteenth century, greatly extending itself both north and south under a series of aggressive rulers, so that it came to cover an area about 2,175 miles (3,500km) long, held together by an impressive road system. But Huyana Capac (1493–1525) founded Quito as a second capital and left a disputed succession between the northern and southern sections of the Empire, which were led respectively by his son Atahuallpa and his half-brother Huescar.

Divisions helped the Spanish gain allies: Atahuallpa was used against Huescar before being strangled in 1533. In addition, Aztec and Inca expansion in the fifteenth century left conquered peoples ready to ally with the Spanish. The Totonacs and the Tlaxcalans welcomed Cortés and he encouraged the rebellion of the ruler of Cempoala in 1519. Having been driven from Tenochtitlán in 1520, Cortés recouped his strength with the help of the Tlaxcalans, and his eventual victory owed much to the role played by about 200,000 Indian allies. Native support was essential in order to match the massive numerical superiority of the Aztecs. Spanish cavalry was effective in the open, but could be countered in urban conflict as in the fighting for Tenochtitlán. The Aztecs captured Spanish weapons, but could not use firearms because they had no gunpowder and lacked the necessary training.

The collapse of centralized authority, especially that of the Incas, was instrumental in the Spanish conquest of both the empires, but this left much of the New World as yet untouched.

LIMITS TO EUROPEAN EXPANSION

The Spanish conquests of some areas like Cuba and New Granada (Colombia) were relatively swift (1511–13 and 1536–39), but others took far longer (map 1). The causes varied, but were usually local resistance, difficult environmental conditions or limited Spanish manpower. This was true both of the northward expansion, which was impeded by the Chichimecas of Mexico, and in much of central America. Cortés sent expeditions to explore Guatemala in 1524 and himself led a costly campaign in Honduras in 1524. Guatemala was conquered by 1542, but the last centre of Mayan power in the Yucatan did not fall until the 1690s. Central Chile was conquered in 1540–58, but the Araucanians, who relied on guerrilla warfare rather than pitched battles, took many decades to subjugate. Spanish control over Florida was limited, while in the Caribbean, the Kulinago of the Lesser Antilles and the Caribs and

Cortés capturing Tenochtitlán. The Aztec city was sited in the middle of a connected series of lakes, and was captured after three months of bitter fighting on the causeways (26 May–13 August 1521). The city was sacked and there was a major massacre.

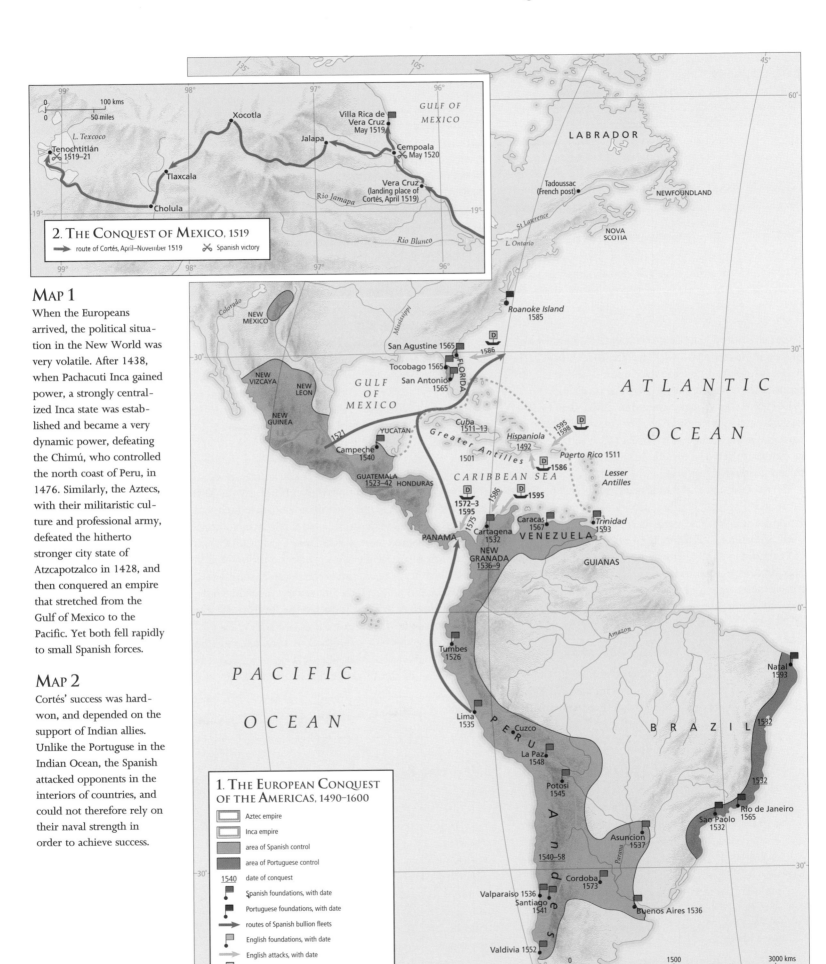

2. THE CONQUEST OF MEXICO, 1519

→ route of Cortés, April–November 1519   ✕ Spanish victory

Tenochtitlán 1519–21
Xocotla
Villa Rica de Vera Cruz May 1519
Cempoala ✕ May 1520
Jalapa
L. Texcoco
Tlaxcala
Cholula
Rio Jamapa
Vera Cruz (landing place of Cortés, April 1519)
Rio Blanco
GULF OF MEXICO

MAP 1

When the Europeans arrived, the political situation in the New World was very volatile. After 1438, when Pachacuti Inca gained power, a strongly centralized Inca state was established and became a very dynamic power, defeating the Chimú, who controlled the north coast of Peru, in 1476. Similarly, the Aztecs, with their militaristic culture and professional army, defeated the hitherto stronger city state of Atzcapotzalco in 1428, and then conquered an empire that stretched from the Gulf of Mexico to the Pacific. Yet both fell rapidly to small Spanish forces.

MAP 2

Cortés' success was hard-won, and depended on the support of Indian allies. Unlike the Portuguse in the Indian Ocean, the Spanish attacked opponents in the interiors of countries, and could not therefore rely on their naval strength in order to achieve success.

1. THE EUROPEAN CONQUEST OF THE AMERICAS, 1490–1600

- Aztec empire
- Inca empire
- area of Spanish control
- area of Portuguese control
- 1540 date of conquest
- Spanish foundations, with date
- Portuguese foundations, with date
- routes of Spanish bullion fleets
- English foundations, with date
- English attacks, with date
- D attacks by Sir Francis Drake

LABRADOR
Tadoussac (French post)
NEWFOUNDLAND
NOVA SCOTIA
L. Ontario
St Lawrence

NEW MEXICO
Colorado
Roanoke Island 1585
San Agustine 1565   D 1586
Tocobago 1565
San Antonio 1565
FLORIDA
NEW VIZCAYA
NEW LEON
NEW GUINEA
GULF OF MEXICO
ATLANTIC OCEAN

1521
YUCATAN
Campeche 1540
Cuba 1511–13
Greater Antilles
Hispaniola 1492
1501
1595 1598 D
Puerto Rico 1511
D 1586
Lesser Antilles
CARIBBEAN SEA

GUATEMALA 1523–42 HONDURAS
1572–3 1595   1586   D 1595
1575
PANAMA
Cartagena 1532
Caracas 1567
Trinidad 1593
VENEZUELA
NEW GRANADA 1536–9
GUIANAS

PACIFIC OCEAN

Tumbes 1526
Amazon
Natal 1593
BRAZIL
1532
1532
Lima 1535
Cuzco
PERU
La Paz 1548
Potosi 1545
Sao Paolo 1532
Rio de Janeiro 1565
Asuncion 1537
A n d e s
1540–58
Valparaiso 1536
Santiago 1541
Cordoba 1573
Parana
Buenos Aires 1536
Valdivia 1552

0   1500   3000 kms
0   500   1000   1500 miles

Arawaks of the Guianas thwarted Spanish attacks and mounted counter-raids with fast, manoeuvrable shallow-draft boats carved from tropical trees. Similarly in Brazil, which they 'discovered' in 1500, the Portuguese made only slow progress at the expense of the Tupinambá and Tapuya. These difficulties continued into the following century, although not all European contacts with the Amerindians were hostile.

North of Florida, contacts were less violent. Large numbers of European ships came to Newfoundland waters to fish, and traders bartered on the Nova Scotia coast for furs, and relations were generally peaceful. In 1534 and 1535 a small French expedition under Jacques Cartier sailed up the St Lawrence in their search for gold and a route to the wealth of the Orient. Their arms impressed the native Americans, but Cartier's expedition suffered badly from scurvy when it overwintered in 1535–36.

Cartier returned in 1541 and established a fortified base, but encountered resistance from the local villages. The French abandoned the base in 1543 and until the 1580s the native peoples prevented European penetration up the St Lawrence. The French preferred to devote their energies to civil war, and in the New World to unsuccessful attempts to challenge the Portuguese in Brazil (1555) and the Spanish in Florida (1562 and 1564). In Brazil, the Tupinambá Indians supported the French.

The dynastic union of Portugal and Spain (1580–1640) prevented colonial conflict between the two leading European maritime powers: their respective spheres of potential control had already been regulated by the Treaty of Tordesillas in 1494. This did not, however, leave any role for other European maritime powers. The chances of a peaceful settlement of competing interests were further reduced by the Reformation and the Wars of Religion, which pitted England and the Dutch against Spain.

ENGLISH RAIDS IN THE CARIBBEAN

English interest in the eastern seaboard of North America was of limited concern to Spain, and in any case the English ventures were unsuccessful. In 1584–89, Sir Walter Raleigh sent a series of expeditions to try to found a colony near Roanoke Island, but the settlement failed to prosper and was abandoned.

Trade and buccaneering in the Caribbean, however, began to challenge the commercial and financial structure of the Spanish empire. Conflict broke out in 1568 when the Spanish repeatedly attacked English ships in the harbour of Vera Cruz. Sir Francis Drake responded by mounting two expeditions in 1571–72 and 1572–73: on the second of these expeditions he successfully ambushed a Spanish mule-train which was crossing the Isthmus of Panama with a consignment of Peruvian silver. Drake circumnavigated the world in 1577–80, and caused havoc on the Pacific coast of South America.

In 1585, war formally broke out between England and Spain, and in 1585–86 Drake took a large fleet to the Caribbean, sacking Spanish bases, including Cartagena and St Augustine, but failing to intercept the Spanish silver fleet. But Spanish defensive measures, including the organization of effective convoys, improved, and Drake's last Caribbean expedition in 1595–96 was a failure. English attempts to establish a powerful Caribbean base were as unsuccessful as Raleigh's 1595 efforts to find the famed golden city of Venezuela, El Dorado.

Thus, rather than seeing military activity in the New World simply in terms of the clash of native and European, it is more appropriate to note the conflicts within both groups. In the sixteenth century, these conflicts did not lead to the major shifts in territorial control that were to occur in North America in the eighteenth century. Instead, English attacks on Spanish interests were generally a matter of raiding, the search for profit rather than permanent control, and accordingly the English forces were small and often private enterprises. The English lacked the structure of bases and permanent land and naval forces necessary for a serious challenge to Spanish control and, as a consequence, the Treaty of London of 1604 that brought peace between the two powers left Spain dominant in the New World, although James I refused to recognize Spanish claims to its commercial monopoly.

WARFARE IN CANADA

Canada provides a good example of nomadic warfare, although, by its very nature, this is poorly documented. In the far north from about AD 1000 onwards, the Palaeo-Eskimos of the eastern Arctic (Dorset people) retreated before the eastward migration of seafaring Neo-Eskimos (Thule people), who hunted with harpoons for bowhead whales. The Thule also used sinew-backed bows, dog sleds, and houses of stone, and early in the sixteenth century established themselves on the Labrador coast; the Dorset were killed, assimilated, or driven into harsher regions.

Meanwhile to the south of the Canadian Shield in south-central Ontario and the St Lawrence Valley, competing native American tribes lived in settled farming communities. Their villages were fortified with exterior and interior palisades which created a series of defendable cul-de-sacs. In the fifteenth century, the Huron conquered and partly assimilated the Iroquois.

PORTUGAL AND SPAIN IN ASIA AND AFRICA

WHILE SPAIN was founding an empire in the New World, the Portuguese established a direct route round Africa to the wealth of the Orient. Their arrival disrupted earlier trading relationships, and the response was often military. The completion of the Reconquista in 1492 led to similar ambitions in the dynamic Spanish kingdom.

THE ADVENT OF PORTUGAL

The Portuguese navigator Vasco da Gama first arrived in Asia, at Calicut in India, on 20–21 May 1498. A foretaste of the difficulties Portugal was later to face in the Indian Ocean was provided by the clashes that occurred en route between his expedition and the Muslims of East Africa, and when, in December 1500, the Portuguese factory-cum-trading post which he had established in Calicut was destroyed after fighting broke out there. The Portuguese were seeking trade, but their arrival disrupted established trading relationships, and conflict was inevitable.

While the Portuguese sought to construct a network of fortified bases in the Indian Ocean, the Mameluke Sultan of Egypt, Qanswah al-Ghawri, took steps to prevent them from challenging the existing trade route from India to Suez. An Egyptian fleet sent in 1507 initially defeated the Portuguese at Chaul (1509), but it was then largely destroyed by Francisco de Almeida in a later battle off Diu (1509, map 1). Meanwhile, the chain of Portuguese fortresses was expanding: in East Africa (Sofala founded 1505, Kilwa 1505, and Mozambique 1507); at the approaches to the Red Sea (Socotra 1507); at the mouth of the Persian Gulf (Ormuz 1514); on the west coast of India (Cochin 1503, Cannanore 1505, Goa 1510, Diu 1534, Bassein 1534); and in the Straits of Malacca (Malacca 1511). This expansion reflected the energy and strategic vision

THE PORTUGUESE NAVY

Portuguese naval strength in the early sixteenth century was based on sailing ships which were strong enough to carry heavy guns capable of sinking the lightly-built vessels of the Indian Ocean. Their heavier armament was crucial in the face of the numerical advantage of their opponents. They were built in the royal dockyards at Lisbon and Oporto, but, as with the Spanish at Havana, the Portuguese also discovered the value of developing a colonial dockyard. This was useful both for constructing vessels from durable tropical hardwoods like western Indian teak, and for repairing warships locally. The Portuguese built a large 800-tonne ship at Cochin in 1511–12, established a major dockyard at Goa in 1515, and developed shipbuilding facilities at Damao and Macao.

The galleon was developed by the Portuguese as a warship able to sail great distances. It was longer and narrower than earlier carracks, with a reduced hull width-to-length ratio, was faster, more manoeuvrable, and capable of carrying a heavier armament. The Portuguese brought galleons into use in the Indian Ocean from the mid-1510s, and there were two in a squadron of twenty-five ships sent to Ormuz in 1520. The galleon came to replace the *nau* or 'great ship', the very large carrack-type vessel on which the Portuguese had initially relied. As early as 1518, the standard armament of a Portuguese galleon was thirty-five guns.

Estimates of the size and distribution of the navy vary, but it seems clear that the majority of Portuguese galleons operated in the Indian Ocean. When the Japanese ruler Toyotomi Hideyoshi planned his invasion of Korea in 1592, he unsuccessfully attempted to hire two Portuguese galleons. Portuguese vessels relied mainly on Asian seamen, but the officers and gunners were Europeans.

Sixteenth-century oceangoing Portuguese ships from Livro das Armadas.

of Alfonso de Albuquerque, the Viceroy of Portuguese India from 1509 to 1515. Alfonso de Albuquerque was the first to appreciate the strategic importance of seapower in the region and the first to apply it systematically. He failed at Aden in 1513, but from Malacca trade routes were developed to the Far East, with bases established at Ternate in the spice-producing Moluccas (1521), Macao in China (1557), and Nagasaki in Japan (1570). These bases were all commercial centres, not major fortified positions like Goa and Malacca.

THE OTTOMAN CHALLENGE

Naval strength was crucial to the position of the Portuguese in the Indian Ocean. When they arrived, no Asian vessels carried cannon, and thus the Calicut fleet was destroyed relatively easily in 1502, and then that of Gujarat in 1528; but the Portuguese lacked the manpower to become a major territorial empire. Albuquerque wanted 'a large well-armed fleet manned by 3,000 European-born Portuguese', but none was sent during the period of the sixteenth century. The population of Portugal, about one million people, was not large, and there were many other emigration opportunities, especially to Brazil. Tropical diseases killed many people who went to India, and there was a shortage of female emigrants.

The Portuguese also had to face major challenges. The expansion of the Ottomans into Egypt (1517) and Iraq (1534) gave this dynamic Islamic power a direct interest in the Red Sea and the Persian Gulf. The Ottoman fleet sent to Diu in 1538 was repulsed, but en route the Turks seized Aden, pre-empting a Portuguese expedition. From bases there and at Basra (captured in 1546) and Suez, the Ottoman admirals Piri Reis and Seydi Ali Reis exerted much pressure in mid-century, sacking the Portuguese base of Muscat in 1552, and then besieging Ormuz. The latter, however, resisted successfully, and an Ottoman fleet was heavily defeated there in 1554.

From the 1560s, Ottoman naval activity in the Indian Ocean declined, although in 1568 an expedition was sent to help the Sumatran Sultan of Aceh against Malacca. As in the Mediterranean after the mid-1570s, a rough division between areas of naval hegemony was thus defined. Although the Portuguese had sent an expedition into the Red Sea in 1541 which raided Suez, their earlier hopes of controlling that sea had to be abandoned, and from there the Turks were able to threaten the Portuguese position on the Swahili coast of East Africa in the 1580s. With the support of Persia, the Portuguese were able to neutralize the Ottoman presence in the Persian Gulf, and, as an imperial force, Ottoman maritime power was essentially restricted to these seas.

ASIAN RESISTANCE

Elsewhere in the Indian Ocean, the Portuguese were challenged by Asian powers. The sultanates of Indonesia, especially Aceh, attacked Malacca on a number of occasions, including 1568. There, as in Indian and African coastal

waters, the heavily-gunned Portuguese vessels, with their deep draught and reliance on sails, were vulnerable to shallower-draught oared boats. Indian (Malabar) and Malay privateers did some damage, but had little effect on large Portuguese vessels in deep waters, and did not threaten their fortresses.

Fortresses could be attacked by local rulers, as were Goa and Chaul in 1571, but many of these rulers lacked naval strength. It was therefore not possible to cut the Portuguese bases off from relief by sea, which proved crucial at both Goa and Chaul. Mughal India was not a naval power, and the Chinese did not send fleets to the Indian Ocean, though they had done so until the 1430s. Chinese naval power would have been sufficient to challenge the Portuguese, and indeed a Chinese naval force did defeat a Portuguese squadron off Tunmán in 1522.

Nevertheless, other states developed naval power and they sought to match the substantial ocean-going cannon-

The Portuguese were initially dependent on Arab and Indian pilots for their nautical charts, but they soon created their own charts that were reasonably accurate. Sixteenth-century Portuguese navigators were at the forefront of navigational expertise. The Diego Homen map of the Indian Ocean (*below*) reflects the greater knowledge made available to Europeans after the Cape of Good Hope was rounded.

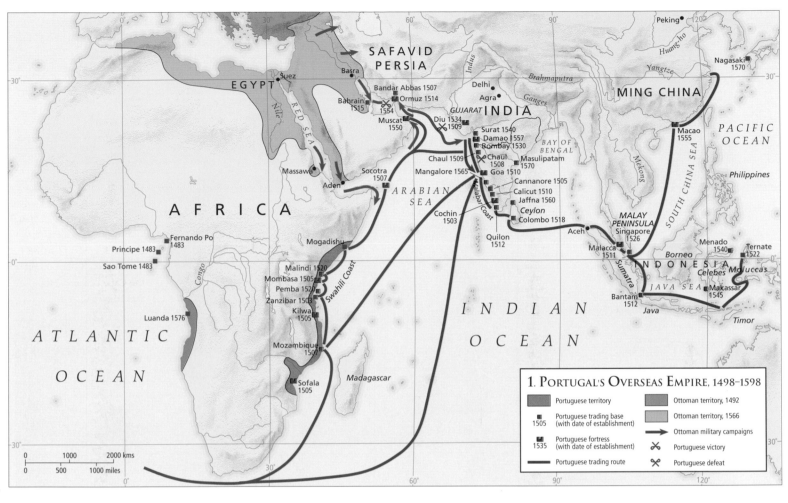

1. PORTUGAL'S OVERSEAS EMPIRE, 1498–1598

■ (dark)	Portuguese territory	Ottoman territory, 1492
■ 1505	Portuguese trading base (with date of establishment)	Ottoman territory, 1566
■ 1535	Portuguese fortress (with date of establishment)	→ Ottoman military campaigns
—	Portuguese trading route	✂ Portuguese victory
		✂ Portuguese defeat

MAP 1

The arrival of the Portuguese in the Indian Ocean disrupted existing maritime routes and relationships. The Portuguese presence was dependent on military success, most obviously in defeating challenges by Mameluke Egypt and the Ottoman Turks. The Mameluke fleet of twelve ships that left Suez in 1507 defeated the Portuguese off Chaul, but was largely destroyed at Diu. The Turks were to be similarly unsuccessful off India, but they closed the Red Sea to the Portuguese, and limited their presence in the Horn of Africa: most cities on the Swahili coast between Mogadishu and Kilwa recognized Turkish supremacy after their naval expeditions of 1585 and 1588.

carrying Portuguese warships. The Sultans of Aceh built vessels that could mount a challenge, and Sultan Alauddin Riayat Syah al-Kahhar (1539–71) sent an embassy to Suleiman the Magnificent in 1574 to seek military assistance for an attack on Malacca. The Ottoman Empire developed economic links with Aceh and provided gun-founders and artillerymen who increased Acehese naval capability.

A VULNERABLE EMPIRE

Thus, towards the end of the century, the Portuguese were increasingly threatened in the Indian Ocean. Ternate in the Moluccas was lost in 1575. In 1589, they had to send a large force to the Swahili coast to check the advance of the Ottomans. In 1593, Fort Jesus was established at Mombasa. These challenges contributed to and reflected imperial overstretch: the problems of an imperial power with limited resources seeking to allocate its efforts between a number of commitments. In the 1590s, after the seizure by the Spanish king of the disputed Portuguese throne, these commitments dramatically increased. The Dutch and the English were both at war with Philip II of Spain, and were therefore anxious to attack his Portuguese colonies.

As in the New World, competition between European powers was to become a major theme, but in contrast to their American situation, the Portuguese in Asia and East Africa had neither control over a large hinterland nor demographic weight. Their military structure, of warships and

garrisons, depended very heavily on reinforcements from Europe and was relatively easy to disrupt. The Dutch caused such disruption between 1598 and 1663, conquering the principal Portuguese bases in the Moluccas in 1605, Malacca in 1641, the bases in coastal Ceylon in 1638–58, and those on the Malabar Coast in 1663. This contrasted with the resilience of the Spanish in the New World and of the Portuguese in Brazil, where after a conflict begun in 1624, the Dutch were finally forced to surrender in 1654. These differing Portuguese fortunes in east and west reflected the strength in the latter of relatively numerous settlers and of a Christianized and acculturated indigenous population.

Nevertheless, the earlier growth of the Portuguese empire in Asia indicated what could be achieved with naval power when a substantial technological gap existed in military capability. Portugal's success also reflected the advantage of seeking colonial gains in areas like the Moluccas and the Swahili and Indian coasts, where there was considerable political fragmentation and so the possibility of creating unopposed new political entities.

THE SPANISH ADVANCE

In 1492, the *Reconquista*, the reconquest of Spain from the Moors by the Christians, culminated in the capture of Granada, Spain's last Moorish state. Over the next seventy years, the *Reconquista* was extended by Spanish interest in gaining territories in North Africa, more specifically ports

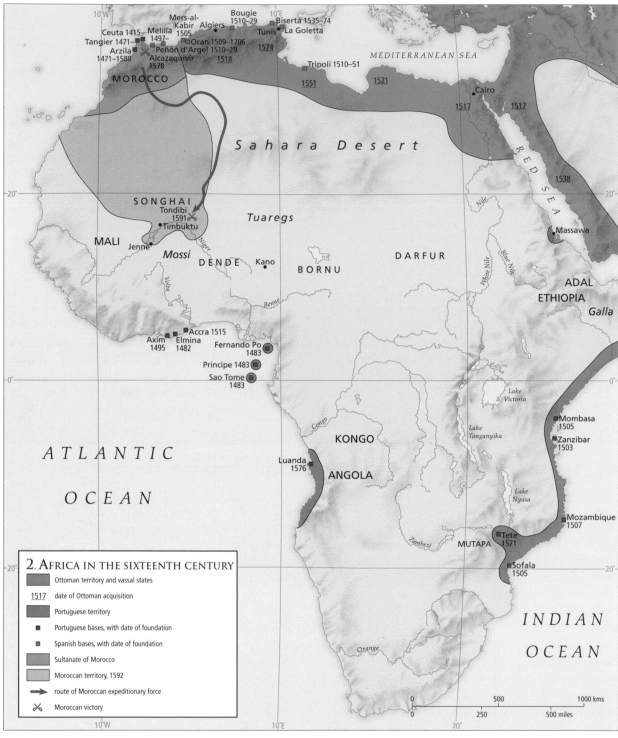

2. AFRICA IN THE SIXTEENTH CENTURY

- Ottoman territory and vassal states
- 1517 date of Ottoman acquisition
- Portuguese territory
- ■ Portuguese bases, with date of foundation
- ■ Spanish bases, with date of foundation
- Sultanate of Morocco
- Moroccan territory, 1592
- → route of Moroccan expeditionary force
- ✗ Moroccan victory

MAP 2

Although the politics of the Mediterranean littoral of Africa directly affected the Sahel (savanna) to the south of the Sahara Desert, as with the Moroccan attack on Songhai, the lands further south constituted a separate world. The Portuguese sought to penetrate the interior in order to develop trading links, and in the 1530s they began to move up the Zambezi, but their success was limited.

from which the trade of the region could be controlled (*map* 2). Spain's interest in North Africa was further aroused by religious concern: the conquest of Granada raised anxiety about the loyalty of the Muslims in Spain and the spectre of foreign intervention on their behalf. This led to decrees (1502, 1525) insisting on baptism or exile, but Spain was left with a substantial minority of *moriscos*, converts whose loyalty was suspect. The Portuguese had similar ambitions on the Morrocan coast, and established a network of bases there. In the late fifteenth century, the Portuguese made an effort to control Morocco; Arzila had been captured in 1471 by a Portuguese force of 400 ships and 30,000 men.

Initially the Spanish enjoyed considerable success in North Africa: their military machine had been well-honed by the long war for Granada and their opponents were weak and divided. Melilla was gained in 1497, Mers-al-Kabir in 1505, Oran in 1509 and Bougie, Tripoli, and the Peñón d'Argel position dominating Algiers, in 1510. The situation deteriorated, however, in the 1520s as the Emperor Charles V devoted more resources to war with France, and as the Muslims took the initiative.

This started with local corsairs, especially Khair al-Din Barbarossa, but after the conquest of Egypt and the suppression there of a rebellion in 1523–24, Suleiman the

Magnificent began to take a greater interest in North Africa and the western Mediterranean. In 1516, the rulers of Algiers had called on Barbarossa to recapture the Peñón. By the time he did so, in 1529, he had also gained control of Algiers itself. The Spanish lost Bougie in 1529. In 1532 Suleiman appointed Barbarossa Grand Admiral of the entire Ottoman fleet. In 1534, he attacked the coast of southern Italy and expelled the pro-Spanish Moorish ruler of Tunis.

In response, a crusade was launched from Europe, and Charles V in person conquered La Goletta and Tunis in 1535. In 1541, he led an unsuccessful attack on Algiers, but his fleet was badly damaged by an autumnal storm. The Ottomans countered by widening their operations in the western Mediterranean. The east coast of Spain was raided in 1529, 1535, and 1540, and, in co-operation with the French, the Ottomans seized Nice in 1543.

BOUNDARIES STABILIZE

Barbarossa died in 1546, but his successor Dragut captured Tripoli in 1551, and turned it into a corsair base under the authority of the Sultan. A Spanish force sent by Philip II to recapture it was crushed at Djerba in 1560. There was more fighting along the North African coast, especially in 1573–74 for control of Tunis, and by 1578 the Spanish held nothing east of Oran.

By this time, Portuguese possessions had been reduced to Ceuta and Tangier, and in the same year Sebastian of Portugal was killed in the crushing defeat at Alcazarquivir when he led an expedition into the interior of Morocco. North Africa did not offer Portugal the economic or military opportunities of the Indies.

The Ottomans also suffered significant reverses. Malta (1565) and Lepanto (1571) marked their failure to dominate the mid-Mediterranean, and the western Mediterranean was too remote to allow regular Ottoman commitment. Crucially, from the Spanish point of view, the *morisco* rising in the Alpujarras mountains of Granada (1568–71) was suppressed with little Ottoman intervention: Selim II was busy elsewhere, more interested in Cyprus and well aware that it would be difficult to act effectively at such a range.

Too much should not, however, be made of physical distance: the Ottomans sent fleets to Indian waters, and overran the Fezzan in 1577. The Moroccans crossed the Sahara to the Niger. Philip II created an empire on which the sun literally never set. Distance was most important when it was also an expression of mental horizons; in the Mediterranean these had expanded in the early decades of the sixteenth century, but closed from the 1570s as both Spain and the Ottoman Empire turned to their other respective concerns, north-western Europe and Persia.

ALCAZARQUIVIR 4 AUGUST 1578

King Sebastian of Portugal's intervention in Moroccan politics was designed to make Morocco a Portuguese client state, free of Ottoman influence. He invaded with some 18–20,000 men and marched into the interior to challenge the Sharif, Abd al-Malik, and his force of about 70,000. Sebastian sought battle at Alcazarquivir, believing that his infantry would successfully resist the Moroccan cavalry. He deployed his infantry units in a deep phalanx, with cavalry on the flanks and artillery in the front. The Moroccan army consisted of lines of arquebusiers with cavalry (including mounted arquebusiers) in the rear and on the flanks.

The Moroccans opened the battle with harrying attacks by horse arquebusiers; the unsupported Portuguese artillery was overrun. The Portuguese infantry fought well, however, and pressed hard on the Moroccan infantry. A second Moroccan cavalry attack pushed back the Portuguese cavalry on both flanks, but the Moroccans again lost impetus. A renewed advance by the Portuguese infantry allowed a gap to open in their left flank, which the Moroccans exploited with great effect. The Moroccan horse arquebusiers then succeeded in destroying the cohesion of the Portuguese rear right flank, and Sebastian's army disintegrated. Sebastian was killed and his entire army killed or captured. The skilful, well-disciplined Moroccan force had won a crushing victory which left Morocco free from European attack until 1842.

The sixteenth-century Portuguese castle at Safi-Beir El Bahar, Morroco.

WARFARE IN THE ORIENT, 1500-1600

IN THE POPULOUS ORIENT, the major powers deployed larger armies than their European counterparts. In Ming China, this reduced the impact of firearms, but in India and Japan military competition and relative wealth permitted extensive re-equipment. Dynamic powers included Vijayanagar and the Mughals in India, the Burmese Toungoo kingdom, and, latterly, Japan.

THE UNIFICATION OF JAPAN

The struggle for predominance between the clans of Japan occupied much of the sixteenth century, and gave great impetus to the quest for military advantage through fire-power. Chinese firearms were in use in Japan before 1543, but from that year better Portuguese muskets, brought initially by castaways, were much more widely copied. Firearms certainly played an important role in war after the Battle of Shinano Asahiyamajo (1555), and at the Battle of Nagashino (1575), musketeers in the army of Nobunaga, of the Oda clan, used volley fire to smash the charges of Takeda cavalry. Such firepower tactics were in use neither in China nor in Europe at the time.

Japan's metallurgical industry could produce muskets in large numbers. These were used by armies under *daimyo* (lords), of whom Nobunaga was the most successful, to defeat local forces in a series of brutal struggles in the 1560s and 1570s. Nobunaga was also most successful in defeating rival *daimyo*, but he was murdered by a vassal in 1582. The succession to his position in central Japan was disputed, but eventually taken by one of his generals, Toyotomi Hideyoshi. By forcing other *daimyo* to accept his leadership, Hideyoshi completed the unification of Japan; this culminated in his 300,000-strong army's conquest of Kyushu in 1587, starving out of the Hojo fortress Odawara in 1590, and successful north-eastern campaign in 1591. After the Shimazu had been defeated in southern Kyushu, Hideyoshi issued an edict in 1588 demanding the surrender of all weapons to the government. This monopolization of the means of violence was matched by the policy of systematically destroying the fortifications of defeated rivals.

WAR IN KOREA

Hideyoshi had long planned an attempt to seize control of China. After the unification of Japan in 1591, he prepared an expedition from Kyushu. Hideyoshi intended to cross the narrow strait between Kyushu and Korea and then march overland to Peking, which he saw as his future capital. The crossing in April 1592 was uncontested, and Japanese forces rapidly advanced on Seoul (*map 1*). Thereafter, they were impeded by increasingly stiff Korean guerrilla resistance,

Toyotomi Hideyoshi (1536–98) rose to prominence as a general of Nobunaga. He completed the unification of Japan and twice invaded Korea.

the advance of massed Chinese forces southwards across the Yalu River, and naval action by the Korean fleet under Yi Sun-sin, culminating in the destruction of the main Japanese fleet in Hansan Bay on 8 July. The Korean victory owed much to the 'turtle ships' – oar-driven, cannon-firing boats that were covered by metal plates to prevent grappling and boarding.

The Japanese defeats led to negotiations. Hideyoshi agreed to withdraw his troops to the Pusan area, but conflict resumed in 1596 when the negotiations broke down. The Japanese fleet was again defeated by the turtle ships in July 1597, and the Japanese expeditionary force, deprived of naval support, lost impetus; in 1598 it was withdrawn. Japan was not to gain control of Korea until 1905.

The Japanese seizure of the Pacific island of Okinawa in 1609 was scant consolation. Shimazu of the Satsuma clan obtained permission to restore the profitable trade with China via the Ryukyu islands. His initial approaches were unsuccessful, so an invasion force of 1,500 was sent to compel Okinawan acceptance of Satsuma suzerainty. Hideyoshi's successor, Tokugawa Ieyasu, concerned at the possibility of Satsuma rivalry with the newly-established Shogunate, ordered the destruction of all large ships in the south-west. Although the Japanese had traded with Southeast Asia in the sixteenth century, in the 1630s they were forbidden to engage in overseas trade. Thus the influence in the western Pacific of the powerful and prosperous Japanese state was limited, and the Portuguese, Spanish, and Dutch nations grew in importance.

CHINA AND SOUTHEAST ASIA

In the 1570s, mobile artillery was developed and the Great Wall adapted for musketeers to resist the resurgent Mongols under Altan Khan, but the military strength of the Ming empire rested primarily on the size of its army – up to half a million in number – and on fortifications. In the 1550s, the Ming had used large numbers of men, armed with traditional weapons – bows, lances, and swords – to capture the Chinese bases of the *wako* (Japanese pirates) who attacked coastal regions. At the end of the century, the size of the army sent to support the Koreans against Hideyoshi was decisive, rather than its level of military technology.

Firearms also played a relatively minor role in Southeast Asia and the East Indies. The possession of muskets was of limited importance unless they were employed in a regular manner to provide concentrated fire. Such tactics required discipline, drill, and a large number of similar weapons, and all these were difficult to provide in such regions. Instead, the emphasis was on individuals' fighting qualities and on warrior elites, rather than on large numbers. Thus, territorial changes in Burma were largely effected by traditional fighting methods. In 1555, the Burmese kingdom of Toungoo, which had overrun Pegu in 1535–41 and territory around Pagan in 1542, conquered the rival kingdom of Ava. The resulting dynamic state expanded considerably in the 1550s and 1560s, capturing Lan Na in 1556 and the Thai capital of Ayuthia in 1564 and 1569 (map 1). A puppet ruler, installed there in 1569, remained in power until a Thai rebellion in 1584.

FIREARMS IN SOUTHERN INDIA

By contrast, firearms were readily adopted by both sides in the struggle between Hindu and Muslim states in sixteenth-century India. Under its dynamic ruler Aliya Rama Raja (1542–65), the Hindu state of Vijayanagar (map 2) maintained its position in the complex politics of the region by deploying armies equipped with artillery manned by Portuguese or Muslim gunners. This policy reflected the same search for a response to Muslim expansion in India

MAP 1

The consolidation of Japanese power under Hideyoshi was followed by a short-lived period of attempted territorial expansion before Japan entered a long era of international quiescence. Ming China was not an aggressive state during this period.

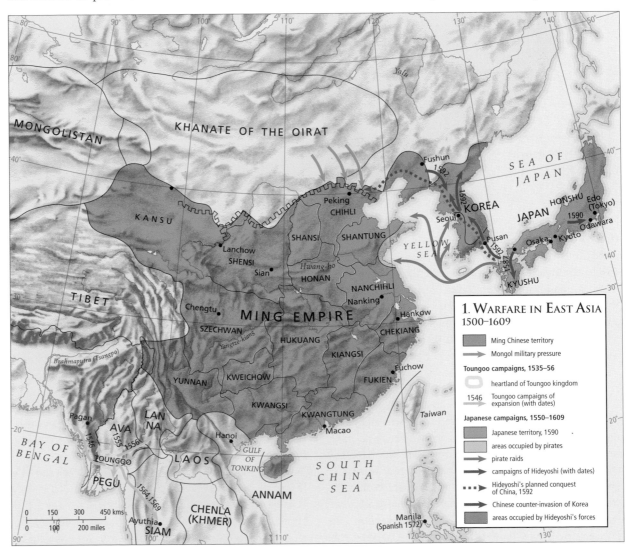

1. WARFARE IN EAST ASIA
1500–1609

- Ming Chinese territory
- Mongol military pressure

Toungoo campaigns, 1535–56
- heartland of Toungoo kingdom
- 1546 Toungoo campaigns of expansion (with dates)

Japanese campaigns, 1550–1609
- Japanese territory, 1590
- areas occupied by pirates
- pirate raids
- campaigns of Hideyoshi (with dates)
- Hideyoshi's planned conquest of China, 1592
- Chinese counter-invasion of Korea
- areas occupied by Hideyoshi's forces

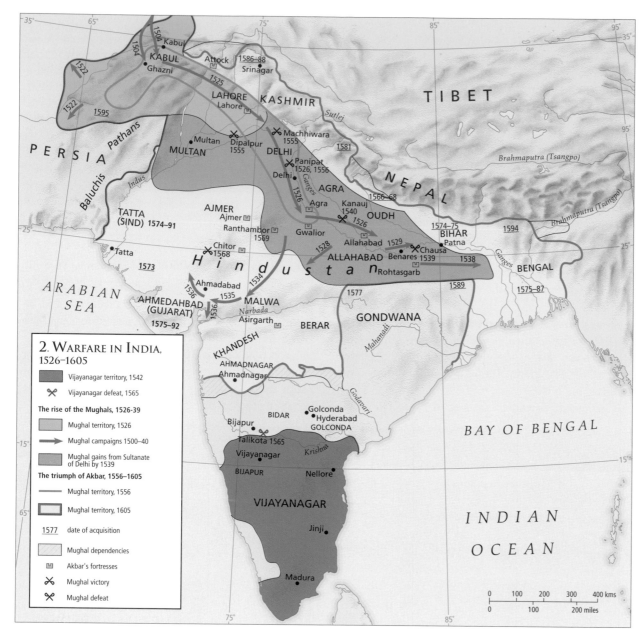

2. Warfare in India, 1526–1605

- Vijayanagar territory, 1542
- ✖ Vijayanagar defeat, 1565

The rise of the Mughals, 1526-39

- Mughal territory, 1526
- → Mughal campaigns 1500–40
- Mughal gains from Sultanate of Delhi by 1539

The triumph of Akbar, 1556–1605

- Mughal territory, 1556
- Mughal territory, 1605
- 1577 date of acquisition
- Mughal dependencies
- Akbar's fortresses
- ✖ Mughal victory
- ✖ Mughal defeat

MAP 2

Babur (1483–1530) launched the Mughal empire. He became ruler of Farghana on his father's death in 1494, and turned towards India from 1515 after his struggle to establish his position in Transoxiana was unsuccessful. His grandson Akbar (1542–1606) greatly expanded the Mughal state. Though he invaded Afghanistan in 1581 and subdued Baluchistan, most of Akbar's campaigns were to the east of the Indus. He dominated northern India but had less success further south in the Deccan.

which had led, earlier in the fifteenth century, to the adoption of improved war-horses and archers. In addition, Muslim mercenaries were hired in the fifteenth century, and Portuguese from the sixteenth. Expenditure on military modernization, accompanied by monetization, helped to transform the economy of Vijayanagar, and Rama Raja in turn benefited from the increasing customs revenue which it generated.

This increased wealth encouraged the Islamic Sultans of the Deccan, especially Husain Nizam Shah of Ahmadnagar, Ibrahim Qutb Shah of Golconda and Ali Adil Shah of Bijapur, to unite against Vijayanagar. At the battle of Talikota in January 1565, Rama Raja was killed and his army was decisively defeated. The city of Vijayanagar was subsequently sacked. Ibrahim (1530–80) then built a new capital at Hyderabad, where he relied upon heavy cavalry, led by the Muslim nobility and supported by landholdings, and upon a European artillery corps financed by the royal monopoly of diamonds, a newly-discovered source of wealth. The

affluent maritime state of Gujarat in western India could similarly afford to adopt the latest in military technology. In the 1530s, its ruler Bahadur Shah developed a large army which was equipped with new cannon manned by Portuguese gunners.

THE RISE OF THE MUGHALS

The Mughals originated in the Central Asian kingdom of Farghana, one of the successor states to the Mongol empire of Tamberlaine. Under their leader Babur, they captured Kabul and Ghazni in 1504, then mounted a series of major campaigns against the predominant power of northern India, the Afghan Lodi Sultanate. The decisive battle was at Panipat on 20 April 1526, in which the Lodi army was destroyed and control of the entire Ganges valley passed to the Mughals (map 2).

After Babur's death, his opium-addicted successor, Humayun (1530–56), was driven out of Hindustan by Sher Khan Sur, an Afghan noble based in southern Bihar.

An Afghan surprise attack at Chausa (1539) led to the rout of Humayun's army, and Sher Khan assumed the title of Sher Shah. The following year, the demoralized Mughal army was defeated near Kanauj. Humayun fled to Tatta (Sind), and in 1544 to Persia. Persian troops helped him drive his brother Kamran from Kabul in 1553, and Humayun then reinvaded India in 1554. Sher Shah had died in 1545 and the surviving Sur regime was weak and divided. Mughal victories at Dipalpur and Machhiwara in 1555 were followed by the recapture of Delhi.

Humayun's successor, his son Akbar, was challenged in 1556 by Himu, a Sur general who captured Agra and Delhi, but was defeated by the smaller Mughal army at a second battle at Panipat. Himu's death prevented a Mughal defeat, and Akbar consolidated his control of the wealthy agricultural heartland of Hindustan in 1557–58, and proceeded to rebuild the empire of his grandfather. From this base, Akbar's power spread in a series of campaigns to include Bengal (1575–76), Kashmir (1585–89), Tatta (1586–93), and Gujarat (1572–73).

Mughal success reflected the energy and determination of Akbar, the divisions among his opponents, the impressive resources of Hindustan and those gained by conquest, and the strength of the Mughal military system. Akbar took an interest in the improvement of his muskets, maintaining a special collection which he tested himself. The infantry were equipped with the arquebus, while the artillery was superior to that of rival rulers. The Mughals also deployed heavy cavalry armed with swords and lances, horse archers, war elephants, and swivel guns borne on animals, and specialized sappers. Akbar anchored his position with a number of fortresses, including Lahore, Agra, Allahabad, and Ajmer.

While gunpowder weaponry was important to Akbar, it also benefited his opponents, and his victories were not easy. Much of his success was due to his military skill and to the strong organization of his state.

FORTIFICATIONS IN ASIAN WARFARE

Fortifications played a major role in warfare in much of Asia, particularly India, Japan, and along China's steppe frontier. They were less developed and important in the East Indies and Southeast Asia. Fortifications were vulnerable to siege artillery. In 1567, the Mughal Emperor Akbar declared a *jihad* (holy war) against the fortified capital of the leading Rajput ruler, Udai Singh, Rana of Mewar. Initial attacks were repulsed and Akbar resorted to bombardment and the digging of mines (tunnels under the walls, filled with explosives). The siege artillery produced breaches in the walls and the city fell on 23 February 1568; all the defenders and 20–25,000 civilians were killed in hand-to-hand fighting. In the following year the major fortress of Ranthambor, held by a vassal of Udai Singh, surrendered after a bombardment by fifteen enormous siege guns which had been dragged by elephants and bullocks to a commanding hill.

Such vulnerability encouraged, in both India and Japan, the construction of less exposed fortifications. In Japan, new-style fortresses used bastions similar to those in Europe or were founded on solid ridges.

The Chinese had no need for such a programme of rebuilding. The earlier use of gunpower in China ensured that their fortified cities had very thick walls capable of withstanding the artillery of the sixteenth century. As a consequence, assault rather than bombardment was the tactic used against fortified positions in early-modern China. This tactic was also well suited to the large forces available: the risk of heavy casualties could be accepted and sieges had to be brought to a speedy close because of the logistical problems of supporting large armies.

Akbar's forces besieging Rai Surjan Hada in Ranthambor, 1568.

OTTOMAN EXPANSION TO 1566

THE FALL of Constantinople in 1453 led to expansion by the Ottoman Turks around the Black Sea and in the Balkans. The armies of Selim I and Suleiman the Magnificent humbled the Persians, the Mamelukes, and the Hungarians, and overran central Europe, while their navy dominated the Mediterranean. Only problems of range, and Russian and Austrian resistance, limited their advance.

THE RISE OF THE OTTOMANS

Originating in Anatolia in the thirteenth century, the Turkish Ottoman state expanded rapidly, helped by the strength of its ruling family, the house of Osman, and by the weakness of its opponents. The Byzantine (Eastern Roman) Empire based in Constantinople was defeated in the struggle to control Anatolia and the Balkans. With the accession of Sultan Mehmed II al-Fatih (1451–81), the Ottomans controlled the majority of both these regions, and in 1453 Constantinople fell to the Ottoman siege artillery (map 1).

Mehmed was defeated outside Belgrade in 1456 by Hungarian forces under Janos Hunyadi, and the Turkish seizure of Otranto in southern Italy in 1480 was only temporary, but the seizure of Trebizond (1461) and the Emirate of Karaman (1468) consolidated Ottoman control of Anatolia, while the capture of Caffa from the Genoese in 1475 established the Ottomans in the Crimea, and was followed in 1484 by the capture of Akkerman at the mouth of the Dniester. The Black Sea was now dominated by the Turks and this gave them control or influence over the rivers that flowed into it, and thus over the lands around the sea.

Although Mehmed's death in 1481 was followed by a struggle for succession which weakened the Turks, the Ottoman Empire continued to make gains. At the fall of the Venetian base of Modon in the Morea in 1500, the Ottoman siege artillery played a decisive role: 22 cannon and 2 mortars fired a total of 155 to 180 shot per day.

THE CONQUEST OF THE MAMELUKES

Under Selim I 'the Grim' (1512–20), major expansion was resumed. The greatest challenges and opportunities lay not in Europe but in Asia. In 1510, the Safavid ruler Isma'il had defeated the Uzbeks in battle near Marv. The skull of the Uzbek ruler Muhammad Shaybni had been set in gold, made into a drinking cup and sent to Isma'il's other major enemy, Selim's predecessor Bayezid II (1481–1512). Support for the Safavids among the peoples of eastern Anatolia threatened Ottoman security, particularly when it prompted rebellions in the area in 1511–12. Selim brutally repressed the rebels, and in 1514 invaded Persia. The initial Safavid scorched earth strategy created major logistical problems

for the Ottoman forces, but Isma'il chose to fight his far more numerous opponents at Chaldiran on 23 August.

The Safavid army was of the traditional central Asian nomadic type: cavalry archers combining mobility with firepower. The Ottomans, however, had made the transition to a more mixed force and had innovative weapons systems. In addition to cavalry, they had infantry equipped with hand guns, and field artillery. Although the Safavids had used cannon in siege warfare, they had none at Chaldiran. The Ottomans won a crushing victory due undoubtedly to their numerical superiority and firepower. But it has also been suggested that it was the cannon that played the crucial role for, chained together, they formed a barrier to cavalry charges. Chaldiran was followed by the capture of the Persian capital, Tabriz (1514), and by a major eastward shift in the Ottoman frontier.

An opportunity for Ottoman expansion southwards had also been created. The defeat of the Persians was a crucial precondition of the Turks' subsequent advances against both Mamelukes and Christians. The Emirate of Dhu'l-Kadr was annexed in 1515, and Selim then achieved the rapid overthrow of the Mameluke Empire: firepower was decisive in the defeat of Mameluke heavy cavalry at the Battles of Marj Dabiq (1516) and al-Rayda (1517). Syria, with its centres of power in Aleppo and Damascus, fell in 1516,

Suleiman the Magnificent besieging Rhodes, 1522. Just over 10 miles (16km) from the Anatolian mainland, Rhodes belonged to the crusading Knights of St John, but had a garrison of only 180 knights and 1,500 auxiliaries. Suleiman launched a formidable campaign to take the well-fortified position. He mounted 20 assaults and fired 85,000 iron and stone shot. The garrison was forced to surrender after it ran out of gunpowder.

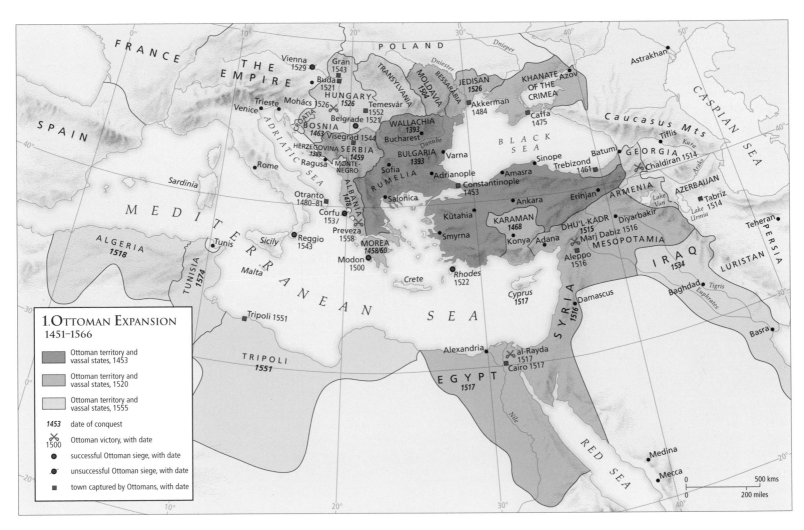

1. **OTTOMAN EXPANSION**
1451–1566

- Ottoman territory and vassal states, 1453
- Ottoman territory and vassal states, 1520
- Ottoman territory and vassal states, 1555

1453 date of conquest

✕ Ottoman victory, with date
1500

● successful Ottoman siege, with date

◓ unsuccessful Ottoman siege, with date

■ town captured by Ottomans, with date

MAP 1

The Ottomans were a major and expanding presence in Europe, Asia, and Africa. Their territorial gains between 1451 and 1566 created an empire larger than any in the region since Byzantium in the early seventh century.

Cairo and Egypt in 1517. Turkish power was thus established on the Red Sea, leading to the acquisition of the Muslim holy places of Mecca and Medina and to subsequent expansion into Aden, commitments in conflicts in the Horn of Africa, and activity in the Indian Ocean.

The conquest of the granary of Egypt and the vital port of Alexandria allowed growth in Ottoman naval strength and rising influence within the Mediterranean. Cyprus became a tributary in 1517, and in 1522 Rhodes was captured from the crusading order of St John, the Hospitallers. The knights, their fortifications strengthened by bastions, resisted assaults and bombardment before accepting reasonable terms of capitulation when their supplies of gunpowder ran out.

SULEIMAN THE MAGNIFICENT

Under Selim's son, Suleiman I the Magnificent (1520–66), Europe again became the main focus of Ottoman attention, although Suleiman's reign also brought the conquest of Iraq (1534), Aden (1538), and Massawa on the Ethiopian coast (1557), and saw Ottoman power spread along the coast of North Africa (map 1). A Mameluke rebellion in Egypt in 1524 was suppressed the following year. The Persians were pushed back in 1533 when Suleiman invaded. The Safavids preferred to avoid conflict, so Suleiman abandoned operations in the harsh climate of Persia and instead

overran northern and central Iraq. Basra and southern Iraq were later taken, expanding Ottoman power eastwards to the Persian Gulf. However, the failure to defeat Persia left control over the southern Caucasus outside Suleiman's grasp. The Persians similarly avoided battle when the Turks attacked in the late 1540s. Azerbaijan was taken in summer advances, only to be retaken by the Persians when the Turks retired during the winter.

Ottoman naval pressure on Europe increased in the Mediterranean, with sieges of Corfu in 1537 (map 2) and Reggio in 1543. To the north of the Black Sea, Ottoman armies crushed a rebellion in Moldavia and conquered Jedisan in 1538. But the most important military theatre was the Danube valley, and Belgrade was besieged in 1521 (map 1). Its small garrison resisted direct assaults, but accepted terms in the face of heavy bombardment.

In 1526, Hungary was invaded: at Mohács on 29 August, the Hungarian feudal cavalry was devastated by Turkish firepower and King Louis II was killed (page 30). Hungary was then overrun, and in 1529 the Ottoman armies advanced to besiege Vienna (map 1). This was the limit of their range, despite the flight of Archduke Ferdinand of Austria. Suleiman did not reach Vienna until 27 September and the city was able to resist assaults until the Ottoman retreat began on 14 October. Campaigning at such a distance from their base caused major logistical problems, as

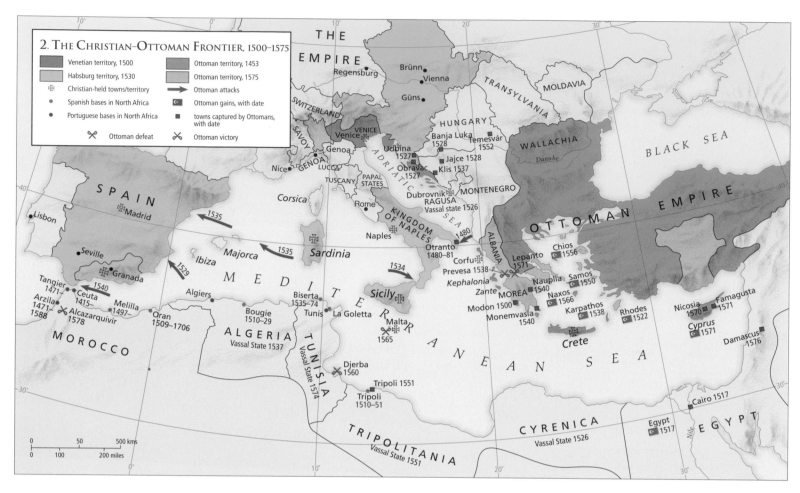

troops and supplies had to move for months before they could reach the sphere of operations, and the onset of winter limited the campaigning season. During the campaign, Ottoman raiders reached as far as Regensburg and Brünn.

Vienna was not besieged again until 1683, but after 1529 pressure was maintained on the frontiers of Habsburg territory, for example with the unsuccessful siege of Güns in 1532 (map 2). This expedition, the first after 1529, was a failure. Suleiman had assembled an enormous army of nearly 300,000 men and hoped that his invasion of Austria would provoke the main Habsburg army into battle. This was not to be, and the widespread devastation achieved by Suleiman's raiders was not matched by any decisive victory. As soon as the Turks withdrew, Ferdinand reoccupied southern Austria and northern and western Hungary. Nevertheless, the campaign was followed in 1533 by a peace that left most of Hungary under effective Turkish control with a frontier that was anchored by new garrisons and fortifications. Gran fell in 1543, Visegrad in 1544, and the peace subsequently negotiated in 1547 acknowledged Ottoman control over most of Hungary. War resumed in 1552 with the Ottoman conquest of Temesvár, but Austrian reluctance to engage in battle and the difficulty of maintaining lengthy sieges at the end of stretched supply lines was yet again to limit Ottoman advances.

Suleiman had brought Ottoman power into central Europe and made it feared throughout the Mediterranean. These were formidable achievements. They may appear limited in contrast to the new global range of Portuguese and Spanish power, but under Suleiman an appreciable portion of the Eurasian heartland was brought together into one state. Not since the mid 630s, when the Arabs advanced through the Byzantine territories of Syria and Palestine, had any empire encompassed the Middle East, Egypt, and much of eastern Europe, and the power of Byzantium had not extended north of the Danube or into Iraq.

Ottoman strength was based upon the resources of a far-flung empire (especially of Egypt and the Middle East), on an ideology which saw war against the non-believer as a duty, and on a society structured for the effective prosecution of such war. The most valuable of the regular troops were the janissaries, recruited from the *devshirme* – a tribute of children levied in the Balkans. Converts to Islam, they were a trained elite corps, paid from central funds, armed with firearms, and increased by Selim I to 35,000 men. The janissaries achieved levels of military professionalism and weaponry advance unmatched in Europe or elsewhere in the Islamic world.

THE AEGEAN AND ADRIATIC THEATRES

The Ottomans increased their naval strength in a number of ways (*map 2*). They consolidated their position in the Morea, acquiring the Venetian bases of Monemvasia and Nauplia in 1540. The Aegean was brought under greater control with the capture of Karpathos and the northern Sporades (1538), and the Duchy of Naxos (1566), all from

MAP 2

The Iberian attempt to continue the *Reconquista* by gaining bases in North Africa, and the dramatic growth of Ottoman naval power, led to bitter conflict in the sixteenth century. Ottoman ambitions extended to North Africa and competed with the determination of the Habsburgs to protect the maritime links between their possessions.

THE SIEGE OF MALTA, 1565

After their surrender of Rhodes in 1522, the Knights of St John were offered new bases in Malta and Tripoli in 1530 by the Emperor Charles V. Tripoli fell to the Ottomans in 1551, but Malta became the principal Christian corsair base in the Mediterranean and a threat to Ottoman trade in the east. It therefore became an obvious Ottoman target, especially when Ottoman power increased on the Barbary coast.

The defeat of a Spanish fleet at Djerba in 1560 increased Malta's vulnerability, and in 1565 Suleiman the Magnificent sent a formidable force of 40,000 against the island. The defenders, under Grand Master Jean de la Valette, a veteran of Rhodes, had only 2,500 trained soldiers to defend the three fortresses of St Elmo, Senglea, and Birgu.

The struggle initially concentrated on St Elmo, which the Ottomans needed to gain to obtain a safe harbour. Landing on 18 May, the Ottoman forces brought cannon ashore and launched repeated attacks, covered by artillery fire: 60,000 shot were fired. The 1,500 defenders of St Elmo used their twenty cannon, firearms, and primitive grenades to repel these attacks, but the walls were destroyed and on 29 June the last of the garrison fought to the death (1).

On 19 May, the Ottoman troops had attacked Senglea and Birgu, gaining a temporary advantage at Birgu. An attack on the Ottoman camp by a small Christian group from Medina raised fears of the arrival of a major relief force, and the Ottomans withdrew. They returned to the attack later (2, 3), but were unable to overrun the rebuilt fortifications and their determined defenders. The Ottoman troops were also hampered by divided leadership, the summer heat, and logistical problems such as the supply of drinking water.

The defenders could only repel the attacks: they were not strong enough to mount a sortie. Unlike the Siege of Rhodes, however, a relief army was in preparation. On 7 September, the Spanish viceroy of Sicily, Don García de Toledo, arrived with 11,000 men, and the besiegers retreated, unwilling to face a new foe. They had suffered perhaps as many as 24,000 casualties; the defenders lost about 5,000, including Maltese levies. The Ottomans never again attacked Malta.

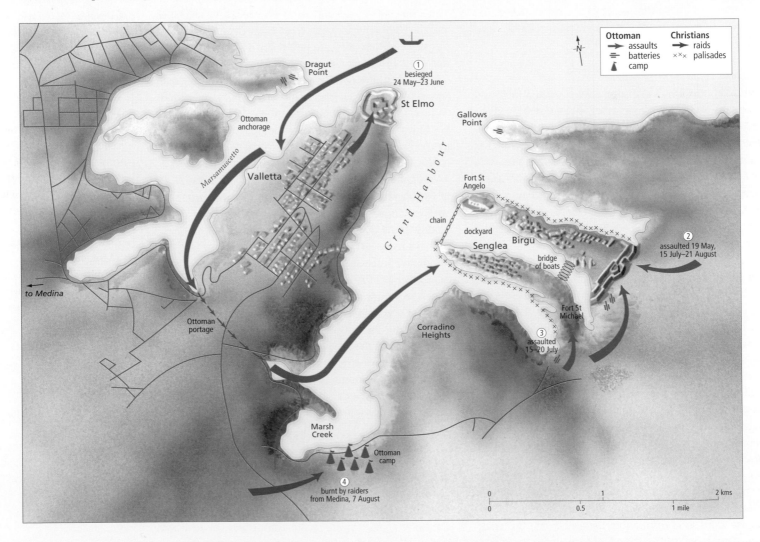

Venice, while Samos (1550) and Chios (1556) were taken from the Genoese. Neither Venice nor Genoa had the capability to protect such exposed positions; this was a far cry from the naval reach enjoyed by both powers during the Middle Ages.

In the Adriatic, the Ottoman Empire also made steady gains. Dubrovnik (Ragusa) became a vassal in 1526, and the spread of Ottoman power in Croatia threatened the hinterland of Venetian Dalmatia. After Mohács, more Croatian fortresses fell: Obrovac and Udbina in 1527, Jajce and Banja Luka in 1528, Klis in 1537. In the Adriatic itself, the Ottomans struck in 1537, invading and ravaging Corfu, but withdrawing without attempting a major siege of the powerful Venetian fortress.

Emperor Charles V, Venice, and the Papacy agreed an alliance in the face of this threat, their combined fleet encountering the Ottoman navy off Prevesa on 28 September 1538. Accounts of the battle vary. In one view the wind fell, causing the Genoese admiral Andrea Doria to hold back the Habsburg fleet for fear of separating his rowed galleys from his sail-driven ships. The Ottoman fleet, under Khair ad-Din, also held back, hoping for just such a separation. Another explanation blamed Doria for leaving the bulk of the action to his papal and Venetian allies, who lost several vessels in what turned out to be a minor defeat. The battle was followed by the Ottoman capture of Castelnuovo on the Adriatic coast in October 1538.

WAR IN THE MEDITERRANEAN

Such a combination of Christian powers was unusual, and the alliance swiftly disintegrated: Charles V did not share the Venetians' concern for Greek waters and the Adriatic, while the Venetians, dependent on grain supplies from the Ottoman Empire, wished to resume commercial links with the Levant, and found the conflict expensive and unrewarding. In 1539, the Ottomans regained Castelnuovo, and Venice suffered serious food shortages. Peace was arranged in the following year, with the Venetians ceding their last bases in the Aegean and the Morea, and promising to remain neutral. After 1540, the focus of conflict shifted from Greek waters and the Adriatic to the waters between Italy and North Africa. The most dramatic episode was the unsuccessful Turkish invasion of Malta in 1565 (*page 27*), when they suffered perhaps as many as 24,000 casualties.

War between Venice and the Ottoman Empire resumed when the Ottomans attacked Cyprus in 1571. This led to the formation of another major Christian league which triumphed at Lepanto in 1571 (*page 29*), but again failed to gain lasting strategic advantage. Venice abandoned the alliance in 1573, while the Ottomans rapidly rebuilt their fleet and in 1574 took Tunis, thus ending hopes of a Habsburg advance in North Africa.

THE HUNGARIAN FRONTIER

On land also, the Ottoman Empire generally retained the initiative in the second half of the century. In 1551, Charles V's brother, Archduke Ferdinand of Austria, sent forces into

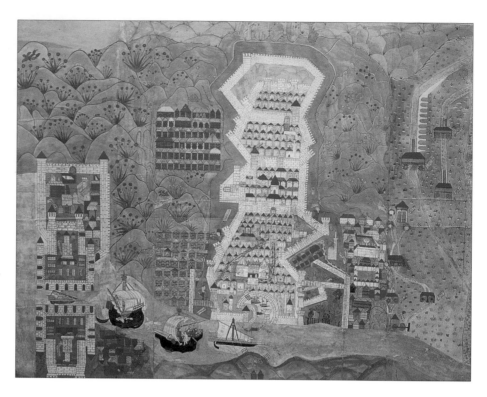

Transylvania, leading to a massive Ottoman response in 1552 which culminated in victories at Szegedin and Fülek and the Ottoman conquest of Temesvár (*map 1*). Ottoman forces were, however, stopped at Erlau. The war continued until 1562, mainly as intermittent border skirmishes with no breakthrough by either power, but Austria then agreed to a peace which left Transylvania in Ottoman hands and required an annual Austrian tribute to the Sultan. Like the Habsburgs, Suleiman was preoccupied by other commitments: peace with Persia was not signed until 1555 and conflicts over the succession led to civil war in 1558–59.

The Ottoman war with Austria resumed after the death of Ferdinand in 1564, again over Transylvania. In 1566, Suleiman in person led his troops to besiege Szigetvár, but Miklos Zrinyi commanded a spirited defence of the city, and Suleiman died before it was successfully stormed.

In both Europe and Asia, the Ottoman armies were close to their limits of effective campaigning, while their opponents had learned how to counter their tactics. Further gains were to be made, most significantly Podolia from the Poles in 1672, but the difficulties of fighting at great distances from bases and the growing effectiveness of Austrian fortifications ensured that there could be no repetition of the early major advances. Both the Austrians and the Persians had learned that the best policy was to avoid major battles, and without these the Ottomans could gain little more.

IVAN THE TERRIBLE'S ADVANCE

The struggle between Christendom and Islam was very wide-ranging. It took place in the plains of Hungary and the mountains of Croatia and Dalmatia, in the Mediterranean, on the North African littoral, in the Horn of Africa, on the Arabian Sea, and across a broad swathe of territory to the north and east of the Black Sea (*map 3*).

A Turkish map of the fort of Lepanto, 1550. Lepanto, a harbour at the entrance of the Gulf of Corinth in Greece, was a Turkish stronghold from 1499.

To the north, the Ottoman Empire reached to the Galician and Ukrainian frontiers of Poland-Lithuania, and further east there were the independent Islamic Tatar Khanates of Kazan and Astrakhan. The Grand Principality of Muscovy had long sought to throw off the 'Tatar yoke'. Under Ivan III (1462–1505), Muscovy conducted a series of campaigns against Kazan (1467–69) and began to take the initiative. Ivan then took advantage of dynastic strife within Kazan and in 1487 his troops placed a sympathetic claimant on the Kazan throne.

Ivan's successor, Vassily III (1505–33), initially maintained good relations with Kazan. But the Crimean Tatars

LEPANTO 7 OCTOBER 1571

After their failure at Malta, Cyprus was an easier target for Ottoman conquest. It was closer to the centres of Ottoman power and its Venetian rulers appeared less formidable than the Maltese-Spanish combination. In 1570, Suleiman's successor, Selim II 'the Sot', sent a force of 116 galleys and 50,000 troops to attack the Venetian fortresses of Nicosia and Famagusta.

The first fell in only seven weeks, but Famagusta, under Marc'Antonio Bragadin, held out until the following August, resisting attacks and defying both bombardment and mining. The Venetians appealed for help to Philip II of Spain, as Spanish resources and leadership were crucial to Mediterranean resistance against the Ottoman Empire. In May 1571, the Holy League of Spain, Venice and the Papacy was organized by Pope Pius V and a fleet was prepared. By then Famagusta had fallen. Short of gunpowder, it surrendered on generous terms similar to those granted Rhodes by Suleiman. But the Ottomans broke the terms, killing the garrison and flaying Bragadin alive.

The Christian fleet under Philip II's illegitimate half-brother Don John of Austria found the Ottoman fleet at Lepanto off the west coast of Greece. The Ottomans had more ships, 270 to 208, but fewer cannon, 750 to 1,815, and Don John had made modifications to his ships to widen their field of fire. He put the Venetians on the left, Gian Andrea Doria on the right, and took the centre himself, adding weight to the line with six Venetian galleasses (three-masted lateen-rigged galley) which were longer and heavier-gunned than galleys. There was no tactical subtlety; Don John relied on battering his way to victory. More than 100,000 men took part in the battle.

Superior Christian gunnery, the fighting qualities of the Spanish infantry who served on both the Spanish and the Venetian ships, and the exhaustion of Ottoman gunpowder, all helped to bring a crushing victory in four hours' fighting. The rams and cannon of the galleasses were held responsible for the sinking of seventy Ottoman galleys, although the cannon were more important.

Ali Pasha, the Turkish admiral, was killed, and Ali al-Uluji, the effective commander of the Ottoman left, fled. The Christians lost 15,000 men, but Ottoman casualties were about twice this number, and their losses included 113 galleys sunk and 117 captured, as well as their cannon and naval stores.

The battle was applauded as a triumph throughout Christian Europe, a decisive victory over a feared foe. However, it was late in the year and the battle could not be consummated by the recapture or Cyprus, let alone, as Don John hoped, by the liberation of Palestine. The Ottomans rapidly constructed a new navy which included galleasses. In 1573, Venice reached a separate peace with the Ottoman Empire, recognizing the conquest of Cyprus and paying an indemnity. Tunis fell to the Ottomans in the following year. Lepanto was decisive more for what it prevented – a possible resumption of the Ottoman advances in the Mediterranean and Adriatic – than for pushing the balance of military advantage towards the Christians.

The Battle of Lepanto, a contemporary painting by Andrea Micheli (Vincentino).

MOHÁCS 29 AUGUST 1526

Twice in the sixteenth century, foolish military initiatives by young monarchs led to the end of their lives and of the independence of important states. Sebastian of Portugal was crushed by the Moroccans at Alcazarquivir in 1578. In 1526, Louis II of Hungary confronted the powerful forces of Suleiman the Magnificent.

Although Suleiman had set off in April 1526, bad weather delayed his crossing of the river Drava until late August. The Hungarians, however, in part due to slow preparations, were divided, poorly led and short of infantry, and they failed either to contest the Drava crossing or to retire to Buda and allow the Ottomans to exhaust their resources in a difficult siege. Instead they deployed behind the Borza, a small tributary of the Danube, and rather than waiting on the defensive, their heavy cavalry advanced.

Suleiman at the Battle of Mohács.

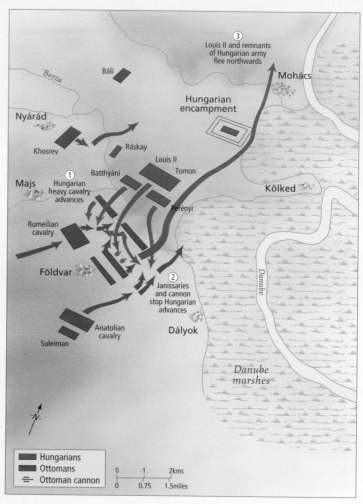

The Hungarian charge (1) pushed back the Ottoman *sipahis* (cavalry) of Rumelia, but halted when Turkish troops advanced on their flank. Louis then led the remainder of his cavalry in a second attack which drove through the *sipahis* of Anatolia, but was stopped by the janissaries and cannon. Their fire caused havoc, and the Hungarians, their dynamism spent, were then attacked in front and rear by the more numerous Turkish forces.

Louis and most of his aristocracy died on the battlefield or in the nearby Danube marshes, Louis drowning while trying to swim across a river in armour, and few of his army escaped (3). Suleiman swept on to Buda, which fell ten days later. The days of independent Hungary were numbered. Louis had no children, and his inheritance was to be contested by his brother-in-law Archduke Ferdinand and by the Ottomans. Suleiman, however, initially decided not to annex Hungary but rather to accept the suggestion by John Zapolya, Prince of Transylvania, who was opposed to the Habsburgs, that he and his supporters be left in control in return for an acknowledgement of Ottoman suzerainty and a payment of tribute. Zapolya was chosen King of Hungary at the Tokay diet in 1527, but the Habsburgs under Ferdinand defeated him in 1527, leading to renewed Ottoman intervention in 1528–29.

MAP 3

Although generally treated as a side-show in the struggle between Christendom and Islam, the Russian overthrow of the Khanates of Kazan and Astrakhan led to a major extension of Russian power, and encouraged fresh interests and commitments that were to be of crucial importance for the history of both Siberia and of the lands round the Black Sea.

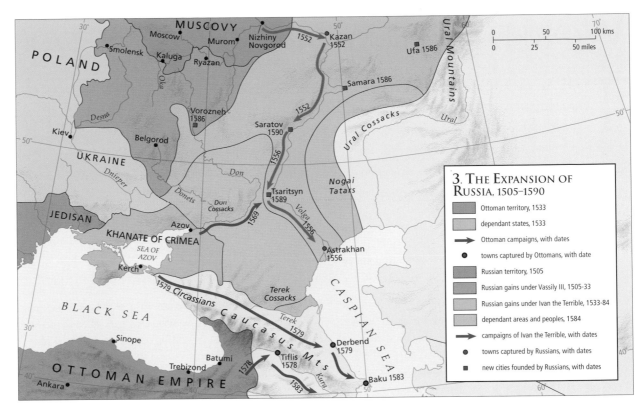

3. THE EXPANSION OF RUSSIA, 1505–1590

- Ottoman territory, 1533
- dependant states, 1533
- → Ottoman campaigns, with dates
- ● towns captured by Ottomans, with date
- Russian territory, 1505
- Russian gains under Vassily III, 1505–33
- Russian gains under Ivan the Terrible, 1533–84
- dependant areas and peoples, 1584
- → campaigns of Ivan the Terrible, with dates
- ● towns captured by Russians, with dates
- ■ new cities founded by Russians, with dates

were supported by the Ottoman Turks, and organized a pan-Tatar league which ousted the pro-Muscovite ruler of Kazan in 1521. He was replaced with Sahib, brother of the Khan of the Crimean Tatars. In the same year, the Crimean and Kazan Tatars advanced on Moscow from the south and the east, and the city was saved only by an attack on the Crimea by the Tatars of Astrakhan. In 1524, the Khan of Kazan acknowledged the suzerainty of Suleiman the Magnificent, but in 1532 Vassily succeeded in installing another pro-Muscovite khan, Djan Ali, who was murdered in 1535 and replaced by Sahib's nephew, Safa-Girey. Relations between Muscovy and Kazan deteriorated, with frequent raids by the Tatar light cavalry. In 1545, Ivan IV 'the Terrible' (1533–84) took the initiative, helped by divisions among the Tatars. After unsuccessful campaigns in 1547–48 and 1549–50, Kazan was overcome in October 1552. The Russians then enforced their power along the Volga by punitive expeditions, finally occupying Astrakhan without a struggle in 1556 (map 3).

The Russians owed their success in part to more advanced weaponry, especially cannon, but there were other important factors. The demographic balance favoured Russia, and there was a clear difference in consistency and quality of leadership. Although during Ivan IV's minority the Russian government was weak and divided, there was little comparison with the situation in Kazan, where the throne changed hands six times between 1546 and 1552. This provided numerous opportunities for Russian intervention, further aided by the divisions between the peoples of the Steppe. The Great Nogai Horde accepted the annexation of Astrakhan, and the Ottoman Turks were too distant and disinterested to intervene, although in 1579 they took Derbend on the Caspian Sea and in 1583 they took Baku.

Kazan was insufficiently strong and was too remote from potential allies to resist the Russians, whose advance to the Caspian Sea and the valley of the Don created a major southward extension of their power. This was of enormous importance to the trajectory of Russian history, ensuring that first the Urals and then Siberia were laid open to their further expansion.

THE USKOKS

The disturbed nature of the frontier between Christendom and Islam allowed a number of free military communities to flourish. The most important were the Barbary Corsairs of North Africa, the Cossacks, and the Knights of Malta. In the Adriatic, the comparable group was the Uskoks of Senj, an Adriatic port under the nominal control of the Habsburg Military Frontier in Croatia. Senj came to play a major role in the incessant Dalmatian conflict, with the Uskoks living entirely on raiding the Turks and, to a lesser extent, the Venetians.

The Uskoks originated in nearby Habsburg territories threatened by the Ottomans, but later they came from all the Croatian-Ottoman and Venetian-Ottoman border areas, their grievances channelled into warfare fuelled by ideals of holy honour and vengeance.

For most of the sixteenth century effective restraint by the Habsburg authorities of Uskok raiding was attempted only intermittently, its benefits to the Military Frontier outweighing its disadvantages. From the end of the 1590s, however, with increased Venetian pressure in the form of port blockades, Uskok actions posed a diplomatic threat. A serious attempt to control Senj was made in 1600–01, and in 1618 the Uskoks were finally expelled by a joint Habsburg-Venetian action.

WORLD MILITARY POWER, 1600-1700

THE SEVENTEENTH century saw a notable increase in the influence of European powers in the world, but this influence was founded on trade as much as military strength, and was limited by inter-European rivalries. A worldwide trend towards greater state power in the second half of the century led to the revival of vigorous, dynamic states both in Europe and elsewhere.

EUROPEAN EXPANSION

In the seventeenth century, more of the world's land surface was brought under the control of European powers, who also strengthened their position on the major sea-trading routes. In Asia, Russian expansion across Siberia to the Pacific brought a vast, little-populated area under European control (page 34). Elsewhere in Asia, European impact was minimal, although in South Asia the Europeans sought trade, not territory (page 17). European penetration was limited even in areas which are generally seen as under European control. The Philippines, for example, are frequently presented in atlases as Spanish from 1570; although Spanish expeditions reached northern Luzon before the end of the sixteenth century, specific documentary reference to a Spanish presence in what is now central Ifugao dates only from 1736, and Spanish military and missionary activity was still sporadic during the nineteenth century. As yet,

despite the establishment of Spanish power in the Mariana Islands in 1668 and the Caroline Islands in 1696, and the development of Spanish cross-Pacific trade between Manila and Acapulco, European contact with the Pacific and Australasia was limited. Although there were a number of European settlements on African shores (page 18), contact with the interior was also limited. There were steady advances in South America by the Spanish and Portuguese, and in North America by the Spanish, English, and French (page 44). In Europe itself, the Turks were pushed back: the Ottoman siege of Vienna in 1683 was unsuccessful and by the close of the century their frontier was pushed back in Hungary, southern Greece, and to the north of the Black Sea (page 92). In the Mediterranean, the Ottoman conquest of Crete brought no major revival in Turkish naval power, and the English, Dutch, and French navies came to play a considerably greater role.

As in the sixteenth century, it would be mistaken to think simply in terms of European versus non-European warfare. Both within and outside Europe, the European powers competed vigorously. Their common concern to dominate trade routes ensured that this competition was often more intense than that between European and non-European powers. Thus the Dutch drove the Portuguese from coastal Ceylon, but failed to do so from Angola and Brazil, while the English drove the Dutch from New Amsterdam, and renamed it New York. Equally, in Africa, the Near East, India, and the Orient, struggles between local powers were more important than those with European states.

MAP 1

1600 was a year of European expansion. In London, for example, an East India Company was founded to trade with South Asia. It was to be the basis of Britain's later empire there. However, the maritime prominence of western European powers and their conquests in the New World had scant impact in the more populous Orient. Japan's attempt to conquer Korea was unsuccessful, but Ming China was soon to be under increasing pressure from the Manchu.

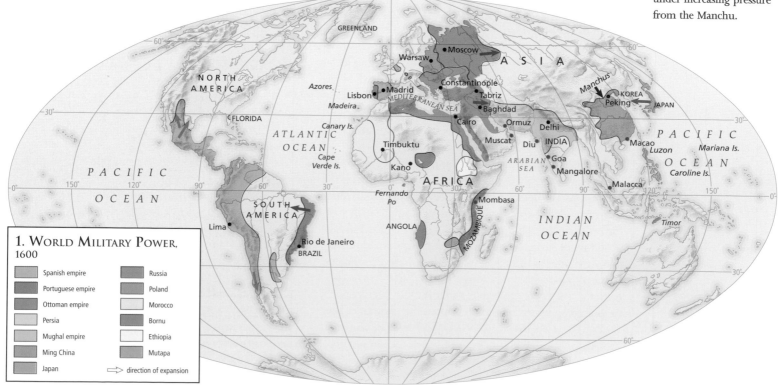

1. WORLD MILITARY POWER, 1600

Spanish empire	Russia
Portuguese empire	Poland
Ottoman empire	Morocco
Persia	Bornu
Mughal empire	Ethiopia
Ming China	Mutapa
Japan	⇨ direction of expansion

Macassar soldiers with blowpipes and poisoned darts from *Voyages and Travels in the East Indies* by Jan Nieuhoff after 1645. Macassar in the Celebes was only finally subjugated by the Dutch in 1669, after protracted struggles. Dutch success owed much to the assistance of the Buginese ruler Arung Palakka.

GROWTH IN STATE POWER

The greater importance of immediate rivalries demonstrates why it is inappropriate to judge military capability against a single measure. Aside from the difficulty of making an overall assessment of a weapons system that could be used in a great variety of circumstances, there is also the question of military effectiveness, widened to include logistics, the permanence of armed forces, and systems of command. In Europe and elsewhere, there was great variety under these heads. Internal political crises in mid-century in a large number of states, including China, the Ottoman Empire, Russia, France, Spain, and Britain, affected their international military strength.

Nevertheless, a worldwide process of domestic growth and consolidation of governmental power is perceptible in the second half of the century. This inevitably led, despite the widespread demographic stagnation and economic problems of the period, to increases in the resources at the disposal of the state, and in the military activity of a number of powers, most obviously France, England, Austria, Russia, the Ottoman Empire, and China. Some of this activity was directed against peoples with looser governmental structures, as with the Chinese in Mongolia and the establishment of the French in Louisiana, but most was deployed against other states with comparable governmental structures. With increases in the size and firepower of armies and navies throughout this period, warfare defined and reflected the relative strengths of states.

PERSIA UNDER ABBAS I

Persia exemplifies the interaction between military capability and administrative reform. Under Shah Abbas I (1587–1629), the Safavid empire acquired a large standing army, based on Caucasian military slaves (*ghulam*), including a 12,000 strong corps of artillerymen with about 500 guns. This force was supportable because of administrative changes allowing troops to be paid directly from the royal treasury, rather than from the revenues of provinces assigned to tribal governors. Abbas enlarged the amount of land he directly controlled, while increasingly *ghulams* became provincial governors, also strengthening the position of the shah. This stronger governmental-military nexus contributed significantly to a series of Persian military successes. Herat was regained from the Uzbeks in 1598, Kandahar from the Mughals and Hormuz from the Portuguese in 1622, and Baghdad from the Turks in 1623. A similar process took place in other states.

Sea battle off Hormuz (Persian, Isfahan style, 1697).

RUSSIAN EXPANSION, 1550-1700

RUSSIAN EXPANSION into Siberia was one of history's most significant European colonizations, enabled by technological advance and limited only by the Ch'ing Chinese of the Amur valley. With the decline of the Poles, the Russians also overcame the Cossacks and took the eastern Ukraine, but expeditions against the Tatars and the Ottoman Khanate of the Crimea were costly failures.

THE CONQUEST OF SIBERIA

Siberia was a vast region inhabited by small numbers of nomadic and semi-nomadic peoples who were well attuned to the hunting, fishing, and pastoral possibilities of their environment. The region was also the world's leading source of fur, and as a result Russian merchants came to take a greater interest in Siberia from the late sixteenth century. The Russian acquisition of the Khanate of Kazan in 1552

was followed by expansion into and then across the southern Urals (map 1). Tobolsk was founded in 1587 and from there Russian power slowly expanded all the way to the Pacific, where Okhotsk was founded in 1648.

This was an advance in which the Europeans enjoyed a definite technological edge. Their opponents had no gunpowder weaponry and indeed many existed at a very primitive level of military technology. The Cossacks used cannon effectively against unco-operative Siberian aborigines and remnants of the Golden Horde along the Tobol and Irtysh rivers. The native peoples were also subjugated by the Russian construction of forts which maximized the defensive potential of firearms and anchored their routes to the Pacific. Furthermore, resistance was weakened by the small size and disorganization of the native population, several of whose mutually hostile tribes even gave the Russians military support. Those who resisted were treated barbarously, and great cruelty was exercised in the extortion of a heavy *iasak* (tribute) in furs. Due to this and to the introduction of new diseases, the native population decreased dramatically. But resistance continued, especially among the Chukchi and Koryaks of Kamchatka, and the Russians made little further progress until the eighteenth century.

CHINESE OPPOSITION

The Russians faced more serious opposition from another direction. Their movement into the Amur valley in the 1640s led to a vigorous response from Ch'ing (Manchu) China, once the Manchus had completed their overthrow of the Ming dynasty (page 40). In 1683, the Chinese ordered the Russians to leave, and in 1685 they successfully besieged the Russian fortress of Albazin. The Russians rebuilt it, only to lose it to a second siege in 1686. The Russian forces were equipped with cannon; while the Manchu forces did not bring such ordnance to the Amur, this technology gap was of little value to the Russians, for the Manchu bided their time and allowed hunger to do its work. Superior Chinese strength could not be resisted, especially at such a distance, and by the Treaty of Nerchinsk of 1689 (the first treaty by which the Chinese recognized another power as an equal), the Russians acknowledged Chinese control of the Amur valley. Chinese demands for a Russian withdrawal beyond Lake Baikal, so that the Russians would abandon their Pacific coastline, were unsuccessful.

Nerchinsk left Russia still in control of a vast extent of territory, which was to be expanded further in the following century as the Russians moved into Alaska and the Aleutians and from there down the western coast of North America. These possessions did not, however, make Russia an active Asian or Pacific power. The concentration of population, resources, and government on the European side of Russia, increased further by Peter the Great's transfer of the capital from Moscow to his new city

'The Habits of the Ostiachen and Kerrgiessen people' from Adam Brand's *Journal of the Embassy to Peking* (1698). Siberian tribes armed with bows and arrows were little match for Russian power.

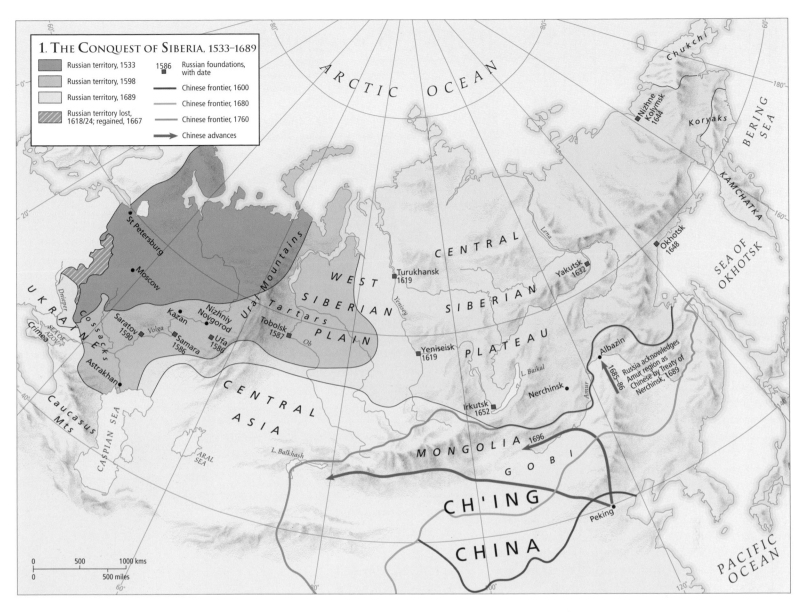

1. THE CONQUEST OF SIBERIA, 1533–1689

▨	Russian territory, 1533
▨	Russian territory, 1598
▨	Russian territory, 1689
▨	Russian territory lost, 1618/24; regained, 1667

1586 ■ Russian foundations, with date
— Chinese frontier, 1600
— Chinese frontier, 1680
— Chinese frontier, 1760
→ Chinese advances

MAP 1

The Russian drive east-wards was a formidable example of rapid overland expansion in the face of a hostile environment. Having been exposed for centuries to pressure from central Asia, the Russians dramatically reversed the relationship, although this brought them into conflict with China.

of St Petersburg, rendered Siberia merely peripheral to the Russian state. Militarily, the geopolitical context of power was amply demonstrated. The hostile nature of the Siberian environment exacerbated the impact of the region's vast distances, and there was no warm-water sea route along the coast.

THE STRUGGLE FOR THE EASTERN UKRAINE

In 1648, the southern frontier of European Russia was still far from the Black Sea. The lands between were under the sovereignty of two powers: Poland, which ruled the Ukraine; and the Khanate of Crimea, which ruled both the peninsula of that name and the lands to the north and east of the Sea of Azov (map 2). Various Cossack groups were also effectively autonomous. In 1648, the Cossacks of the Ukraine, under the leadership of Bogdan Khmelnitsky, rebelled against the Poles. Initial success could not be maintained, and the Cossacks turned to Alexis I of Russia for help, swearing allegiance and signing the Treaty of Pereiaslavl in 1654. This led to war between Poland and Russia, at the end of which the Truce of Andrusovo (1667) gave Russia

control of Kiev and Left Bank Ukraine (east of the river Dnieper). The settlement agreed at Andrusovo was challenged by the Cossacks, with more serious opposition coming from the Ottomans and from their Crimean allies.

THE RUSSO–OTTOMAN WAR, 1677–81

In 1677, the Turks invaded the Ukraine, bombarding the important Dnieper fortress of Chigirin with 36-lb (16.4kg) shot and 80-lb (36.4kg) mortar bombs. The Russian garrison resisted for long enough to permit the arrival of a relieving army, but in 1678 the Ottomans advanced again, and this time the Russians were forced to evacuate Chigirin, blowing up the fortress during their retreat.

Traditional Russian musketeer units, the *streltsy*, fared badly in these campaigns, and the artillery, though numerous, was ill-equipped and mismanaged. But the Russians fought well and limited the Ottoman advance. At the price of an annual tribute to the Khan of the Crimea, Russia retained Left Bank Ukraine and Kiev in the Treaty of Bakhchisarai (1681). The Ottomans were already planning to concentrate their resources on Vienna (*page 95*).

A seventeenth-century engraving showing the Grand Duke of Moscow and the Great Cham of Tartary.

MAP 2

As in the Far East, Russian expansion led to a clash with another aggressive power. The Turks and their Tatar allies proved troublesome foes, and although Peter the Great captured Azov, it proved impossible to conquer the Crimea.

GOLITSYN IN THE CRIMEA

The Ottoman failure at Vienna in 1683 led to renewed Russian expansion. Strengthened in 1686 by confirmation of the Andrusovo terms in the Treaty of Eternal Peace with Poland, Russia became committed to war with the Ottoman Empire. The leading minister, Prince Vasily Golitsyn, led two campaigns to the Crimea in 1687 and 1689.

The 1687 campaign was hampered by a vast baggage train. Several hundred heavy cannon were difficult to move speedily, and each Russian soldier had to carry many months' food. There were no supplies on the steppe, and Tatar fires denied the horses forage. Golitsyn was forced to turn back, still 130 miles (210km) from Perekop. He constructed a fortress, Novobogoroditskoe, at the confluence of the Dnieper and the Samara.

Ottoman defeats by the Austrians, and fear that Russia would gain nothing from peace, led Golitsyn to embark on a second Crimean campaign. After the problems of 1687, he was determined to advance earlier and faster, but was delayed by rivers swollen with spring snowmelt. However, his army of about 112,000 reached the river Karachakrak by 3 May 1689; this was the point of maximum advance in June 1687. From 15 May, the Tatars attacked repeatedly, but the Russian formations held, and on 20 May Golitsyn's army reached Perekop, at the entrance to the Crimean peninsula. There was, however, no food or water to be found outside the city, and the Tatars refused to leave their defences and to engage in battle. Golitsyn once again withdrew to Novobogoroditskoe on 11 June. Up to 35,000 men died during the retreat, which prompted the fall of Golitsyn and his lover the Regent Sophia, and the rise of Peter the Great. Under Peter, Russian attention shifted from the Crimean peninsula to the exposed, strategic Tatar city of Azov, finally captured in 1696.

2. THE RUSSIANS ADVANCE SOUTHWARDS, 1648–1700

- Polish frontier, 1648
- Russian territory, 1648
- Russian territory, 1667
- 1687 Russian advances, with date
- Russian fortresses
- Ottoman empire
- Turkish gains from Poland, 1676
- 1677 Turkish advances, with date

THE APOGEE OF MUGHAL INDIA, 1605–1707

MILITARY CAMPAIGNS under Jahangir and Shah Jahan brought new territories under Mughal rule, and Safavid Persia was challenged for control of central Asia. Under Aurangzeb, the empire expanded to include almost the whole of India, but a long war against the emergent Hindu Maratha state of the western Deccan indicated growing opposition to the Mughals.

THE EMPIRE OF SHAH JAHAN

Under Akbar's successor Jahangir (1605–27), the most immediate threat to Mughal power was from Jahangir's son Khurram, the Rana of Mewar, who was harried into capitulating after a system of positions had been created in the hills of Rajasthan which had hitherto been thought inaccessible by the Mughals. From 1612, in the valley of the Brahmaputra, the Ahom, a Shan people originally from

Seventeenth-century Indian elephant armour. Elephants played a role in a number of battles, but were vulnerable to firearms. Mughal commanders often directed operations from their war elephant, for example Dara Shukoh at the battle of Samuagarh in 1658.

upper Burma, proved a more formidable challenge, not least because all their resources were mobilized for war. This was a riverine and jungle terrain very different from Rajasthan, and Ahom fighting techniques were well adapted to it. They relied on infantry, armed with muskets or bows and arrows, used flexible tactics, including surprise night attacks, and rapidly created fortified positions based on bamboo stockades. In the Himalayas, however, the powerful fortress of the Raja of Kangra was taken in 1618. To the south, the Mughals sought expansion in order to gain new sources of men and money. After a decade of conflict, the army of Ahmadnagar was crushed near Jalna in 1616, but neither Bijapur nor Golconda were willing to accept Mughal supremacy.

Fratricidal conflict in the 1620s led to the reign of Shah Jahan (1628–58), and Mughal expansion continued (map 1). The Mughals made gains in the Deccan, and Bijapur and Golconda were forced to accept the status of Mughal vassals (1636). In Sind, a network of small forts manned by cavalry and musketeers further extended Mughal power.

Nevertheless, to the north, a Mughal attempt to recover their ancient homeland of Ferghana from the Uzbeks was unsuccessful. The Uzbeks were the Mughals' ancestral enemies, ruling Bukhara and Samarkand north of the Oxus and Balkh and Badakhshan to its south. Benefiting from an Uzbek civil war, a Mughal army of 60,000 was instructed to restore the exiled ruler Nazar Muhammad Khan as a tributary, or to annex the state; they occupied Balkh in 1646 with scant opposition. The following year, Mughal field artillery and musketeers competed with the more mobile Uzbeks in indecisive combats. However, the Mughals found it impossible to obtain adequate supplies from the harsh region, and in late 1647 Prince Aurangzeb evacuated Balkh. On his retreat through the snowbound Hindu Kush mountains he suffered many losses, and the Mughals decided to secure a strategic frontier line from Kashmir through Kabul to Kandahar. This was seen as essential to prevent any invasion of India from central Asia.

Kandahar had been regained from the Persians in 1638 when the Persian commander, fearing execution by his sovereign, surrendered. After the Mughal failure in Balkh, however, Shah Abbas II recaptured Kandahar in 1649. Mughal attempts to regain it in 1649, 1652, and 1653 all failed. It was difficult to campaign effectively so far from the centre of Mughal power, and success had to be achieved before the harsh winter. Mughal siege artillery was also of poorer quality and less accurate than the Persian cannon, and the latter inflicted heavy casualties on their besiegers. In 1653, three specially cast heavy guns made breaches in the walls of Kandahar, but the onset of winter and logistical problems made it impossible to exploit them. The Mughal attempt to dominate much of central Asia as well as India had failed.

Nevertheless, the Mughals were successful in other difficult regions. In the Himalayas, Garhwal fought off the Mughals in 1635 but submitted to a second expedition in 1656. Lesser Tibet, or Baltistan, was conquered in 1637 after a difficult expedition over hazardous mountain passes by 12,000 men, who had to carry all their supplies with them as the route was largely barren. In Assam, a fierce war with the Ahom in 1636–38, in which the Mughals won a major battle at Burpetah (1637) and lost a second near Kajali (1638), led to a compromise which preserved Ahom independence but advanced Mughal authority to Kamrup. Both sides made extensive use of river boats with bow-mounted cannon.

Shah Jahan ruled a massive empire with a spectacular new capital at Shahjahanabad (Delhi). In 1647, the historian Abdul Hamid Lahori listed Mughal military strength as being 200,000 stipendiary cavalry, of whom 7,000 served at court, and a central army of 40,000 garrisoned musketeers and gunners, 10,000 of whom were posted with the emperor. This army was supported by the great and rising revenues of the government. However, little attention was devoted to artillery or to the quality of firearms.

AURANGZEB AND THE MARATHAS

Shah Jahan's final illness led to a war over the succession between his four sons. Their armies were similar, the crucial elements being cavalry and artillery, and victory was the reward for superior tactics or better fighting qualities. The early morning surprise attack that led to the defeat of the Bengali forces of Muhammad Shuja near Benares in February 1658, demonstrated the former, while Aurangzeb's victories at Dharmat (February), and Samuagarh (29 May) displayed the latter. At Samuagarh, the crucial battle of the war of the Mughal succession, Aurangzeb's generalship and his well-disciplined cavalry and cannon defeated the repeated Rajput cavalry attacks of his elder brother, the designated heir Dara Shukoh.

As a consequence of Samuagarh, Aurangzeb (1658–1707) gained possession of Shahjahanabad, where he crowned himself Alamgir or 'world-seizer'. After his coronation, he routed the outnumbered and outgunned forces of his second brother Shuja, before defeating Dara again in a bitter three-day battle at Deora near Ajmer in March 1659. Dara fled, but was betrayed by Malik Jiwan, an Afghan chief with whom he had taken refuge. In August 1659, Aurangzeb had Dara killed and heavily defeated Shuja at Tanda after a fierce campaign involving flotillas on the river Ganges; Shuja was killed when he sought refuge with the King of Arakan. The third brother Murad, who had joined with Aurangzeb to defeat their father's forces at Dharmat, was imprisoned in June 1658 and executed in 1661.

Having triumphed over his brothers, the aggressive Aurangzeb sent an army which forced the Ahoms to sue for peace (1663), seized Chatgaon in an amphibious expedition (1664), and annexed the forested chiefdom of Palamu (1661). Any interest in expansion into Central Asia diminished with a series of Pathan tribal revolts. That of the

Yusufzai in 1667 was suppressed, but the Afridi, who rebelled in 1672, successfully ambushed Mughal armies in 1672, 1673, and 1674. Aurangzeb was able to restore order only by lavish payments and the construction of new fortresses. His problems led him to concentrate on the Deccan, and this was also encouraged by challenges in the area. In the western Deccan around Poona, Shivaji Bhonsla (1627–80), leader of the Marathas, a Hindu warrior caste, was creating a powerful state; by the 1660s he commanded 60,000 troops, substantial revenues, and important fortresses. In 1665, a major advance by Aurangzeb's forces under the Hindu Rajput, Jain Singh, forced Shivaji to accept an agreement which conceded most of the fortresses, but relations rapidly deteriorated, and in 1669 he asserted his independence by recapturing the fort of Sinhagad. In 1670, Shivaji sacked the major port of Surat and pressed the Mughals onto the defensive in west-central India. In the following year he drove them from their surviving bases around Poona and advanced into first Bijapur and then Golconda. The Marathas were able to hold their own against Mughal heavy cavalry and field artillery thanks to their own cavalry's superior mobility.

In 1677, Shivaji successfully invaded the Carnatic, and when he died in 1680 he left a powerful position in the Maratha homeland and a strong presence elsewhere. Unable to defeat the Marathas in the early 1680s, Aurangzeb turned to conquer the two Deccan sultanates. A lengthy siege of the massive walls of Bijapur ended with its surrender in 1685 when Mughal trenches reached the ramparts. Two years later the 4-mile (6.4km) walls of the fortress of Golconda were invested by Aurangzeb. After a lengthy siege, the city finally fell through betrayal.

In 1689, Shivaji's heir, Shambhaji, was captured and killed, and the Maratha state was annexed by the Mughals. Maratha resistance continued, however, under Shambhaji's brother Rajaram and subsequently under his young son Shivaji II. Aurangzeb spent his last years combatting the Marathas. The massive hill fortress of Jinji held out against Mughal siege until 1698; ultimately Aurangzeb was helped by the divisions among his enemies.

The Marathas relied on lightly armoured horsemen and musketeers who supported themselves by raiding. Their mobile and decentralized style of fighting system was crucial in enabling them to resist Aurangzeb effectively. The Mughal emperor finally declared a holy war against the Marathas, and in 1699 launched a systematic attack on their hill fortresses: thirteen fell, most after the bribery of their commanders. Maratha armies were not strong enough to relieve the fortresses, and Aurangzeb covered his siege forces with mobile field armies, as Louis XIV did in Europe.

In terms of weaponry, seventeenth-century Indian warfare was not innovative. Adoption of the flintlock was slower than in Europe, and the bayonet was not used. Mughal India failed to keep pace with European advances in artillery, especially in cast iron technology. There were clear signs of political and military over-extension in Aurangzeb's later years. Aside from their failure to destroy Maratha strength, the Mughals were defeated in the Battle of Itakhuli (1682) by the energetic new King of Ahom, Gadadhar Singh, and his flotillas, and the Mughals had to accept the Manas river as a frontier. A serious revolt in 1696–98 challenged Mughal rule in Bengal, but was eventually suppressed. From the mid-1680s, there were growing problems with the Jats, although when their stronghold of Sinsini was captured in the early 1690s the situation was temporarily stabilized.

Nonetheless, the ability of the Mughals to maintain their dominance of northern India even when Aurangzeb and most of his army were engaged in protracted conflict with the Marathas was significant. Whatever the deficiencies of the Mughal regime in the Emperor's last years, European rulers would have considered themselves fortunate to wield such power.

The Mughals had failed to develop as a naval power. Their attempt to advance their north-western border had also been unsuccessful. They had not challenged Uzbek control of Bukhara and Samarkand and had been unable to hold Balkh but, despite this, the Uzbeks were not able to repeat the earlier success of the Mughals against the Lodi Sultanate in the 1520s.

In comparative terms, the Mughals were far more successful in the seventeenth century than the Ming, and were appreciably more successful than the Ottoman Turks. Mughal armies had to adapt to a bewildering variety of environments, from the equatorial heat and humidity of the forested Brahmaputra valley to the arid plains and snowy mountains of central Asia. Their troops, military system, and generalship proved equal to the challenge.

MAP 1

Mughal expansion was, in some respects, more impressive than that of the Russians in Siberia and the Manchus in Mongolia and Sinkiang, because it brought control over well-developed and populous polities. Mughal India was, however, very much a land power. The most intractable problems were on the Persian (Safavid) and Uzbek frontiers, and also in the Deccan: the latter led to repeated campaigns against Bijapur, Golconda, and the Marathas. The Ahoms of Assam were also difficult opponents who could not be decisively defeated.

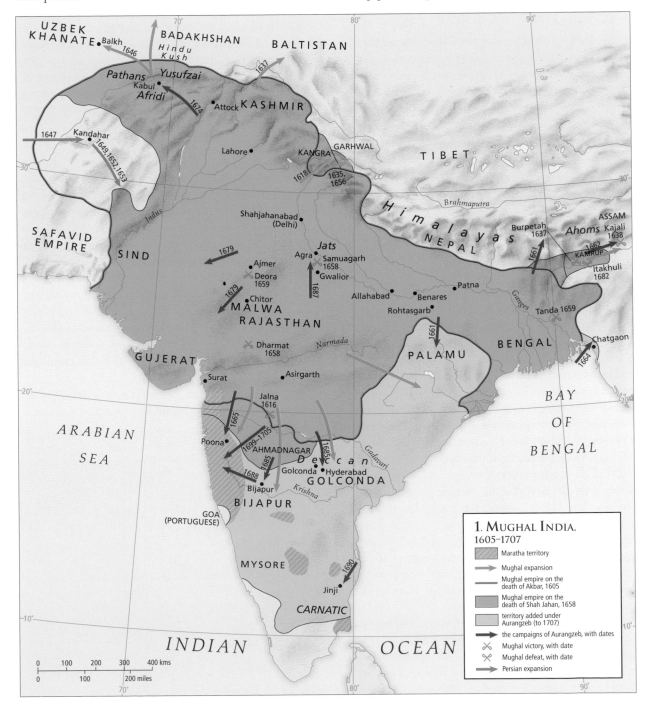

THE FALL OF MING CHINA

WEAKNESS in the Ming empire in the first half of the seventeenth century was accompanied by the emergence of south-eastern Manchuria as a major military power. Profiting from rivalry between Chinese warlords and from captured weapons technology, the Manchus gained control of China, overcame a pro-Ming rebellion, and established a dynamic new dynasty.

THE RISE OF THE MANCHUS

In the 1590s, the Ming had been able to send massive armies to help the Koreans against Japanese invasion (*page 20*). But in 1644 the last Ming emperor, the weak Ch'ung-Chen, committed suicide. The following dynasty, the Ch'ing (1644–1911), was established by a non-Chinese people, the Manchus. The fall of the Ming, however, was due not to foreign conquest but to a crisis produced by internal instability and disorder. From 1582, there were weak emperors, increasingly arbitrary central government, and oppressive taxation. This encouraged both rebellion and a quest for power among ambitious leaders. Major rebellions included one in Fuchow (1607) and the White Lotus uprising in Shantung (1625). From 1628 there was a major series of rebellions in central China, and from 1636 these spread to include much of the north. Out of this chaos, two regional warlords emerged.

In the early 1640s, Chang Hsien-Chung (1605–47) dominated the Yangtze valley and the eastern plain, and from 1644 established himself in Szechwan. Li Tzu-Ch'eng (c.1605–45), a former bandit, was more powerful in the north; from 1641 he controlled Shansi, Hupeh, and Honan, and in 1644, helped by supporters within the walls, captured Peking (25 April) and crowned himself emperor.

His ambitions, however, were thwarted by the Manchus. They were originally based in the mountains of south-eastern Manchuria, expanding under Nurhachi (1559–1626), with the aid of some Chinese, to dominate the lands to the north of the Great Wall in the early seventeenth century. Nurhachi developed a strong cavalry army based on horse archers and used this to gain control of most of northern Manchuria by 1616. In 1618 he attacked the Chinese, capturing Fushun and defeating a far larger army at Sarhu. Liaoyang and Mukden fell in 1621, but in 1625 the Ming used cannon to repel an attack on Ningyan. From 1625 the Manchu capital was at Mukden.

Under Abahai (1626–43) and Dorgon (1643–50) the Manchus continued dynamic expansion (*map 1*). After invasions in 1627 and 1636–37, Korea was reduced to vassal status, and Inner Mongolia became a dependency in 1633. In 1629 the Manchus captured Chinese artillerymen skilled in casting Portuguese cannon, and by 1631 the captives had made them about forty. Plundering expeditions into northern China in 1632 and 1634 were followed by a major invasion in 1638–40 which captured many cities in Shantung and Chihli. The Ming loss of Chinchow was followed by the defection of Hung Ch'eng-Ch'ou, who became a Manchu general and captured Hankow (1645) and Nanking (1646), and pacified Fukien (1646).

Li Tzu-Ch'eng's coup against the Ming provoked the Manchus to intervene and proclaim a new dynasty. Wu San-Kuei (1612–78), who commanded the largest Chinese army on the northern frontier, refused to submit to Li and instead supported the Manchus. Li was crushed by the Manchu cavalry at the Battle of the Pass (Shanghai-Kwan) on 27 May 1644, then abandoned Peking, and was pursued into Shensi and Hupeh and killed (October 1645). Chang Hsien-Chung was defeated and executed by the Manchus in 1647.

CHALLENGE IN THE SOUTH

Ming resistance was continued in the south by Emperor Chu Yu-sung, who was based at Nanking, but his loyalist officials lacked the necessary expertise to hold off the Manchus. Most of the country fell rapidly to the Manchus: the north and east in 1644–45, Szechwan in 1646, Canton in 1650, and much of the south by 1652, although their position was challenged by Cheng Ch'eng-Kung (known to Europeans as Coxinga) who, with the profits of piracy and trade, had developed a large fleet based on Fukien and amassed an army of over 100,000 equipped with European-style weapons. In 1656–58, he regained much of southern China for the Ming, but in 1659 failed to take Nanking, and the Manchus advanced into Fukien. In the same year they gained Yunnan.

Deprived of his mainland bases, Coxinga turned his attention to Taiwan, which had not previously been Chinese

The centre of the Chinese world: a view of the Imperial Court at Peking during the Manchu period. The last Ming emperor, Ch'ung-Chen, committed suicide in the court complex.

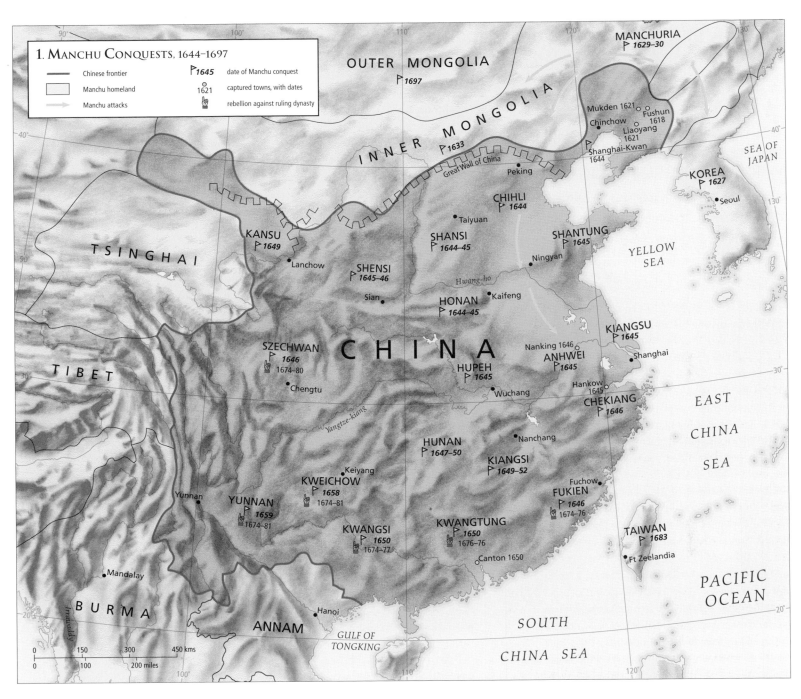

1. MANCHU CONQUESTS, 1644–1697

⎯⎯ Chinese frontier	⌷ *1645* date of Manchu conquest
▢ Manchu homeland	○ *1621* captured towns, with dates
→ Manchu attacks	✊ rebellion against ruling dynasty

MAP 1

The most populous state in the world fell rapidly to a newly-emerged power that displayed a successful combination of determination, political skill, and military decisiveness. North China fell comparatively rapidly, but it was necessary to make repeated campaigns in order to conquer southern China.

and was still largely under Dutch control. Coxinga invaded the island in 1661 with a force of 25,000 men and 300 junks, and after a 9-month siege, in which he employed 28 European-style cannon, he took the Dutch base of Fort Zeelandia. Attempts were made from Batavia to relieve the outnumbered garrison, but they failed, and Fort Zeelandia surrendered after the walls of its Utrecht redoubt collapsed under heavy fire. In 1662, Coxinga was succeeded by his eldest son Ch'eng Ching, who consolidated his father's position. After his death in 1680, the family was divided and in 1681 was badly defeated by a newly-constructed Chinese navy. Taiwan surrendered in 1683 after the Manchu fleet defeated the nearby Pescadores pirates.

This was the last stage in the suppression of the Rebellion of the Three Feudatories, a rebellion begun in December 1673 by powerful generals who were the governors of the

southern and western provinces. By 1677, the rebellion had been confined to the south-west, where the most important of the rebels, Wu San-Kuei, the governor of Yunnan and Kweichow, died in 1678; order was restored in his former provinces in 1681 and Taiwan, which had supported the rebellion, was conquered. Free of domestic problems, the Ch'ing government conquered Outer Mongolia in 1696–97. The long reign of K'ang-hsi (1661–1722) was a period of consolidation. After the 1680s, there was no major internal disorder and revenues improved.

Warfare in China demonstrated the close relationship between the political and the military. Manchu success owed much to the continuity they maintained in important aspects of Ming society. As with other civil conflicts, politics was crucial to military strategy, while the quality of military leadership was all-important in politics.

CONFLICT IN SUB-SAHARAN AFRICA

AFRICAN WARFARE *in the seventeenth century featured a variety of conflicts between African states, between native Africans and Europeans, and between the non-African powers themselves. The spread of firearms was accompanied by greater emphasis on missile tactics and by a growth in armies, but the most dynamic powers remained African rather than colonial.*

INTER-AFRICAN CONFLICT

Across the Sudan, Islam had a major impact on warfare by offering an ideological justification for the seizing of territory and people and by strengthening links with North Africa, a source of firearms and horses. Thus, at the beginning of the century, Mai Idris Aloma used weapons from Tripoli and Tunis and captured slaves by raiding to turn Bornu into a major power. Bornu was later undermined by the Tuareg, but further east three other states developed in the Sudan: Baquirmi, Darfur, and Wadai. These states likewise used their military strength to acquire slaves which they sent to North Africa.

The development of African states owed much to the leadership of individual rulers. In Madagascar, the Sakalava became important under Andriandahifotsi (c.1610–85) and his son Andrianmanetriarivo (c.1685–1718), while in the centre of the island the Kingdom of Merina developed: it was given cohesion by a sacred monarchy, force by firearms, and purpose by warfare for slaves. Fasilidas (1632–67) and Iyasu the Great (1680–1704) maintained Ethiopia as a significant power, while to the north of Lake Victoria the kings of Buganda expanded their influence.

African warfare was transformed by the increasing preponderance of firepower over hand-to-hand combat and by a growing use of larger armies; the armies of the major states began to campaign over long distances. In West Africa, prior to the use of firearms armies fought in close order, with javelinmen in the front line and archers behind, providing overhead fire. The javelins could be thrown or used as pikes and the javelinmen were also equipped with swords, and therefore able to fight as individuals in 'open' order. Shock warfare prevailed. Lacking shields, the archers were essentially support troops, and the bow lacked the prestige of the javelin and sword.

From the mid-seventeenth century on, the role of archers increased in Akwamu and Denkyira, inland states of West Africa, and as firepower became more important this led to a more open formation and a wider battle frontage, with archers in the front line flanking the javelinmen. Thus missile tactics came to prevail in West Africa before the widespread use of firearms. This had social implications: war-

fare based on shock tactics was selective in its manpower requirements, but in Akwamu and Denkyira all males fit to bear arms were eligible for conscription. The new military methods spread, for example to Asante in the 1670s. Javelinmen came to play a tactical role subordinate to that of the bowmen, and between the 1660s and the 1690s the javelin was discarded as a military weapon, becoming (like the halberd in Europe) essentially ceremonial. In turn, the bow was supplanted by the musket.

THE SPREAD OF FIREARMS

Firearms came into use in Africa over a long timespan. The use of firearms was first reported in Kano in the fifteenth century, but a regular force of musketeers was not organized there until the 1770s. In the forest interior of West Africa, muskets replaced bows in the 1690s and 1700s. On the West African coast, the Asebu army of the 1620s was the first to include a corps of musketeers, their guns being supplied by the Dutch. Muskets replaced bows in the 1650s to 1670s, but the tactical shift towards open-order fighting did not come until later: musketeers were used as a shield for the javelinmen, and tactics centred on missile warfare were slow to develop in the coastal armies. Firepower increased in the 1680s and 1690s as flintlock muskets replaced matchlocks, but bayonets were not used.

The new emphasis on missile weapons, bows, and later muskets, interacted with socio-economic changes, in particular with the transformation of peasants into militarily effective soldiers. This development led to the formation of mass armies and to wars which lasted longer and took place over much wider areas. This new warfare led to the rise of Asante and Dahomey and maybe to the late seventeenth-century expansion of Oyo.

COLONIAL WARFARE

Struggles between African and non-African peoples were most important in the Portuguese colonies of Angola and Mozambique. The Portuguese sought to penetrate up the Zambezi towards the kingdom of Mutapa in modern Zimbabwe. In both areas, however, the limitations of Portuguese musketeers were revealed. Their slow rate of fire and the open-order fighting methods of their opponents reduced their effectiveness, and the Portuguese failed to maintain their position on the upper Zambezi. In Angola, the Portuguese were effective only when in combination with African soldiers; indeed the Portuguese army in Angola was essentially an African force with European officers and some European troops.

When they were left without African light infantry, Portuguese forces could be destroyed, as by Queen Njinga of the Ndongo at the Battle of Ngolomene at Kweta (1644), but the combination of Africans and European infantry, with its body armour and swordsmanship, was effective, as in the eventual Portuguese victories over Njinga at Cavanga (1646), and over Kongo at Ambuila (1665). On the other hand, the impact of firearms on the shield-bearing Kongo heavy infantry was decisive at the Battle of Mbumbi (1622). Yet on the whole, the Portuguese were no more effective with flintlocks than they had been with matchlocks, and the role of their firearms should not be exaggerated; indeed the expanding Lunda state did not use muskets until the mid-eighteenth century.

A long series of wars against the Kingdom of Ndongo, begun in 1579, ended in stalemate for the Portuguese in the early 1680s. The Portuguese victory over Kongo at Ambuila has attracted attention, but Portugal's real opportunity was provided by a serious civil war in Kongo, and Kongo did not collapse rapidly as the Aztecs and Incas had done: Portuguese efforts to overcome it had a long history. On the East African coast, the Portuguese base of Fort Jesus at Mombasa, built in 1593–96, fell in 1631 to a surprise storming by Sultan Muhammad Yusif of Mombasa, and the Portuguese failed to regain it in 1632; they were able to return only when the Sultan abandoned the fortress.

EUROPEAN RIVALRIES

There were several important conflicts between non-African powers. The struggle for dominance on the Guinea coast was especially acute during the period of Anglo-Dutch antagonism between the 1650s and 1670s. Earlier, the resumption of war between the Spanish and the Dutch in 1621 had also involved Portugal, which was then ruled by the King of Spain. In 1637, a Dutch fleet took Elmina, the leading Portuguese base on the Gold Coast. In 1641, Fernando Po, Luanda, and Benguela followed, but in 1648 they were recaptured.

On the East African coast, the Portuguese were affected by the rise of Omani naval power, not least because the Portuguese military presence was scanty: they were short of men, ships, and money. In 1661, the Omanis sacked Mombasa, avoiding Fort Jesus; in 1670 they pillaged Mozambique but were repulsed by the fortress garrison; and in 1678 the Portuguese successfully besieged Pate but then withdrew in the face of an Omani relief force. Fort Jesus finally fell after a lengthy siege in 1698.

The military history of Africa in the seventeenth century was similar to that of other parts of the world. Very varied military systems co-existed and competed, but there were also important shifts, in particular towards larger armies in which missile weapons played a major role. European impact was largely indirect, in the form of supplies of guns. African states were not naval powers, and the principal challenges by sea came from Europe and from Oman.

MAP 1

Conflict between Europeans and Africans was most marked in Angola and modern Zimbabwe. The empire of Mutapa split into a number of states which became Portuguese vassals, but there were serious risings in 1631 and in 1693. Changamira of Butua drove the Portuguese from the plateau, and they retreated to Tete.

The French fort at Gorée, an important base for trade in slaves and gum.

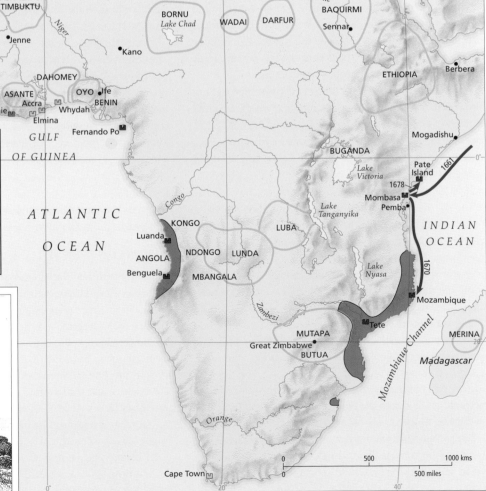

THE STRUGGLE FOR NORTH AMERICA

THE SEVENTEENTH century was a period of European expansion in North America, with the creation of French colonies in Nova Scotia and the St Lawrence valley and of English colonies along the eastern seaboard. Europeans faced serious difficulties: America was an unknown continent, the numbers of Europeans were limited, and the Native Americans were determined opponents.

EUROPEANS AND NATIVE AMERICANS

Conflict between Native Americans and English settlers on the eastern seaboard of North America in the seventeenth century was sporadic and localized, but emphasizes the lack of any clear military advantage on either side. In 1622, the local tribes launched a surprise attack designed to wipe out the colony established in Virginia in 1607. They were repelled only after 347 people, a fifth of the colony's population, had been killed. From the 1640s, the spread of firearms among the native peoples made them even more effective opponents of the English colonists: the rising in New England of 1675, King Philip's War, was suppressed with considerable difficulty. Some Native American tribes learned to use bastions as early as the 1670s. The military balance in the region was not to shift significantly in favour of the Europeans until the following century.

The Spanish also advanced north in the seventeenth century. The pueblos of the upper Rio Grande were conquered in 1598, becoming the isolated colony of New Mexico, and over the following century the province of New Vizcaya expanded north to meet it. Lower California was also brought within the Spanish orbit, and in 1696 a garrison was established at Pensacola in Florida.

The most powerful tribe in the St Lawrence region in 1600 was the Mohawk, and they resisted French expansion for much of the century. The French established a trading post at Tadoussac at the mouth of the Saguenay river over the winter of 1600–01, and another at Québec in 1608, but their participation in the lucrative fur trade necessitated their involvement in local wars; Samuel de Champlain, leader of the French expeditions, took the side of the Huron against the Mohawk. In 1626, the Mohawk attacked Dutch settlers in the Hudson valley, who were trying to trade to the north of the St Lawrence, and defeated a force of Dutch and Algonquian Mohicans. In 1645, Mohawk attacks forced the French to abandon Fort Richelieu, established at the mouth of the Richelieu river in 1642.

The growing presence of Europeans and the greater commercial opportunities they provided for the native peoples led to an increase in warfare between the tribes, and to growing European involvement in it. The French had ini-

tially refused to supply firearms, but the Dutch provided them, and as warfare increased in scope, restrictions on the supply of firearms decreased. In the early 1640s, the French began to sell muskets to baptized native allies to strengthen them against the Mohawk, who themselves traded freely for Dutch muskets after agreements in 1643 and 1648.

By 1648, the Mohawk had amassed at least 800 muskets, and in the late 1640s they had sufficient firepower to destroy their traditional enemies, the Huron, Petun, and Nipissing tribes. It proved impossible to unite their opponents: whereas the Mohawk, like the other Iroquois, fought on a tribal or confederacy basis, the Huron fought, and were destroyed, village by village.

Having failed to provide the Huron with adequate support, the French suffered further Iroquois attacks after war resumed in 1658, and trade from the St Lawrence to the interior was blocked. In 1665, however, the French government sent 600 men to 'exterminate' the Iroquois. The new force built five forts from the mouth of the Richelieu river to Lake Champlain, and the four western Iroquois tribes negotiated peace. The isolated Mohawk left negotiations too late, and in 1666, 600 regulars, 600 militiamen and 100 Indian allies led by Alexandre de Prouville de Tracy burned the four major Mohawk villages and their crops and forced them to accept terms.

Thereafter, French trade, influence, and power expanded. The construction of Fort Frontenac (1673) and Fort Niagara (1676) on Lake Ontario took the French presence westwards, but in the early 1680s the English encouraged the Iroquois to resume hostilities: in 1684, the French were compelled to withdraw protection from the Illinois and Miami tribes. Reinforcements arrived from France in 1685 and 1694 and the French, with their native allies, took the initiative, destroying the Mohawk villages in a bold winter raid in 1693 and those of the Onondaga and Oneida in 1696. Left isolated by the Anglo-French peace of 1697, the Iroquois came to terms with the French in 1701.

THE NATURE OF THE STRUGGLE

Many Native American tribes were happy to trade with the Europeans, but all were disinclined to lose their lands to them. The natives were better attuned to fighting in the unmapped hinterland, and their general lack of fixed battle positions made it difficult for the Europeans to devise clear military goals. Furthermore, as experts with bows and arrows, the eastern American peoples were adept in missile warfare, and thus were more readily able to make the transition to muskets. These factors combined to reduce any significant advantage in military technology the settlers might have possessed.

Ambushes and raiding played a vital role in fighting in the interior. Major raids, such as those of the French and their allies on the Seneca in 1687, or of the Iroquois near

MAP 1
Although increasingly active along the Atlantic seaboard and the Gulf of Mexico, European penetration into the interior of North America was limited (*opposite*), and most Native Americans had never seen a European.

Native American weapons, such as this metal tomahawk, proved deadly in close-quarter fighting in North America. The Native Americans also used firearms acquired from Europeans, inflicting terrible losses. A Native American in combat chose a specific opponent, aimed directly at that individual, and used acquired abilities in marksmanship to kill or wound him.

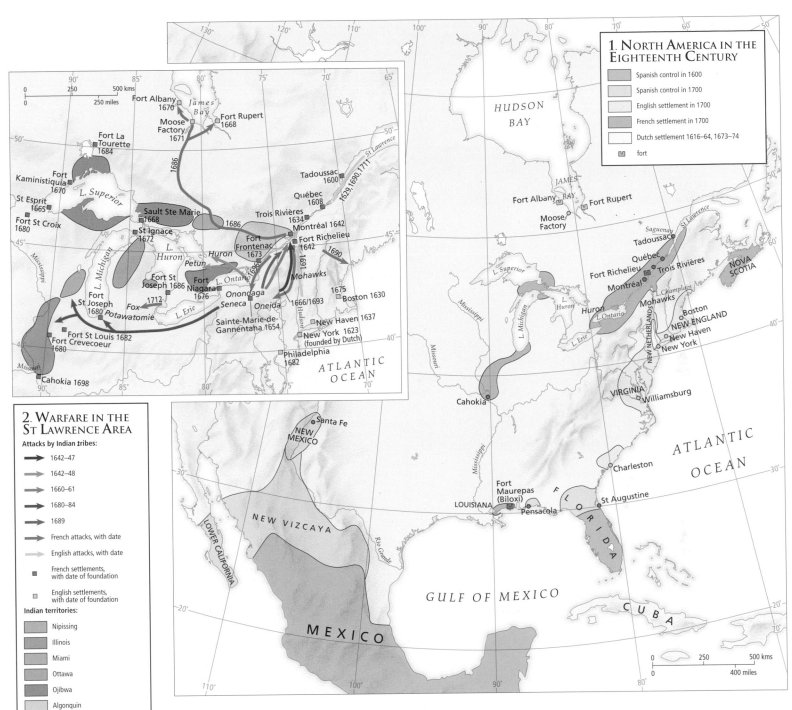

1. NORTH AMERICA IN THE EIGHTEENTH CENTURY

- Spanish control in 1600
- Spanish control in 1700
- English settlement in 1700
- French settlement in 1700
- Dutch settlement 1616–64, 1673–74
- fort

2. WARFARE IN THE ST LAWRENCE AREA

Attacks by Indian tribes:
- 1642–47
- 1642–48
- 1660–61
- 1680–84
- 1689
- French attacks, with date
- English attacks, with date
- French settlements, with date of foundation
- English settlements, with date of foundation

Indian territories:
- Nipissing
- Illinois
- Miami
- Ottawa
- Ojibwa
- Algonquin

Fox   Indian tribe

MAP 2

The Iroquois proved a formidable obstacle to the French but were eventually forced to come to terms with them in 1701 (*above, inset map*). French expansion from the St Lawrence led to the construction of posts in the Great Lakes region.

Montréal in 1689, destroyed food supplies vital for campaigning. Fortresses were important because they could resist and harass raiding parties, but they did not guarantee control. In 1658, the French garrison of Sainte-Marie-de-Gannentaha fled when warned of imminent attack.

As in Siberia (*page 34*), rivalries among the native populations were crucial in the struggle between the natives and the settlers. The Iroquois were pushed out of southern Ontario by the Ottawa and Ojibwa in the late 1690s, while near Detroit, the French allied with the Ottawa and Potawatomie against the Fox in 1712.

Unlike Siberia, however, there was also competition and conflict between the European powers. In the 1690s, the Spanish sought to block French ambitions in Louisiana, while in 1664 the English captured New Netherland from the Dutch. But the most important rivalry was between the English and the French: in 1629, Québec was starved into surrender by an English force, though it was returned in 1632; the two powers competed in Nova Scotia and in the Hudson Bay area; in 1686, the French struck overland against the English on James Bay where 105 men captured Moose Factory, Fort Rupert, Fort Albany, and 50,000 prime beaver which were crucial to the English fur trade. The English recaptured Fort Albany, but attempts on Québec failed in 1690 and 1711.

Nevertheless, the population of English North America was growing far more rapidly than that of its French counterpart, and this was to be of great importance when the struggle between the two powers became more intense in the mid-eighteenth century (*page 146*).

II

WARFARE IN
EUROPE, 1490-1600

Europen warfare is generally thought of in terms of struggles between states, and this was certainly the most important level of conflict. However, it is also important to note the degree of 'popular' warfare in the period. The best-known instance of this is the German Peasants' War of 1524–5, a major conflict motivated by social tension and economic discontent, encouraged by the volatile atmosphere in Reformation Europe. In France, there were a series of peasant risings in 1593–4 directed against seigneurial abuses, and in favour of the end of the French Wars of Religion. Though the French peasant bands were sometimes numerous, over 5,000 strong in some cases, they were generally defeated by professional forces. These conflicts are an important reminder of the role played by irregular forces in the warfare of the period. Urban elements also played an important role in sixteenth-century conflict; on the Day of the Barricades, 12 May 1588, Henry III was expelled from Paris, despite his force of 4,000 Swiss guards.

Yet this was also a period of growing governmental strength and sophistication. This was most apparent at sea, where fleets far larger and more powerful than those of the fifteenth century were created and maintained. It was also obvious in the ambitious fortification programmes, which entailed considerable expenditure. Fortifications designed to cope with artillery were first constructed in large numbers in Italy, and the techniques of these bastioned works were then spread by Italian architects. Cities, such as Florence in 1534, Ancona in 1536, and Genoa in 1536–8, acquired new-style fortifications, clear signs of the impact of artillery. Although the limited mobility and slow rate of fire of cannon did not prevent them from playing a crucial role in sieges and at sea (where the mobility of ships compensated for the immobility of cannon), they were less important in battle. The crucial firearms there were hand-held, but, although important, they were not yet sufficiently developed to drive cutting, stabbing, and slashing weapons from the field.

WARFARE IN RENAISSANCE ITALY

EUROPEAN WARFARE *was revolutionized by gunpowder in the fifteenth century, a development seen as one of the crucial shifts from medieval to modern times. In the Italian wars which brought the century to a close and continued for the first half of the next, the search for the most effective means of employing gunpowder weapons led to a remarkable period of tactical experimentation.*

THE IMPACT OF GUNPOWDER

Knowledge of gunpowder was brought from China to Europe in the thirteenth century, although the path of diffusion is unclear. In the following century it was used in cannon, and in the fifteenth century in hand-held firearms. Between 1380 and 1525 gunpowder led to the supplanting of earlier missile weapons, particularly the crossbow and longbow. It also brought major changes in battlefield tactics, fortification techniques, and siegecraft, and, more generally, in training, logistics, and military finance. Outgunned powers, such as Moorish Granada, were overcome by better-armed opponents, and cannon came to play a greater operational role in campaigns.

The Italian Wars (1494–1559) saw the working through of these themes. Gunpowder technology had played a role in earlier conflicts, as with the use of cannon in the French defeats of the English at Formigny (1450) and Castillon (1453), the closing battles of the Hundred Years' War, and handguns became effective from mid-century, as in the Burgundian wars against the Liégeois, and the Swiss and Burgundian wars of 1475–77. The arquebus, a handgun in which the powder was ignited by a length of slow-burning match, was developed in the 1420s and 1430s; by 1450 the Burgundians and the French had them in large numbers. The arquebus was used in Italy with devastating effect.

The wars in Italy arose partly from the instability of the Italian peninsula, which was divided among a number of states, but also from a new willingness of outside powers

RAVENNA 11 APRIL 1512

The formation in October 1511 of the anti-French Holy League to drive the French from Italy led to a resumption of Franco-Spanish hostilities. The French, under Gaston de Foix, besieged Ravenna, and a Spanish relieving force took up a nearby defensive position. To force them to attack, the French artillery bombarded the Spanish, finally prompting a Spanish cavalry charge. This was repelled by French cavalry, but Spanish arquebusiers, sheltered by a parapet, defeated an advance by French crossbowmen. German pikemen (*landsknechts*) in French service were more successful, but were forced back by Spanish swordsmen. Finally, the French cavalry, supported by artillery, exploited gaps in the Spanish defensive system to turn the flank of the swordsmen, although the Spanish infantry maintained cohesion and retreated successfully. The French had won, largely thanks to superior co-ordination of the various arms of their forces. Casualties in the battle were heavy – about 4,000 in the French army and 9,000 in the Spanish. The battle represented a remarkable competition of different weapons systems, reflecting the state of flux in weaponry in the period and also the degree to which perceived `national' differences determined fighting methods. The Swiss and Germans were noted as pikemen, equally formidable in offence and defence, but vulnerable to firearms and tactically less flexible than the Spanish swordsmen (or sword-and-buckler men). The latter had a considerable advantage in close-quarter fighting: they could get under the pikes by pushing them up with their shields Ravenna also demonstrated the importance of firepower. The first two hours of the battle were taken up by an artillery duel, and it was French artillery fire that provoked the Spanish to charge.

An engraving of the Battle of Ravenna indicates the continued importance of cavalry.

to intervene. Initially the most important was France, whose Valois monarchs, in particular Louis XI (1461–83), had strengthened their government and extended their territorial control within France, especially through the defeat of England and Burgundy. The French had a standing (permanent) army, the first in western Europe for a dynasty ruling a 'national' state, and an impressive train of artillery on wheeled carriages; with these Charles VIII of France marched on Naples in 1494–95.

Charles VIII' capture of Naples aroused opposition from within Italy, from Maximilian I (the Habsburg ruler of Austria and Holy Roman Emperor) and from Ferdinand of Aragon, ruler of Sicily. Charles was forced to withdraw,

although an attempt to cut off his retreat failed at Fornovo (1495), where the Italian forces had numerical superiority but were poorly co-ordinated.

In 1499, Charles' successor Louis XII invaded Italy and seized Naples. The value of the new weapons was most clearly demonstrated at Cerignola (1503), a battle which arose from the inability of Louis and Ferdinand to settle their differences over the partition of the kingdom of Naples. The Spanish were commanded by Gonzalo of Córdoba (the 'Great Captain') who had greatly increased the number of arquebusiers in his army. He held his men in defence behind a trench and parapet which stopped the attacking French cavalry, exposing them and their infantry first to

MAP 1

The first stage of the Italian wars saw France unable to sustain an initial advantage and confronted by the rising power of Spain. Charles VIII's initial advance both aroused opposition within Italy and led to Spanish intervention. Much of the conflict took place in the strategic Duchy of Milan, and in nearby areas of northern Italy.

Spanish fire and then to a successful counter-attack. Córdoba's revival of the long-lost art of field fortification had been used to devastating effect.

COMPETING WEAPONS SYSTEMS

Cerignola was the first in a series of battles in which a variety of weapons, weapon systems, and tactics were tested in the search for a clear margin of military superiority. Thus at Novara (1513), advancing pikemen competed with artillery. French cannon inflicted heavy casualties until overrun by the experienced Swiss pikemen, thanks to the weakness of the French position – they had not had time to entrench – and the inferior quality of the French pikemen.

Military power in Italy was increasingly dominated by France and Spain, which alone had the resources to support major military effort. In contrast, other powers, particularly Venice (defeated by France at Agnadello in 1509), Milan, and the Swiss, took less important and less independent roles. The stronger states played a major part in what can be seen as the 'military revolution' of the period. This is customarily presented in terms of new weapons technology, for example the spread of new artillery-resistant fortification techniques. However, the potential of handguns was still very limited, and too close a focus on gunpowder weapons makes it easy to overlook the importance of the pike, which transformed infantry tactics. The pike was useless as an individual weapon, but was devastating en masse in disciplined formations. This led to a need for trained, professional infantry, far superior to most medieval levies. Handguns were used in conjunction with pikes until about 1700, though the ratio in which they were normally employed during the period changed significantly in favour of the former.

The decisiveness of artillery in siege warfare was lessened by the improvement in fortification techniques, and cannon were still of limited value in more mobile battles.

The ability of European states to finance military activity increased in the late fifteenth and early sixteenth centuries, with their greater political consolidation, administrative development, and economic growth, as populations recovered from the fourteenth-century Black Death. But for many states this process was to be challenged from the 1520s onwards as the impact of the Protestant Reformation increased domestic divisions.

During the sixteenth century, there were some further improvements in firearms. The musket, a heavier version of the arquebus, capable of firing a heavier shot further, was used on the battlefield from the 1550s. It was a cumbersome weapon which required a portable rest to support the barrel. From the 1520s, the wheel-lock mechanism also spread. Unlike the arquebus, which required a lighted fuse, the wheel-lock musket relied on a trigger-operated spring which brought together a piece of pyrites or flint and a turning steel wheel. The contact produced sparks which ignited the gunpowder.

The wheel-lock mechanism was more expensive and more delicate than the matchlock, but was better suited to the needs of the cavalry, as it required only one hand to operate. Wheel-lock mechanisms worked the cavalry carbine and the horse pistol, the latter weapon being used in the tactic of the *caracole*, in which lines of cavalry advanced in order and fired their pistols before wheeling away from the enemy. This tactic proved effective against stationary unsupported infantry, but was useless against mobile and energetic cavalry.

Aside from new equipment, another major cause of increasing military expenditure was new fortifications, for example the rebuilding of Verona and the new citadel of Turin. Cannon were most effective against the stationary target of high walls, so fortifications were consequently redesigned to provide lower, denser, and more complex targets, the new system known as the *trace italienne*. Bastions, generally quadrilateral, angled, and at regular intervals along all walls, were introduced to provide effective flanking fire, while defences were lowered and strengthened with earth. Stronger defences, which also provided secure artillery platforms, obliged attacking forces to mount sieges with more extensive lines of blockade and therefore to employ larger numbers of troops.

Fortresses and sieges featured importantly in the Italian Wars, and in all the warfare of the period. A series of unsuccessful sieges marked the limits of Ottoman advance. Charles V's unsuccessful Siege of Metz in 1552 led to his loss of strategic impetus. Fortresses were significant as a concrete manifestation of control over an area. It is striking how many battles were related to attempts to relieve sieges. However, the expense of constructing, maintaining, and garrisoning such positions was a major burden, one of the many ways in this period in which war pressed heavily on state budgets.

While elaborate suits of armour continued to be produced, in this case in Italy in the 1550s, mounted squadrons of pistol men became more effective in mid-century, and they did not tend to wear full suits of armour. In 1552, German horsemen armed with pistols defeated the French as Saint-Vincent. Such horsemen also pressed the Swiss square at the Battle of Dreux (1562), but they were eventually driven back.

THE FRANCO-HABSBURG WARS, 1521-1559

THE ELECTION of Charles, Duke of Burgundy, King of Spain, and Archduke of Austria as Holy Roman Emperor in 1519 seemed to confirm the worst French fears of Habsburg hegemony. Francis I declared war in 1521, but further French campaigns brought a succession of defeats at the hands of the most effective military system in western Europe.

MAP 1

The struggle between Valois and Habsburg led to conflict across much of western Europe, with especially intense fighting in Italy, Flanders, and along France's eastern borderlands. The Habsburgs emerged victorious.

FIELD FORTIFICATIONS AT BICOCCA

As at the end of the fifteenth century, geography and politics ensured that the main theatre of conflict between France and the Habsburgs would be northern Italy. The French declaration of war was followed by the loss of Milan in November the same year and by a major defeat at nearby Bicocca on 24 June 1522.

Bicocca was a battle in which the limited control of commanders over their forces played a major role. The French commander Odet de Foix, Marquis de Lautrec, was in a powerful position, besieging Pavia with a larger army, and thus obliging the Habsburgs to attempt a hazardous relief operation. But he was short of funds and his core troops, Swiss mercenaries, were under only limited control. The Habsburg relief army, under Prosper Colonna, was entrenched close to Pavia, and Lautrec hoped to cut its supply routes, thus forcing Colonna into the open. The Swiss, however, demanded an immediate attack on Colonna's position in order to gain booty.

The increased emphasis on fortification that had become a feature of the Italian Wars can be seen clearly in Colonna's position. Behind a sunken road was a parapet manned by four lines of arquebusiers backed by pikemen. Cannon were well-sited in a series of bastions. Lautrec appreciated that this would be a difficult position to take and proposed to bring up artillery to prepare for his attack.

The Swiss refused to wait and, in two squares, their 8,000 men advanced. They took heavy losses from cannon and arquebuses, losses which mounted as they struggled to scale the parapet. Those who did so were driven back by *landsknechts* (German pikemen). Having lost 3,000 men, the Swiss returned home; their subsequent caution at the Battle of Pavia was attributed to their losses at Bicocca.

The Swiss losses fuelled the anti-mercenary propaganda campaign launched by the leading Swiss Protestant, Ulrich Zwingli, who had served as an army chaplain. Lautrec was left without an effective army and the French position in northern Italy collapsed.

RENEWED FRENCH EFFORTS

The French regained Milan in late 1524, but were again defeated nearby, at Pavia (*page 52*). The captured Francis I of France signed the Treaty of Madrid on Charles V's terms but, once released, claimed that his agreement had been extorted and resumed hostilities in 1526. After a heavy defeat at Landriano (1529), Francis accepted the Treaty of Cambrai, abandoning his Italian pretensions.

War resumed in 1536, but proved indecisive, and the Truce of Nice was negotiated in 1538. In 1543, Francis attacked Charles in the Low Countries and northern Spain; in the following year, the French won the Battle of Ceresole in Piedmont. Although the infantry were well-matched, the superior and more numerous French cavalry defeated their opponents and the *landsknechts* withdrew, their casualties over twenty-five per cent. The relatively immobile artillery played little role in the battle. In 1544, Charles and his ally Henry VIII of England invaded France, forcing Francis to accept terms. In 1546, the Duke of Alba led Habsburg forces against the Schmalkaldic League of German Protestants, defeating them at Mühlberg in 1547.

1. FRANCO-HABSBURG WARS, 1521–1559

Habsburg possessions

French gains

✂ Habsburg victories

✂ Habsburg defeats

PAVIA 25 FEBRUARY 1525

The strategic importance of Lombardy ensured that the Battle of Bicocca was followed by a further major action in the same area. A renewed French siege of Pavia led to an engagement which brought rivalry between Francis I and the Habsburgs to a climax.

A Spanish relief army dug in facing the French siege lines. The French were weakened by the detachment of a column to attack Naples and by the desertion of 6,000 Swiss. Encouraged by their

the Swiss pikemen in French service was thrown back by the arquebusiers. Finally, a combination of Spanish pikemen and arquebusiers defeated the renegade 'Black Band' *landsknechts*, whose French service was illegal under the constitution of the Empire. At the close of the day, Francis himself was captured.

Tapestry depicting the battle of Pavia, Brussels 1525–32.

resulting numerical advantage and pressurized by their dwindling finances, the Spanish attacked quickly. They achieved surprise by breaching the French lines in the dark and, having placed themselves across French communications, adopted a defensive position to await French counter-attacks.

The Spanish – with arquebusiers on the flanks and pikemen and cavalry in the centre – faced a French cavalry attack. The French defeated the Spanish cavalry but were held by the Spanish pikemen and cut to pieces by arquebus fire. Then an advance by

Pavia was a battle decided by the combination of pikemen and arquebusiers fighting in the open rather than depending on field fortifications. Artillery had played little part. On the Spanish side, the novel skirmishing tactics of the Marquis of Pescara's light infantry were effective. The battle was decisive in the short-term, enabling Charles V to invest Francesco Sforza with the Duchy of Milan, but in 1526 Francis repudiated the terms extorted from him and organized the League of Cognac to renew his challenge to Charles in Italy.

Francis' successor Henry II formed an alliance with the German Protestant opponents of Charles, and seized Metz, Toul, and Verdun in 1552. Charles' attempt to regain Metz, at the head of 59,000 men, failed. It was foolish to mount a major siege in wintertime. Both sides were fielding far larger forces than their predecessors'. Charles V had 148,000 men under arms around Metz, in Germany, the Low Countries, Italy, Spain, and facing the Turks. Henry II had armies in eastern France and Italy, and was able to force Charles to abandon the Siege of Metz by seizing Hesdin in Flanders.

After a truce in 1556, the French invaded Italy in 1557, but then a Spanish advance into France from the Low Countries led to their important victory at St Quentin (10 August 1557).

Henry II was defeated again at Gravelines on 13 July 1558, abandoned by his German allies, and alarmed by the spread of French Protestantism. By 1559, he was bankrupt and forced to accept the Treaty of Cateau-Cambrésis, under the terms of which Spain was left in control of Milan, Naples, Sicily, and Sardinia. The Habsburgs had won the Italian Wars.

ANGLO-CELTIC WARFARE, 1513-1603

T HE SIXTEENTH century was the last in which two states, England and Scotland, shared the mainland of Britain, and although there were periods of co-operation, they sometimes fought. There was war in Ireland, as England's rulers strove to consolidate their power, and civil conflicts in both Scotland and England generated by aristocratic, religious, regional, and economic rivalries.

ANGLO-SCOTTISH WARS

After the Battle of Flodden, negotiations in 1514 secured peace between England and Scotland until 1542, when Henry VIII attacked Scotland in order to cover his rear before a projected invasion of France. A Scottish counter-invasion was crushed at the Battle of Solway Moss (1542), while at Ancrum Moor (1545), an English raiding force was defeated.

Nevertheless, English pressure on Scotland continued, increasing under the Duke of Somerset, who from 1547–49 acted as Lord Protector of Henry's infant successor, Edward VI. Somerset sought to establish both Protestantism and English influence in Scotland, and to break traditional Scottish ties with France. In 1547, he invaded at the head of 16,000 troops (map 1). At the Battle of Pinkie, the Scottish army, at least 25,000 strong, principally pikemen, was badly battered by English cannon and archers, with over 6,000 killed to 800 English. Somerset exploited the victory by taking a large number of positions where he established garrisons, but this policy did not make English rule popular, proved ruinously expensive, and in 1549 had to be abandoned in the face of French intervention.

The heavy defeats at Flodden and Pinkie suggest that the Scots were not in a position to challenge the English field army. Their diverse forces lacked the ability to act as a coherent unit, and some individual sections, especially the Highlanders, were disinclined to accept the discipline of

FLODDEN 9 SEPTEMBER 1513

The Franco-Scottish alliance, renewed in 1512, brought Scotland and England to renewed war in 1513. Henry VIII had sent troops to Gascony in 1512 and invaded France in person the following year, winning the Battle of the Spurs. James IV of Scotland, irritated with his brother-in-law for a number of reasons, including disputes over Border raids, fulfilled his commitment to France by invading England with the largest force that had hitherto marched south. James crossed the Tweed at Coldstream on 22 August 1513 with about 26,000 men, including a French contingent intended to encourage the use of new military methods. Wark, Norham, and Ford castles fell rapidly, the strong Norham to James' artillery. The English under the Earl of Surrey advanced with about 20,000 men. In comparison with the troops then fighting in Italy, this was a militarily 'conservative' force, although this was not to make it less effective. There were archers and billmen, not arquebusiers and pikemen, and the English had few cannon.

James responded to Surrey's approach by taking a strong defensive position on Flodden Hill, but Surrey marched round the Scottish flank, putting himself between the Scots and the route to Scotland. James took a new defensive position on Branxton Hill (1). Casualties from English cannon fire encouraged the Highlanders and Borderers in the Scots army to advance, but, after a bitter struggle, the English line held (2). The Scottish centre was then ordered to advance, but their pikemen were unable to develop momentum in attack (3), and the more mobile English billmen defeated them, rather as Spanish swordsmen had been

effective against pikemen at Cerignola in Italy in 1503. The Scottish centre was further pressed as other English troops, victorious over the Scottish right, attacked it in the rear (4). James IV and at least 5,000 – and possibly as many as 10,000 – of his subjects were killed, along with much of the Scottish nobility; English casualties were far fewer, although still substantial.

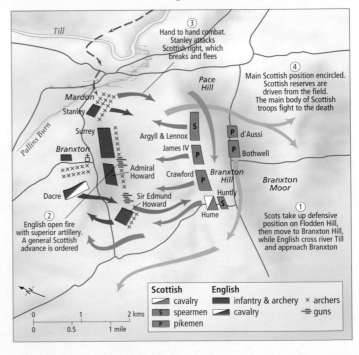

remaining on the defensive under fire. Also, the Scots always had less firepower than the English. In addition to their historical inability to match English archery, the Scots lacked the resources, expertise, and experience to match them in gunpowder weaponry.

Yet these disadvantages did not mean that Scotland was ripe for conquest. The English faced serious problems in locating and sustaining suitable allies in the complex mix of Scottish politics, and there were also significant military difficulties. England was far stronger than Scotland in population and financial resources, and had the English been able to maintain and support a permanent military presence in lowland Scotland, then the Scottish Kingdom would have been gravely weakened. However, as Scotland did not yield the funds for its occupation, the impossibly high cost of maintaining enough garrisons would have fallen upon England. The centre of English power was far to the south, and in Scotland it was challenged by another distant power, France. Scotland was not to be conquered until 1650–52, years in which France was distracted by civil conflict and another foreign war.

CONFLICT WITHIN ENGLAND

The Tudor regime in England faced a number of serious rebellions in the sixteenth century. The dissolution of the monasteries by Henry VIII was very unpopular and led to a major rising in the north, the unsuccessful Pilgrimage of Grace (1536–37). Hostility to the spread of Protestant practices played a major role in the widespread uprisings in southern England in 1549. Also of importance was opposition to landlords, especially to their enclosure of common land and to their high rents, which resulted notably in Kett's Rebellion in East Anglia. The Catholic revolt in the southwest was primarily directed against Protestantism, and the local gentry failed to suppress it. Professional troops from outside the region had to be used, and slaughter in battle and in execution claimed a proportion of the region's

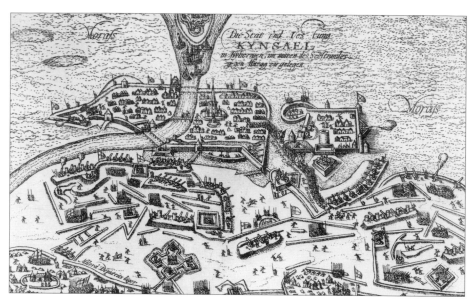

population similar to that lost by the United Kingdom during the First World War. Elizabeth I's church settlement and the flight to England of Mary, Queen of Scots, led to the unsuccessful Northern Rebellion of 1569.

These rebellions faced important political and military disadvantages. Political ambiguity about the notion of rebellion ensured that there was often a fatal confusion of purpose. Militarily, the untrained amateur forces raised in the rebellions were no match for the professional troops that the government could deploy, as was demonstrated on 27 August 1549 when John Dudley, Earl of Warwick, cut Kett's Rebellion to pieces at Dussindale. The rebels tended to lack cavalry, firearms, and cannon; such forces could not challenge the government if it had firm leadership and the support of an important portion of the social elite. It was only in Scotland that the situation was different. There, Mary Queen of Scots, a weak and discredited monarch, faced opposition from a group of powerful Protestant aristocrats and was forced to abdicate in 1567.

The Siege of Kinsale was the culminating clash in the struggle for Ireland. Kinsale, occupied by Spanish forces under Don Juan del Aquila (1601-02), was a modern fortress with low, thick walls, and bastions designed for defence against artillery, on which the English besiegers relied. An Irish relief attempt under Hugh O'Neill was defeated on 24 December 1601, and Kinsale later surrendered.

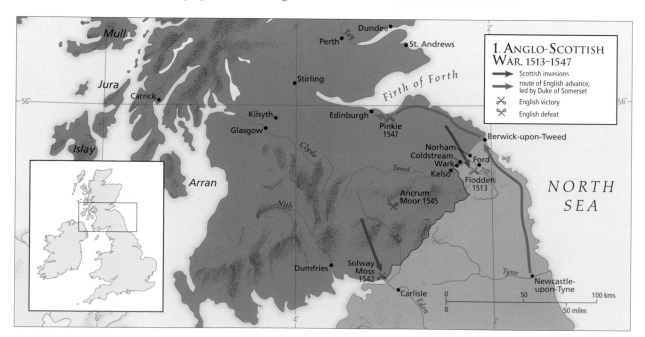

MAP 1
Despite much expense and effort, neither the Tudors nor their Stuart rivals made decisive gains from their conflict in the first half of the sixteenth century. Subsequent English advantage owed more to divisions within Scotland.

1. ANGLO-SCOTTISH WAR, 1513–1547
→ Scottish invasions
→ route of English advance, led by Duke of Somerset
✕ English victory
✕ English defeat

WARFARE IN IRELAND

In 1490, the English Crown wielded only limited power in Ireland. As Lord of Ireland, the monarch had important claims of overlordship, but control was restricted to The Pale, the area around Dublin. The Reformation transformed the situation: Henry VIII was concerned about the risk of Papal or Spanish intervention, and in 1541 had himself proclaimed King of Ireland. Under his successor, Edward VI, the 'plantation' of areas outside The Pale with English settlers began. This increased the security of the Crown's position, although the expropriation of Gaelic landowners was naturally unpopular. The pace of plantation increased from the late 1560s, and English rule became increasingly military in character and intent, leading to fresh attempts to extend and enforce control. These in turn provoked rebellions, culminating in a major Gaelic uprising in Ulster in 1595. This was ably led by Hugh O'Neill, Earl of Tyrone, who also sought support from the 'Old English' – English settlers who were Catholics. He raised a substantial army of 10,000 men, and extended the rebellion into Munster.

The character of the fighting in Ireland was different from that in much of western Europe and is a useful reminder of the variety of types of European warfare. From mid-century, firearms, in the form of the arquebus, had been widely introduced into Ireland, but in the 1560s, Shane O'Neill's forces had still relied principally on traditional weapons like axes, bows, javelins, and swords.

Hugh O'Neill's men, by contrast, used modern firearms, the musket and its smaller counterpart, the caliver, and were as well-armed as the English. Many had been trained in the Spanish army, and O'Neill trained his entire force in the use of pikes and firearms. The wooded and boggy terrain of Ulster was well-suited to guerrilla conflict, and at Clontibret in 1595 O'Neill successfully ambushed an English army. Three years later, at Yellow Ford, another English force was attacked while on the march. Musket fire combined with charges led to 1,500 English casualties. The Earl of Essex was sent with a major force in 1599, but the Irish avoided battle.

In 1600 the English sent a more effective leader, the new Lord Deputy, Charles, Lord Mountjoy. He decided to campaign in the winter in order to disrupt the Irish logistical system, trying to immobilize the migrant herds of cattle which fed the Irish army. Mountjoy brought a new English savagery to the conflict and also enjoyed numerical superiority. However, his attempt to invade Ulster was defeated at the Battle of Moyry Pass (2 October 1600) by O'Neill's use of musketeers protected by field fortifications.

English fears of foreign intervention were realized in September 1601 when Philip III of Spain sent 3,500 troops to Kinsale to support O'Neill. Mountjoy responded by blockading Kinsale, but his force was rapidly weakened by sickness. O'Neill's relieving force, instead of blockading Mountjoy, decided to attack him. On 23–24 December, however, the night march on Mountjoy's camp was mishandled, and on the morning of 24 December, O'Neill, unusually, lost the tactical initiative, allowing Mountjoy to move first. O'Neill also deployed his men in the unfamiliar defensive formation of the Spanish *tercio* (square), which proved cumbersome to the Irish. The English cavalry drove their Irish counterparts from the field, and the Irish infantry retreated, those who stood being routed. The Irish lost 1,200 men, but, more seriously, the pattern of victory was broken and O'Neill surrendered in 1603.

The Nine Years' War in Ireland provides evidence of the strength of the Irish combination of traditional Celtic tactical methods and modern firearms. It also reveals the folly of seeking to transform such a force into soldiers fighting on the standard western European pattern and, in particular, of requiring them to maintain the tactical defensive. Until 1601, O'Neill combined a strategic defensive – protecting Ulster – and a tactical offensive; the switch in strategy proved fatal.

But O'Neill was pitted against a powerful state, with a more sophisticated military and logistical organization and with naval support. The Irish could live off the land and use the terrain, and they benefited from 'modernity' in the form of muskets, but their weak command structure inevitably reflected the problems of a people competing with a state.

MAP 2

The attempt under Henry VIII to assimilate Gaelic Ireland was replaced by his successors' policy of the 'plantation' of districts with English settlers. This increased the Crown's security, but naturally the expropriation of Gaelic landowners was unpopular, and from the late 1560s English rule became increasingly military. By 1603, Ireland had been conquered, and thereafter it was contested as a unit.

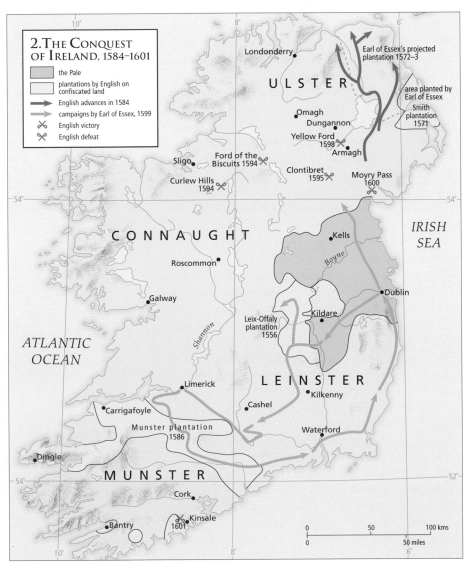

2. THE CONQUEST OF IRELAND, 1584–1601

- the Pale
- plantations by English on confiscated land
- English advances in 1584
- campaigns by Earl of Essex, 1599
- English victory
- English defeat

THE WARS OF RELIGION, 1547-1610

THE REFORMATION led to widespread conflict in Germany, France, and the Low Countries. A high level of popular involvement resulted in a struggle which was often brutal, with atrocities and retaliation on both sides. It was also a war of sieges, especially in the Low Countries, where the Protestant Dutch rebels held off a powerful Spanish army.

EUROPE POLITICIZED

The Reformation helped to change the political environment of much of Europe, and provoked much conflict, both domestic and foreign. In the British Isles, France, the Low Countries, the Empire, and the Austrian Habsburg territories, states and societies were riven by conspiracy, the search for assistance from foreign co-religionists, and regional, social, and factional differences exacerbated by religious antagonism. It was a political world in which everything was seen to be at stake because of the prospect of state-directed religious change. Peasants revolted against their lords, as in the German Peasants' War of 1524–25 and also in Austria in 1594–97, and rulers were assassinated or removed by revolt. Two successive kings of France, Henry III and IV, were killed in 1589 and 1610, Mary, Queen of Scots and Sigismund Vasa of Sweden were stripped of their power in 1567 and 1598, and Philip II of Spain was deposed by the rebellious Dutch provinces in 1581.

War broke out first in Germany, where the opposition of the Protestant princes fatally weakened the power of the Emperor Charles V. In 1531, they created the Schmalkalden League to defend Protestantism and, after attempts at religious reconciliation at the Diets of Augsburg (1530) and Regensburg (1541) had failed, the Schmalkaldic War began in 1546. Charles used a Spanish army to defeat Elector John Frederick of Saxony at Mühlberg on 24 April 1547. The Elector was captured, and two months later the other Protestant leader in opposition, Philip of Hesse, surrendered. Charles had been helped by the neutrality of France and by the support of Protestant princes who hoped to benefit personally: Maurice of Saxony and Margrave Alcibiades of Brandenburg-Culmbach. The victory therefore reflects the combination of military and political factors characteristic of the Wars of Religion.

Charles exploited his victory to dictate peace terms at the 'armed Diet' of Augsburg (1548), but the failure to produce a lasting religious settlement, divisions between Charles and his brother Ferdinand, intervention by the new King of France, Henry II, and the opportunism of Maurice of Saxony, led to a French-supported rising in 1552 which drove Charles from Germany. Peace followed in 1555.

THE FRENCH WARS

In 1562, it was the turn of France. The French Wars of Religion led to a collapse of royal authority, social strife, and foreign intervention, especially by Spain, England, and Savoy. The Wars lasted until the Edict of Nantes of 1598, resuming during the reign of Louis XIII, and ending in royal victory in 1629. Their origins lay in the fragility of the French monarchy after the death of Henry II following a jousting accident in 1559. His weak successors, Francis II (1559–60), Charles IX (1560–74), and Henry III (1574–89), were unable to control the factionalism of the leading nobility, a factionalism exacerbated by the struggle between the Catholics and Huguenots (Protestants).

The Wars involved numerous battles and sieges (map 1). Huguenot defeats in the 1560s at Dreux (1562), St Denis (1567), Jarnac and Montcontour (1569) stopped the Protestant advance. Foreign intervention on their behalf had little impact, and on 10 October 1575 at Dormans, the Catholic leader, Henry Duke of Guise, defeated an English-financed German army under John-Casimir of the Palatinate marching to support the Huguenots.

The years 1577–84 were generally peaceful, but in 1585 conflict resumed once the Protestant Henry of Navarre became heir to the throne. The Guise family turned to Philip II for support, and a war over the succession began. Guise defeated another English-financed German army at Auneau (1587), and Henry III was driven from Paris by a pro-Guise rebellion (1588). Henry's desperate response, the murder of Guise in Blois in December 1588, did not solve the problem. The Catholic League turned against the King, whose power was soon restricted to a section of the Loire valley, and Henry III was assassinated when he attempted to besiege Paris (1589).

Henry of Navarre's eventual victory was again a product of military and political factors. His victories at Arques (1589) and Ivry (1590) enabled him to gain the initiative. At Ivry his cavalry defeated their opponents by employing a charge rather than the anticipated pistol duel. Henry was also helped by his enemies' political divisions, not least over whether a Spanish succession was acceptable, and by their lack of unified leadership, while his willingness to become a Catholic again (1593) was important in winning allies. In 1594, Henry was at last able to enter Paris, which had successfully defied his siege after Ivry, and in January 1596 the League was dissolved.

Spanish intervention had helped to prolong the conflict, relieving besieged Paris in 1590 and Rouen in 1592, and other Spanish forces operated in Brittany and southern France. Henry defeated a Spanish army invading Burgundy at Fontaine-Française (5 June 1595), but Spanish troops operating from the Low Countries captured Cambrai (1595), Calais (1596), and Amiens (1597). Like England's actions in Scotland, the Spanish had discovered the problems of

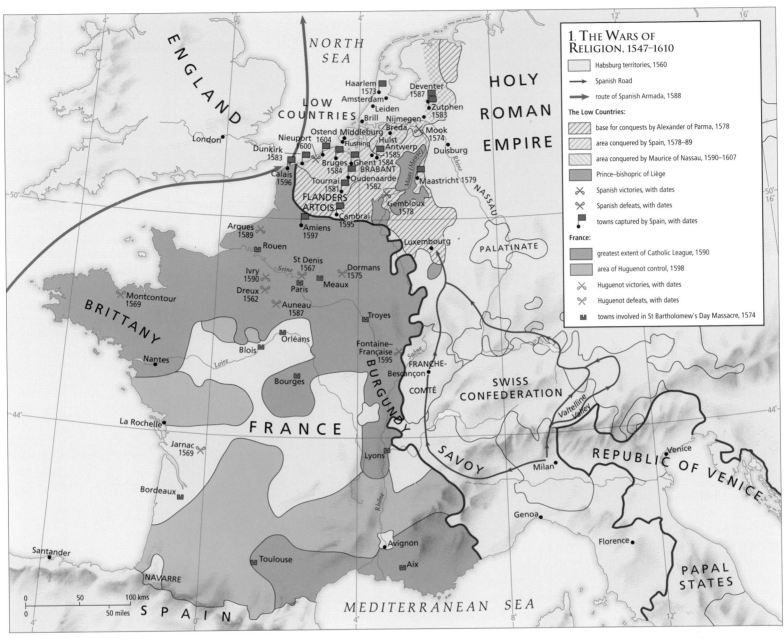

1. THE WARS OF RELIGION, 1547–1610

Habsburg territories, 1560

Spanish Road

route of Spanish Armada, 1588

The Low Countries:

base for conquests by Alexander of Parma, 1578

area conquered by Spain, 1578–89

area conquered by Maurice of Nassau, 1590–1607

Prince–bishopric of Liège

Spanish victories, with dates

Spanish defeats, with dates

towns captured by Spain, with dates

France:

greatest extent of Catholic League, 1590

area of Huguenot control, 1598

Huguenot victories, with dates

Huguenot defeats, with dates

towns involved in St Bartholomew's Day Massacre, 1574

MAP 1

The interrelated struggles in France and the Low Countries ended with the defeat of Philip II, both in his attempt to suppress the Dutch Revolt and in his aim to prevent the accession of Henry IV in France. Spain, however, displayed its military power, not only in its successful reconquest of the southern half of the Low Countries, but also in its ability to affect the course of the bitter civil conflict in France.

intervening in the domestic affairs of another state, but their powerful military machine ensured that when peace came, by the Treaty of Vervins (2 May 1598), the terms of Cateau-Cambrésis (1559), which had recognized Spanish predominance in western Europe, were repeated.

THE DUTCH REVOLT

The revolt of the Dutch provinces under William of Orange against imperial rule also revealed the strength of the Spanish military machine. Philip II's unpopular religious and fiscal policies and his neglect of the Dutch nobility led to riots in 1566–67 which ended only when Spanish policy changed. A powerful Spanish army under the Duke of Alba strengthened Spanish control in the late 1560s, but in 1572 Alba had to turn south to deal with a threatened French attack and an actual invasion under Louis of Nassau. This allowed the Sea Beggars, a rebel fleet of Dutch privateers, to seize the Zeeland towns of Brill and Flushing (April 1572). When the threat of French attack was ended by the killing of the

Huguenot leaders in the St Bartholomew's Day Massacre (23–24 August 1572), Alba was able to re-establish Spanish power over most of the Low Countries, but he was delayed by a seven-month siege of Haarlem (December 1572 to July 1573). Short of money and ships, he was unable successfully to contest coastal waters or to regain Zeeland.

Under Alba's replacement, Luis de Requeséns, the Spanish Army of Flanders reached a peak strength of over 80,000 men in 1574 and retained its battlefield superiority, destroying Louis of Nassau's army at Mook (Mookerheyde) on 14 April 1574, and killing both him and his brother Henry; but the coastal regions proved far harder to control. The Dutch captured Middleburg in February 1574 and the siege of Leiden (May–October) ended when the Dutch breached the dykes, flooding the region and forcing the Spanish to retreat. Unable to suppress the rebellion, the Spanish turned to negotiation, a course encouraged by Philip II's bankruptcy which in 1576 led the army to mutiny and sack Antwerp. The Catholic nobility of the Walloon south were

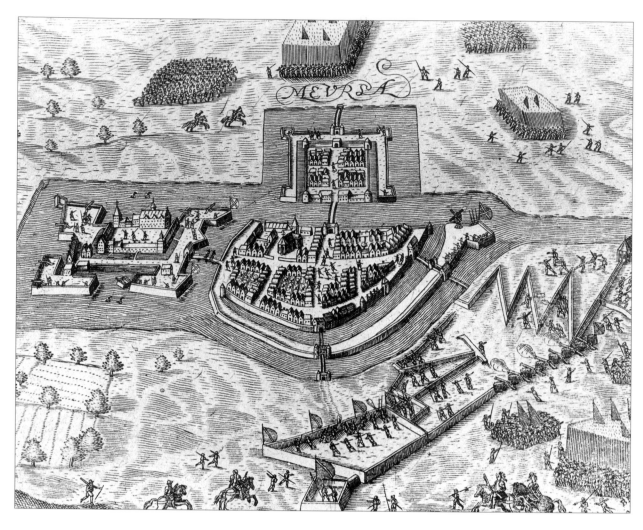

In 1597, Maurice of Nassau advanced in the Lower Rhineland capturing a number of fortresses including Moers, west of Duisburg. His objective was to give the Dutch room for manoeuvre, create a buffer zone of fortified positions, and cut Spanish supply and communication links, particularly along the Rhine and with the north-eastern Low Countries. Dutch siege warfare, directed by Simon Stevin, who was the Quartermaster-General of the army, was both well-organized and successful.

keen to reconcile themselves with Philip II and to restore social discipline. Requeséns' successor, Don John of Austria, the victor of Lepanto, won a victory at Gembloux (1578), again demonstrating Spanish superiority in battle: having defeated the Dutch cavalry, the Spanish horse were able to catch the Dutch infantry unprepared and to inflict heavy casualties. Don John's successor and nephew, Alessandro Farnese, Duke of Parma, continued to woo the southern nobles and signed the Treaty of Arras with the southern provinces in 1579.

Parma was also an able general, and he captured many rebel towns in the south: Maastricht (1579), Tournai (1581), Oudenaarde (1582), Dunkirk (1583), Bruges (1584), and Ghent (1584). On 17 August 1585, Antwerp also fell after a fourteen-month siege that had won the attention of Europe. Parma pushed north across the 'river line' of the Rhine and Maas, taking Zutphen (1583) and Deventer (1587). From 1585 the English, under the Earl of Leicester, intervened on behalf of the rebels, but this proved no bar to Parma, whose opponents had become disunited and war-weary.

However, the Spanish Army of Flanders was hampered in its efforts to overcome the Dutch, first by the need to prepare for an invasion of England (1588), and then from 1590 by the need to intervene in France to prevent the collapse of the Catholic League; in 1590, Parma took 11,000 men into France; and in 1592, 30,000 men. Archduke Albert led the Spanish army into Artois in 1597. The Dutch benefited by going onto the offensive from 1590, although the Spanish returned to the attack after the war in France finished in 1598. The Dutch commander, Maurice of Nassau, took Breda by suprise in 1590 before making major gains in Brabant. Deventer, Hulst, and Nijmegen fell to Maurice of Nassau in 1590, and in 1592 he made major gains at the expense of the Spaniards in the north-east. This was a war of sieges, not battles, but in 1600 Maurice was victorious at Nieuport (1600), where Dutch cavalry charged and routed the unprepared Spanish infantry after they had driven back the Dutch infantry. Nevertheless, Maurice was unable to exploit the situation, and the new Spanish commander, Ambrogio Spinola, captured Ostend in 1604 after a very lengthy siege. Spinola crossed the river line to invade the north-east of the United Provinces, as the rebel state was now known. However, this promising military situation was cut short by Spanish bankruptcy in 1607, and a twelve-year truce was negotiated in 1609.

The wars in the Low Countries indicated the dual importance of battles and sieges. If an army could not be faced in the field, it could attack fortresses as it chose, as Parma demonstrated in his actions in the 1580s. Equally, a lengthy siege could so delay operations that the strategic initiative would be lost.

THE STRUGGLE FOR THE BALTIC (I), 1500-1595

THE BREAKUP of stable political units around the Baltic at the end of the fifteenth century and the emergence of Russia and Sweden as significant rival powers led to a series of wars in the region, characterized by sieges, tactical flexibility, and systematic devastation. The Baltic also witnessed the first modern naval war, between Sweden and Denmark.

RUSSIAN EXPANSION

The Baltic region was the major source of European ship-building materials, and an exporter of copper, iron, and grain. It became unstable in the sixteenth century for a number of reasons. In 1523, the Union of Kalmar, which had bound Denmark, Norway, Sweden, and Finland together under one crown since 1397, finally collapsed, and in its place two opposing states, Denmark-Norway and Sweden-Finland, came to compete for hegemony in the north. The expansion of Muscovite power towards the Baltic threatened the stability of its eastern shores: Novgorod fell to the Russians in 1478, Pskov in 1510. The Reformation opened the question of the fate of the extensive lands of the crusading orders, the Teutonic Knights and the Livonian Order. It also separated Catholic Poland and Orthodox Lithuania from Protestant Denmark and Sweden.

The Battle of Oland (30–31 May 1564) was an important episode in the bitter Swedish-Danish struggle of 1563–70. The Swedes lost their new flagship, the *Mars*, after repeated attacks by the Danish ships and their Lübeck allies under Herlof Trolle. The *Mars* was successfully boarded on the second day of the battle, caught fire, and blew up. Both fleets then withdrew for repairs.

Pressure from Russia was constant. In 1492, the fortress of Ivangorod was built opposite the town of Narva, bringing Russian power to the borders of the Livonian Order. In 1500, Ivan III went to war with Lithuania, threatening Smolensk, and defeating the Lithuanians on the river Vedrosha. The Livonian Order came to the aid of the Lithuanians but were defeated at Helmed. In 1502, Ivan besieged Smolensk without success, but he advanced the Russian frontier to the Dnieper before peace was negotiated in 1503. War resumed in 1507–8 and 1512–15, and Vasily III captured Smolensk in 1514. His son Ivan IV sought to gain the lands of the Livonian Order, capturing Narva (1558) and Polotsk (1563), but being defeated by the Lithuanians at the Battle of Chasniki (1564).

In place of the weaker states that had formerly opposed Russian advances, Ivan now had to face both Denmark and Sweden in the eastern Baltic and the powerful Poland-Lithuania and Ukraine which formed a permanent union in 1569. Reval put itself under Swedish protection in 1561 and successfully resisted Russian sieges in 1570–71 and 1576–77. Ivan conquered most of Livonia in 1575–76, but his army was crushed by the Poles and the Swedes at Wenden (1578), the Swedes fording a deep stream under cover of their field artillery. The Swedes then drove the Russians from Kexholm (1580) and, under the able French mercenary Pontus de la Gardie, crossed the frozen Gulf of Finland and seized Wesenberg (1581). On 6 September 1581, Pontus stormed Narva, slaughtering the entire population, and by the end of the year the whole of Estonia had been regained. Stefan Bátory, King of Poland, retook Polotsk (1579), captured Velikiye Luki and Cholmin (1580), and unsuccessfully attacked Pskov (1581). In 1582, Ivan was forced to make peace with Poland and in 1583 he signed a three-year truce with Sweden, later extended to 1590: Ivan had to give up his gains.

In 1590, the Russians again attacked Sweden, recapturing Ivangorod. A Swedish attempt to besiege Novgorod in 1591 failed. Fighting extended to the White Sea coast, where the Swedes failed to take Kola in 1590 and 1591. By the Treaty of Teusina (1595), Russia abandoned claims to Estonia and Narva and ceded Kexholm (Eastern Karelia) to Sweden, while Sweden gave back Ingria, which had been occupied since the truce of 1583.

DANISH-SWEDISH WAR

Elsewhere in the Baltic, there was conflict between Denmark and Sweden, including a long period of war from 1501 to 1520 when the Oldenburg kings, who ruled in Denmark and Norway, tried to gain control over Sweden. In 1517, Christian II started a series of intensified attempts to gain

control over Sweden. In 1524, the Danes recognized Gustavus Vasa as King of Sweden. Gustavus joined Frederick I of Denmark in defeating Lübeck and resisting an attempt by Christian II to regain the Danish throne (1534-36), but in 1563 the two powers went to war. Sweden's sole outlet to the North Sea, Älvsborg (Gothenburg), fell to the Danes in 1563, prompting Erik XIV of Sweden to seek a new route through southern Norway. Trondheim fell to the Swedes in 1564, much of southern Norway was overrun in 1567 and Oslo was taken, but the Swedes were held at Akershus. From 1565 until 1569 the Swedes held Varberg, to the south of Älvsborg.

Erik relied on native troops, which he transformed by training them in the combined use of pikes and firearms in linear formations. He made the pike the basis of offensive infantry tactics. Frederick II of Denmark used German mercenaries who were usually more successful, severely defeating the Swedes at Axtorna: Erik's troops fought well there but were poorly commanded. The Danish army managed to advance as far as Norrköping in late 1567 before being forced to retreat by the weather.

At sea, 1563–70 saw the first modern naval war between sailing battle fleets in European waters, as Denmark and Sweden fought for control of the invasion routes. The Danes were supported by the semi-independent German city of Lübeck – no longer the great sea power it had been but still able to make an important contribution. Both sides sought to destroy the opposing fleet, and seven battles were fought between 1563 and 1566. The Swedes, under Klas Kristersson Horn, with their modern bronze artillery, systematically used stand-off gunfire to block Danish boarding tactics: sheer weight of metal was decisive. Both navies expanded greatly, and in the late 1560s the Swedes may have had the largest sailing fleet of the period. Both sides were exhausted by 1568, and peace was agreed without any territorial gains to either side.

Warfare on land in the Baltic involved relatively few battles. Sieges were more important, while devastation was used to reduce opponents' fighting capability. This conflict is far more than a footnote to the history of European warfare, being an important reminder of the growing prominence of Sweden and Russia. The tactics employed were less formalistic than those developed in western Europe, and the troops sometimes less specialized in weaponry, but their warfare was well-suited to the eastern European military circumstances of great distances and small populations.

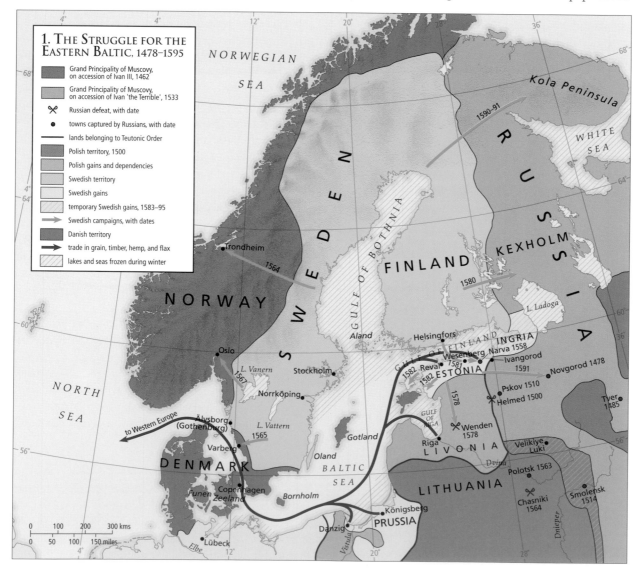

MAP 1

Warfare in the Baltic took place over great distances. The Eastern Baltic lands were bitterly contested, and Denmark and Sweden waged a lengthy struggle on the eastern shores of the Baltic, in Norway, southern Sweden, and at sea.

NAVAL WARFARE IN EUROPE, 1500-1600

NAVAL WARFARE entailed a commitment of resources which was often greater than that required for warfare on land. The failure of Philip II's huge and costly attempt to mount an invasion of England in the summer of 1588, and of subsequent expeditions, both Spanish and English, demonstrate the limits of sixteenth-century seapower.

THE LOGISTICS OF NAVAL WARFARE

The wooden warship equipped with cannon, whether driven by sails, muscle-power, or both, was the single most costly, powerful, and technologically advanced weapons system of the entire early modern period. The construction, equipment, manning, supply, and maintenance of a fleet required considerable financial and logistical efforts. Warships and equipment were durable, a heavy capital investment requiring maintenance; they therefore demanded not only technologically advanced yards for their construction, but also permanent institutions to manage them.

Warships provided effective mobile artillery platforms, and an individual vessel might carry the heavy firepower capacity comparable to that of an entire army. The trading wealth unlocked by the 'Age of Discoveries' encouraged the development of naval power to both protect and attack long-distance trade routes. Warships were also the most effective means of attacking distant hostile bases. In European waters, the strategic commitments of many powers involved maritime links, as for example between Spain and both Italy and the Low Countries, or Sweden and the eastern Baltic.

The sixteenth century saw the establishment and growth of state navies and the greatly increased use of heavy guns in sailing warships: heavy guns were carried in the Baltic from the early 1510s, and by English and French warships in the same period. Carvel building (the edge-joining of hull planks over frames) began to replace clinker (over-lapped planks) construction in about 1500, contributing significantly to the development of hulls which were stronger and better able to carry heavy guns. Also, their sizes grew: there were warships of up to 2,000 tons (2,032 tonnes) displacement from early in the century. The English *Henry Grace à Dieu* (also known as Great Harry) had a 1514 specification of 186 guns and 1,500 tons (1,524 tonnes)

A painting by Agostino Tassi or Buonamico (1565–1644) shows a ship under construction at the leading Tuscan port of Livorno. The painting illustrates the large quantities of wood required for shipbuilding, and the immensity of the task posed by the construction of large warships using largely un-mechanized processes. The capital investment required was formidable, but ships generally had a life of only twenty to thirty years.

deadweight. The French, Scottish, Maltese, Danish, Swedish, Spanish, Lübeck, and Portuguese navies all included ships of comparable size during the course of the century.

Medieval naval warfare had been dominated by boarding, and this continued to play a role. The rising importance of firepower, however, led to a shift towards stand-off tactics in which ships did not come into direct contact and boarding became impossible. The Portuguese were the first systematically to exploit heavy guns to fight stand-off actions against superior enemies, a development often incorrectly claimed for the English at the time of the Armada. In northern Europe, the shift towards stand-off tactics can be seen by contrasting the Anglo-French war of 1512–14, in which the fleets fought in the Channel in the traditional fashion, with the gunnery duel in which they engaged off Portsmouth in 1545. This shift had important implications for naval battle tactics – though truly effective ways of deploying naval firepower were not found until the next century – and it further encouraged the development of warships primarily as artillery platforms. Forged-iron guns were dangerously unreliable, while the manufacture of large cast-iron weapons was beyond the technological scope of the period, but from mid-century firepower was increased by the development of large guns cast instead from lighter, more durable, and workable 'brass' (actually bronze). Simultaneously, improvements in gunpowder increased their range.

THE ENTERPRISE OF ENGLAND

'I am come amongst you…not for my recreation and disport, but being resolved, in the midst and heat of battle, to live or die amongst you all, and to lay down for my God and my kingdom and for my people, my honour and my blood, even in the dust. I know I have the body of a weak and feeble woman, but I have the heart and stomach of a king, and of a king of England too, and think foul scorn that Parma, or Spain, or any prince of Europe, should dare to invade the borders of my realm.'

Elizabeth I's speech to the troops assembled at Tilbury in 1588 to repel a Spanish invasion is famous. She stressed both her dedication to and her identification with England, and her remarks were not idle ones: four years earlier, the other Protestant champion and opponent of Philip II, William of Orange, leader of the rebel United Provinces against the Catholic Empire, had been assassinated.

Had the Spanish forces succeeded in landing in England, Elizabeth's resolution would have been sorely tried. The Spanish Army of Flanders, led by Alessandro Farnese, Duke of Parma, was the most effective army in Christian Europe, while the English defences were inadequate: poor fortifications, insufficient trained troops, and meagre supplies. The rapid and successful Spanish advance under Parma's predecessor, the Duke of Alba, on Lisbon in June 1580 was an impressive display of military effectiveness: Lisbon surrendered on 25 August 1580, and the far-flung Portuguese empire passed into the hands of Philip II of Spain. It is scarcely surprising after the events of 1588 that Providence

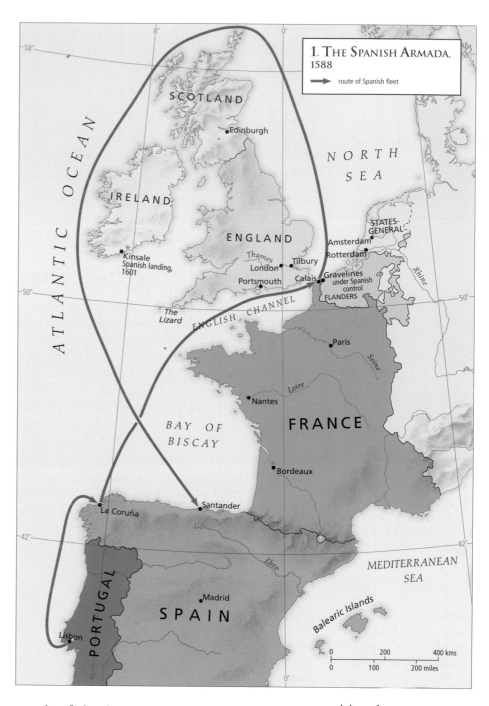

1. THE SPANISH ARMADA,
1588

→ route of Spanish fleet

was identified with a victory which owed as much to luck and to the winds as to the heroism of Elizabeth's navy.

The Spanish failed to co-ordinate adequately two disparate plans: one for an amphibious invasion of England from Spain by the Duke of Medina-Sidonia's fleet, and the other for a crossing from the Spanish Netherlands by Parma's army. They were also delayed by the immensity of the necessary preparations and by Sir Francis Drake's spoiling raid on Cadiz in April 1587. On 28 May 1588, the Armada of 130 ships and 19,000 troops left Lisbon, instructed to proceed up the Channel and then cover Parma's crossing.

Storm damage necessitated refitting in La Coruña, and it was July before the slow-moving fleet appeared off The Lizard, on the southern Cornish coast. The Spanish warships then headed for Calais, maintaining a tight formation to protect their more vulnerable vessels, and harried by

MAP 1

Spanish naval power was deployed in northern Europe in an unsuccessful attempt to tackle the Dutch Revolt, but the Armada of 1588 was of a totally new order of magnitude – part of a bold plan for an invasion of England. Anglo-Spanish naval hostilities contrasted with the minor role of naval forces in the French Wars of Religion.

Robert Adams drew and Augustine Ryther engraved a series of ten plates showing the progress of the Armada. They were published in 1590, dedicated by Ryther to the English commander Lord Howard of Effingham. The appearance of the work, sold by Ryther in his London shop, reflected pride in the English achievement.

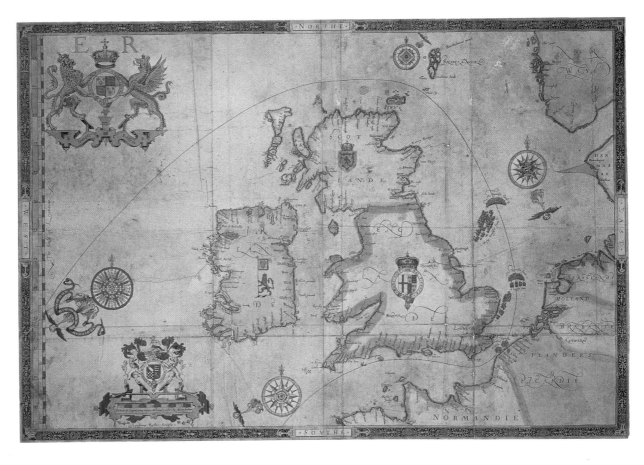

long-range English gunnery. This did little damage, and during nine days of engagements the Spanish retained their formation. However, with the advantage of superior sailing qualities and compact four-wheeled gun-carriages, which allowed a high rate of fire (many of the Spanish guns were on cumbersome carriages designed for use on land), the English fleet suffered even slighter damage, and was most endangered by a shortage of ammunition. When Medina-Sidonia anchored off Calais, he found that Parma had been able to assemble the transport vessels necessary to embark his army for England, but that they could not come out until after the English and Dutch squadrons had been defeated.

Painting of the English fireships approaching the Armada, by the Dutch painter Hendrik Cornelisz Vroom (1566–1640).

The Spanish formation was disrupted by an English night attack using fireships, and the English fleet then inflicted considerable damage in a running battle off Gravelines. The galleons of the Portuguese navy, in Spanish service and experienced in stand-off gunnery, bore the brunt of the battle.

A strong south-westerly wind drove the Armada into the North Sea. With no clear tactical objective after Parma's failed embarkation, the disappointed Spanish commanders ordered a return to Spain via the hazardous north-about route around the British Isles. A succession of violent and unseasonal storms lashed the fleet as it passed north of Scotland and down the west coast of Ireland; ship after ship was smashed or driven ashore, and only a remnant of the fleet reached Spain.

The loss of so many trained and experienced men was a serious blow for the Spanish, but the fleet was rapidly rebuilt. Spain was able to send fleets against England again in 1596 and 1597: both expeditions were stopped by storms, but the English themselves found it difficult to win lasting naval victory. In 1589, Drake mounted a successful attack on La Coruña, destroying Spanish warships, but in other respects the expedition was a failure. Lisbon could not be taken, an attempt to intercept the returning Spanish treasure fleet off the Azores, and a raid on Cadiz in 1596 were also unsuccessful. The English fleet was driven back by storms, and suffered much damage in the process.

Both the Armada and Drake's 'Counter-Armada' illustrate the limitations of naval power in this period, not least its vulnerability to storms, the problems of combined operations, and the heavy supply demands posed by large fleets.

III

WARFARE IN
EUROPE, 1600-1680

In 1671, on a visit to Rochefort, Louis XIV went to sea for the only time in his life; by way of contrast, he frequently accompanied the army campaigns in the first half of his reign. Although governments sought to develop their naval strength, the prestige of naval warfare was less than that of land for monarchical states; warfare on land was easier to accommodate to the aristocratic mores and practices of society and government in this period, brought *gloire* to monarchs and was effective against domestic rebellions as well as foreign foes. Thus in 1620, Louis XIII of France led his army to distant Béarn in south-west France in order to coerce the local Huguenots (French Protestants) into accepting royal authority and Catholicism. He succeeded without fighting, but in 1621 the royal forces encountered resistance. The fortified town of St Jean d'Angely fell after a month-long siege, exposing the Huguenot stronghold of La Rochelle to attack, but Montauban successfully resisted a siege that decimated the besiegers though disease and desertion. The following year a Huguenot army was destroyed at the Ile de Riez south of Nantes, while Louis marched through west and south France, capturing numerous positions before the Huguenots accepted terms that removed their rights to have garrisons. La Rochelle, the last Huguenot stronghold, was besieged and starved into surrender in 1627–8. Thus, although the French royal army of the period was relatively small and weak by the standards of neighbouring Spain, it was able to bring an effective end to a major challenge to the military, political, and religious authority of the Crown.

Rulers did not only seek military strength in order to confront rebellion. They were also taking part in a competitive international situation that had become more volatile as a result of the dangers and opportunities presented by the Reformation. This situation lent new urgency to the English attempt to dominate Ireland at the turn of the century, and reached its apogee in the Thirty Years' War, that affected much of western and central Europe in 1618–48. That crisis acted as the focus and culmination of the struggles between Catholic and Protestant, Holy Roman Emperor and German princes, Spain and France.

THE THIRTY YEARS' WAR, 1618-1648

THE THIRTY YEARS' WAR was effectively a Europe-wide civil war which brought together several different conflicts: an Austrian Habsburg attempt to assert authority in the Empire, hostilities in the long war between Spain and the Dutch, rivalry between France and Spain, and a dynastic struggle within the Vasa family between the rulers of Sweden and Poland.

THE ADVENT OF GUSTAVUS ADOLPHUS

The war initially began as a rising in 1618 against Habsburg authority in Bohemia (*map 1*). This was crushed by superior forces at the Battle of the White Mountain outside Prague (1620). Habsburg authority was then reimposed and Bohemia was re-Catholicized.

The Bohemians had offered the throne to Frederick, Elector Palatine, and in 1620 Spanish troops from the Army of Flanders under Spinola overran much of the Lower Palatinate, helped by units from Bavaria, which also annexed the Upper Palatinate. War resumed between the Dutch and the Spanish in 1621, and the Dutch then encouraged opposition to the Habsburgs in Germany. Emperor Ferdinand II entrusted his troops to a Bohemian military entrepreneur,

Albrecht von Wallenstein, who defeated Ernst, Count of Mansfeld, at Dessau (April 1626). At Lutter in August 1626, Christian IV of Denmark was defeated by Tilly, Maximilian of Bavaria's experienced general. After Lutter, Wallenstein marched to prevent Bethlen Gabor, Prince of Transylvania, from advancing on Vienna. He and Tilly then drove the Danes from northern Germany, defeating a counter-attack at Wolgast (August 1628) and forcing Christian IV out of the war (1629). Wallenstein's freedom of action as an individual commander contrasted markedly with the greater state control of military affairs fifty years later.

Ferdinand dominated the Empire until the Swedish intervention, but he failed to use this period to win support and consolidate his position. French mediation rescued the King of Sweden, Gustavus Adolphus (1611–32), from an indecisive war with Poland (*page 73*) in September 1629, and the following July he landed at Peenemünde (*map 2*). He overran Pomerania and Mecklenburg, and then advanced south into Brandenburg in April 1631. The brutal sacking of Protestant Magdeburg after it was stormed by Tilly (May 1631) helped to lead Brandenburg into Gustavus' camp. The Swedes followed Tilly into Saxony, and crushed him at Breitenfeld (*page 69*), leading many German Protestant princes to rally to Sweden. Gustavus then advanced into central Germany, taking Würzburg (October) and Frankfurt (December), while the Saxons took Prague (November).

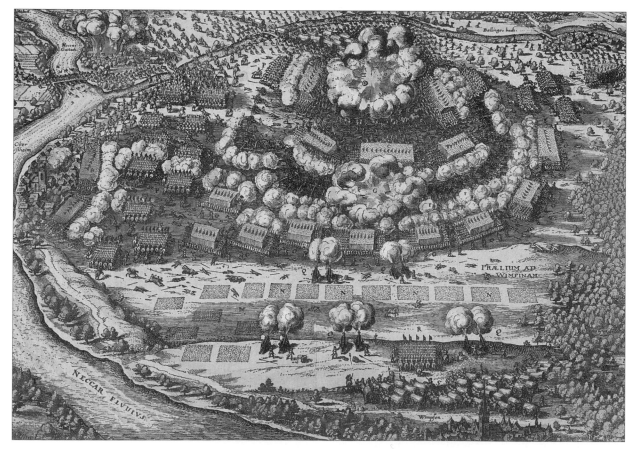

On 6 May 1622 at Wimpfen, the army of the Bavarian-led Catholic League under Tilly and a Spanish force under Don Gonzalo Fernández de Córdoba defeated an army under George of Baden-Durlach that was seeking, on behalf of Frederick V of the Palatinate, to prevent the conquest of the Lower Palatinate. Baden's army was heavily defeated and by late 1622, both Heidelberg and Mannheim, the two leading cities in the Lower Palatinate, had fallen.

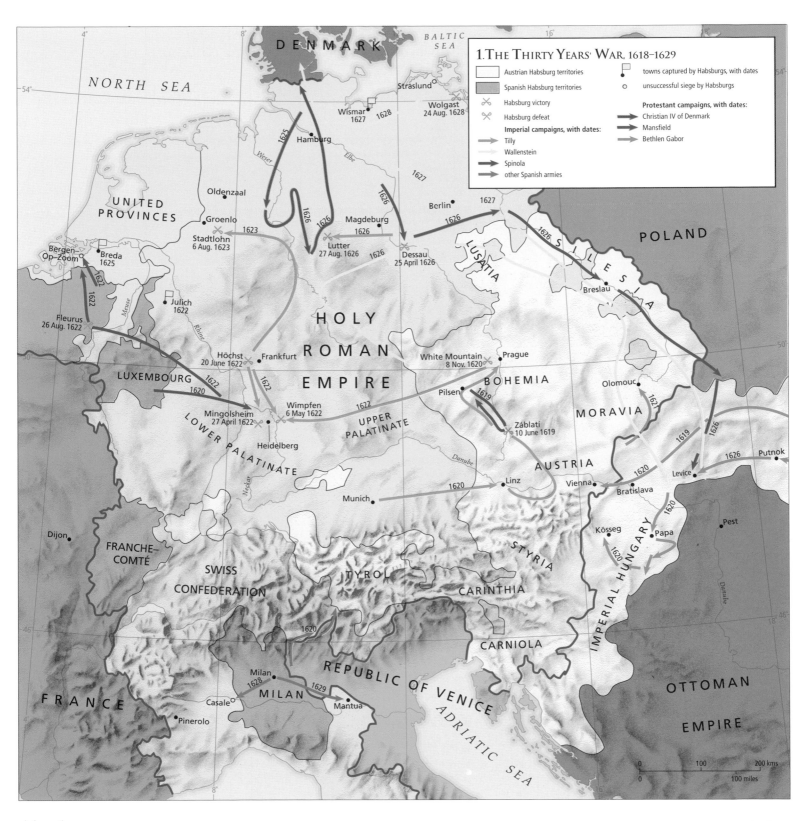

1. THE THIRTY YEARS' WAR, 1618–1629

Austrian Habsburg territories

Spanish Habsburg territories

✗ Habsburg victory

✗ Habsburg defeat

Imperial campaigns, with dates:
Tilly
Wallenstein
Spinola
other Spanish armies

☐ towns captured by Habsburgs, with dates

○ unsuccessful siege by Habsburgs

Protestant campaigns, with dates:
Christian IV of Denmark
Mansfield
Bethlen Gabor

MAP 1

The 1620s were the years of Habsburg advance. Both the Bohemian Protestants and German opponents were crushed, the Dutch were defeated, and Habsburg power extended to the Baltic.

In 1632, Gustavus planned to overrun Bavaria and then conquer Austria. Tilly was killed at the river Lech in an unsuccessful attempt to prevent the invasion of Bavaria, the Swedes crossing under powerful artillery cover, and Munich fell on 17 May. Ferdinand II reappointed Wallenstein as overall commander, and his threat to Saxony led Gustavus to return northwards. The Swedes were unable to drive Wallenstein's forces from a heavily fortified position at the Alte Veste, where Gustavus was unable to use either cav-

alry or artillery, and the Swedish army lost heavily from desertion encouraged by supply problems in the devastated countryside. Wallenstein, convinced that the campaign was over, began to disperse his troops. Gustavus attacked the Imperialists at Lützen (*page 69*), a fog-shrouded and largely inconclusive battle in which both sides lost about one-third of their strength and Gustavus was killed.

The increasingly independent Wallenstein was killed by some of his own officers on the orders of the Emperor

(February 1634), and at Nördlingen (September) an Austro-Spanish army heavily defeated the Swedes.

THE FRENCH INTERVENTION

The defeat at Nördlingen led to the Swedish loss of southern Germany, a settlement of German problems by most of the German princes (1635), and France's entry into the war to resist Habsburg hegemony (*page 75*). The Swedes continued to fight, however, and at Wittstock (October 1636) defeated an Austro-Saxon army, then overrunning Brandenburg and invading Saxony. In 1637, the Swedes were pushed back to Pomerania, but in 1638 they drove the Austrians into Silesia. In 1639, they advanced as far as Prague, but were unable to capture the city. In 1640, the juncture of French and Swedish troops at Erfurt, their first combined operation, had no strategic consequences. The Swedish commander Torstensson took Olomouc (June 1642) and defeated the Austrians at the second Battle of Breitenfeld (November), but the outbreak of war with Denmark (1643–45) led him to postpone his proposed march on Vienna.

In 1645 the Swedes, French, and Transylvanians planned a joint attack on Vienna. Torstensson was successful at Jankov (March 1645), and the French victorious at Allerheim near Nördlingen (August), but neither could maintain their advances. In 1647, the Swedes and French invaded Bavaria and their joint army defeated the Austro-Bavarians at Zusmarshausen (May 1648). As the war ended, the Swedes were besieging Prague.

THE MILITARY REVOLUTION

Swedish victories in the Thirty Years' War are cited as evidence of a European military revolution in which the rise of larger, permanent, professional state forces led to tactical innovations. These changes centred on a rise in the firepower of infantry weapons.

The Dutch introduced broader and shallower troop formations which permitted more soldiers to fire at once, and in the 1590s they maintained continuous fire by using a volley technique. Count Maurice of Nassau, Commander of the Dutch army, had been impressed by Aelian's account of the drill of the Roman javelinmen and slingers, and he proposed six rotating ranks of musketeers. Count Maurice of Nassau also adopted paper cartridges containing a pre-prepared amount of powder, thus increasing each musketeer's rate of fire. The process of retraining was helped in 1599 by funds to equip the entire field army with weapons of the same size and calibre, while its reorganization into smaller units helped improve the mobility of the Dutch infantry.

However, the importance of mercenaries (the vast majority, for example, of Gustavus' troops in Germany) and the hiring of foreign officers helped to ensure a universality of tactics. Whereas the Dutch had earlier used the rotation of ranks of musketeers defensively (having fired, they retired to reload while colleagues took their place), Gustavus used rotation offensively, the other ranks moving forward through

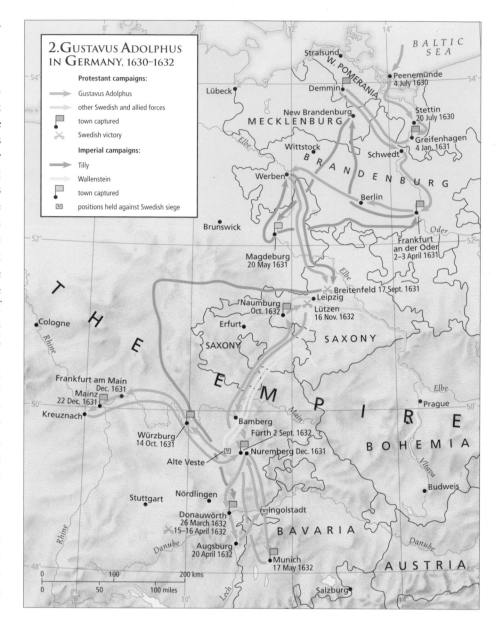

stationary reloaders. He also equipped his infantry units with mobile small cannon and trained his cavalry in a shock charge pressed home with swords in the manner of the Polish cavalry, rather than with pistol fire at short range.

VICTORY IN BATTLE

Battles were usually won by experienced and motivated troops whose dispositions had been well-arranged and, if forces were evenly matched, they were either inconclusive encounters or were determined by other factors, such as terrain, the availability and employment of reserves, and the results of cavalry encounters on the flanks. Such encounters could lead to the victorious cavalry attacking the enemy infantry in flank or rear, as at the Spanish defeat in 1643 at Rocroi (*page 75*). The more innovative linear formations, only five or six ranks deep, were far more vulnerable to flank and rear attack than the long-established columns, or *tercios*. Duke Bernard of Saxe-Weimar, a German prince who served Sweden in 1630–35 before transferring with the army he had raised to French service, won a number of

MAP 2

Gustavus Adolphus was not the first ruler who sought to resist the Habsburgs in the early seventeenth century, and there was no reason to believe that he would be any more successful than Christian IV of Denmark. However, the Swedish army was an experienced and well-honed war machine and Gustavus was a general of great ability and flexibility. Despite his tactical and strategic grasp, his campaigns demonstrated the difficulty of maintaining a consistent pattern of victory.

BREITENFELD 17 SEPTEMBER 1631

Breitenfeld was a crushing victory which established Gustavus Adolphus, King of Sweden, as the leading general of the Thirty Years' War. The Imperialist army under Jean 't Serclaes, Count of Tilly, was defeated just north of Leipzig by Gustavus' Swedish veterans and their allies, the less experienced forces of John George, Elector of Saxony.

The Imperialists were outnumbered, and were outgunned by the more mobile and numerous Swedish artillery. The Saxon infantry on the Swedish left quickly broke when attacked (1), but the flexible and well-disciplined Swedish infantry formations under Gustav Horn in the centre of Gustavus' line were able to halt Tilly's attack with musketry and artillery fire (2). The Swedish cavalry on the other flank overcame their Imperialist opponents and drove them from the field before turning on the Imperialist centre (3). Tilly's infantry, exposed to artillery, infantry, and cavalry, took a heavy battering before retreating.

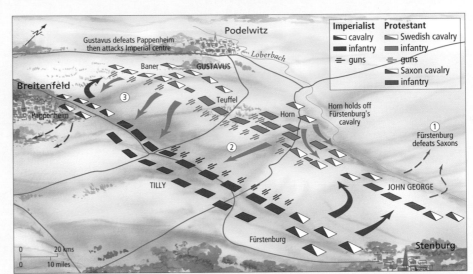

Imperialist casualties were 7,600 killed, compared to 1,500 Swedes and 3,000 Saxons; over 7,000 Imperialist soldiers were also taken prisoner during their retreat from the battlefield, and all of Tilly's artillery was lost. Tilly retreated west over the Weser, leaving Bohemia and the Main valley exposed to Saxon and Swedish advances.

LÜTZEN 16 NOVEMBER 1632

Lützen was a bitterly fought battle in which each side had about 19,000 men. Wallenstein remained on the defensive, deepening a ditch to the front of his position. A mist delayed the Swedish attack, giving the Austrian cavalry commander, Pappenheim, time to add his 3,000 cavalry to Wallenstein's army, taking it up to about 19,000 strong. The Swedes eventually won a cavalry battle on their right after Pappenheim, who had initially turned the tide there, and had seven horses shot from under him, was mortally injured by a cannonball (1). In the centre, the Swedish infantry, led by Gustavus, who was shot in the arm but pressed on, pushed back the opposing musketeers, holding a ditch at the front of Wallenstein's position, but was unable to drive back the main Austrian line. Gustavus died in the mêlée, shot three times (2). Wallenstein stabilized the situation on his left by sending Ottavoi Piccolomini and his cavalry reinforcements there, but at the close of the battle the Swedes on their left captured the village of Lützen and the nearby Austrian artillery that had commanded the battlefield from a rise, and Wallenstein retreated under cover of darkness. Both sides lost about one-third of their strength and Wallenstein retreated to Bohemia, leaving the Swedes in control of Saxony.

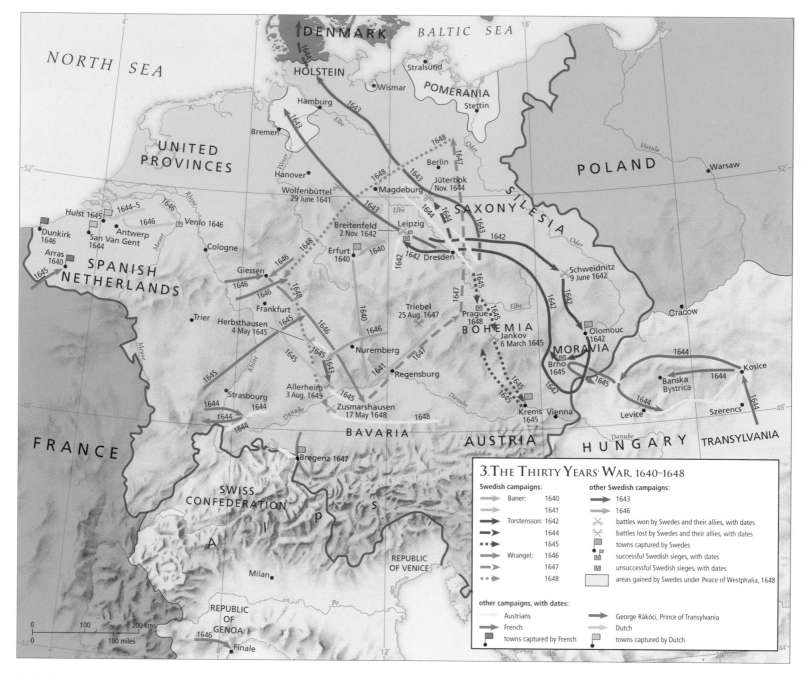

3. THE THIRTY YEARS' WAR, 1640–1648

Swedish campaigns:

Baner:	1640
	1641
Torstensson:	1642
	1644
	1645
Wrangel:	1646
	1647
	1648

other Swedish campaigns:

	1643
	1646
✂	battles won by Swedes and their allies, with dates
✂	battles lost by Swedes and their allies, with dates
◼	towns captured by Swedes
	successful Swedish sieges, with dates
	unsuccessful Swedish sieges, with dates
	areas gained by Swedes under Peace of Westphalia, 1648

other campaigns, with dates:

	Austrians
	French
◼	towns captured by French
	George Rákóci, Prince of Transylvania
	Dutch
◼	towns captured by Dutch

battles by manoeuvre, but did not adopt Dutch-style tactics or formations. At Jankov (6 March 1645), the Swedes under Torstensson, supported by Hessian troops, were initially unable to defeat roughly equal Austrian forces, but succeeded by outmanoeuvring and attacking them from the rear. The Austrian army was destroyed, and the Swedes thus benefited from the tactical flexibility of their more experienced force. The Emperor fled Prague for Graz the day after the battle.

Victory tended to go to larger and more experienced armies, like the Spanish, Swedes, and some of the Austrian and Bavarian units, rather than simply to those which adopted new, Dutch-style tactics. At the White Mountain (1620), there were 28,000 men in the army of the Catholic League against 21,000 Bohemians and German Protestants; at Breitenfeld (1631), Gustavus Adolphus outnumbered his opponents by 42,000 to 35,000; at Nördlingen (1634),

there were 33,000 Catholics to 25,000 Protestants; and at Rocroi (1643), 24,000 French to 17,000 Spanish.

In terms of manpower, Breitenfeld was the largest battle of the war, and exceptionally so for a conflict in which field armies were rarely more than 30,000. Gustavus' victory was due to his numerical superiority, to the resilience of his Swedish forces despite their Saxon allies' collapse, and to his defensive position from which his superior artillery could attack Tilly's army. At Gustavus' next battle, Lützen, Wallenstein ordered his cavalry to copy the Swedes; the two forces were each 19,000 strong and, partly for that reason, the engagement was essentially inconclusive.

The uncertain outcomes of most of the campaigns were due largely to difficulties in the supply of men, money, and provisions; to the strength of fortifications; to the size of the disputed areas; and to the security of the key centres of Vienna, Paris, The Hague, and Stockholm.

MAP 3

The latter stages of the war saw wide-ranging campaigns in which control over much of Germany, especially Saxony, was bitterly contested. Despite her commitment against Spain, France also sent a number of armies across the Rhine and, although they were not always successful, they contributed to the heavy military pressure on the Austrian Habsburgs.

EUROPE AND THE TURKS, 1593-1664

THE STRENGTH and flexibility of the Ottoman military system became apparent in the century after Suleiman's death in 1566. The war with Poland (1620–21) was a fast-moving confrontation involving light cavalry and fortified camps. The Austro-Ottoman conflict (1593–1606) was a war of sieges around the Danube valley, while the war of 1663–64 was decided by a major battle.

SIEGES AND REVOLTS

War broke out between the Ottoman Empire and Austria along the Danube after large-scale border raids by irregulars on both sides led in 1592 to the intervention of regular forces (map 1). The Austrians renounced the peace treaty and attacked, routing an Ottoman army at Sissek (June 1593). In 1594, Prince Michael of Wallachia revolted against Ottoman rule. In the following year, the Austrians reversed initial Ottoman gains in northern Croatia, capturing Gran (September 1595) and threatening Bosnia. Ottoman forces overran most of Wallachia, but guerrilla activity and a severe winter forced them out, leading to a revolt in Moldavia.

In 1596, Mehmet III took personal charge of the army, the first sultan to do so since Suleiman. With over 100,000 men, he captured Erlau after a long siege, and at Mezö Kerésztés (October 1596), with a significant advantage in artillery, he outflanked and defeated the Austrians. Thereafter, the Turks took the initiative in the summer season, in both Hungary and Wallachia, but found it difficult to sustain their position during the winter.

Ottoman political problems, however, corroded army discipline and the Austrians were able to surprise and capture Raab (March 1598). In 1599, while the Ottoman army remained immobile due to instability in Constantinople, Michael of Wallachia overran first Transylvania and then Moldavia, but Ottoman-Polish action in 1601–05 restored Ottoman suzerainty. Under a new commander, Lala Mehmet Pasha, Ottoman forces regained Pest (1604), and took Gran and Visegrad (1605). Austrian policies of Catholicization prompted resistance, with Ottoman support, in Hungary and Transylvania. Peace was restored in 1606.

THE WAR OF 1663–64

War resumed in 1663 as a result of Habsburg efforts to challenge Ottoman dominance of Transylvania. The Grand Vizier, Fazil Ahmet, advanced in 1664, being met near St Gotthard by the Austrians under Montecuccoli, who sought to block any Ottoman advance on Graz or Vienna. The Austrians were supported by German contingents and by French troops sent by Louis XIV. The Ottoman forces, prevented from advancing across the river Raab, lost their cannon, but avoided a rout. The war was terminated swiftly

MAP 1

The wars of 1593–1606 and 1663–64, although bitter struggles, were less decisive than the earlier wars by which the Turks gained and subsequently lost Hungary. The situation was particularly serious for the Turks in 1594 when Prince Michael of Wallachia rebelled, and again in 1599–1600 when Michael conquered Transylvania and Moldavia.

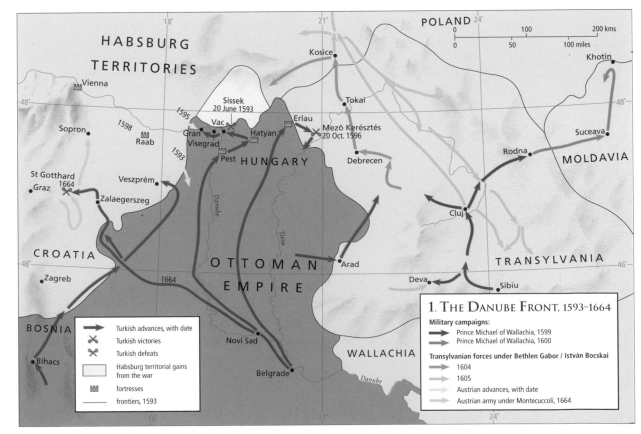

THE WAR FOR CRETE 1645-1669

A major war began in the Mediterranean in 1645 when the Ottomans invaded the Venetian possession of Crete in response to pirate raids. Sultan Ibrahim (1640–48) assembled a massive force of 400 ships and over 100,000 soldiers, and landed on the island on 24 June 1645. Canea was rapidly captured, but the siege of the capital Candia began in 1648 and lasted until 1669.

The Venetians sent reinforcements, including 33,000 mercenaries from Hanover, Celle, and Brunswick, while political divisions undermined the Ottoman war effort. The Venetians blockaded the Dardanelles in 1648, leading to the overthrow of the Sultan, and again from 1650. An Ottoman fleet which evaded the blockade was defeated off Naxos (1651), and in June 1656 the Venetians largely destroyed the Ottoman navy off the Dardanelles. The vigorous Mehmet Köprülü, who became Grand Vizier in the subsequent political crisis, rebuilt the fleet, and the blockade was broken in 1657. Köprülü's successor, Fazil Ahmet Pasha, personally led a renewed effort to take Candia in the mid-1660s. The Ottoman fleet cut off the flow of reinforcements from Europe, and in 1669 a quarrel between the Venetians and their European allies in the garrison led the latter to retire and forced the Venetians to capitulate.

by the Peace of Vasvar (1664), with an Austrian agreement to respect the Ottoman position in Transylvania.

OTTOMAN LOGISTICS

The Ottoman Empire faced formidable logistical problems in the Danube valley. During the war of 1593–1606 an efficient supply system moved food from Hungary, Wallachia, and Moldavia to the front. The supply line through Hungary was helped by the rivers that flow north-south: beyond Belgrade, men, supplies, and equipment were transported along the Danube or the Tisza. Troops could march the 600 miles (965km) from Constantinople to Buda in six weeks, drawing for provisions on forty depots. Magazines were set up by the army establishment in the conflict zone. The soldiers were well-fed, receiving meat regularly, and the pay was not generally in arrears, in marked contrast with most of Europe. The 'Ottoman road' from Constantinople to Buda and beyond ensured that Ottoman military administration was more efficient than other European powers.

St Gotthard was the major battle in the Austro-Turkish war of 1663–64. In 1661, Habsburg forces under the Italian Raimondo Montecuccoli had intervened in Transylvania to assist a rebellion against the Turks. This was unsuccessful and provoked Turkish attacks on Austria. Montecuccoli repelled the 1663 attack and checked the invasion in 1664 at St Gotthard.

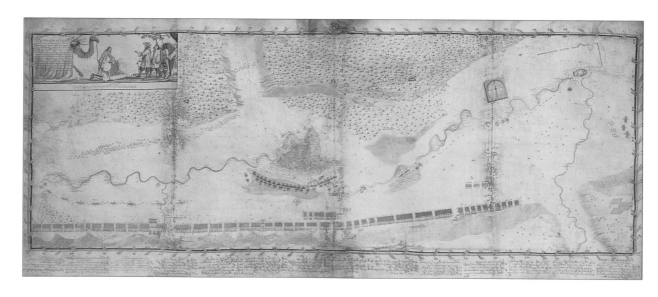

POLAND AT WAR, 1617-1667

EASTERN EUROPE *was a major field of conflict in the seventeenth century as Austria, Poland, Russia, Sweden, and the Ottoman Empire all sought territorial advantage over their rivals. Russia continued to seek a Baltic coastline, while the Swedes sought to dominate the eastern Baltic. This conflict turned Poland into a battleground for much of the century.*

THE IMPACT OF SWEDEN

Gustavus Adolphus of Sweden attacked Poland in 1617–18, 1621–22, and 1625–29, capturing the important Baltic port of Riga (1621) after a siege in which he used creeping barrages (systematically advancing artillery bombardment). He overran Livonia in 1625. These campaigns ensured that the Swedes were battle-hardened when Gustavus invaded Germany in 1630 (*page 66*).

Encounters with the Swedes led both Poland and Russia to experiment with new military ideas. In 1632–33, the Poles created musketeer units, replacing the earlier arquebusiers, and attempted to standardize their expanding artillery. Imitating the Swedes, the Poles introduced 3- to 6-pounder (1.4–2.7kg) regimental guns between 1633

and 1650. The Russian government, conscious of Swedish developments and dissatisfied with the *streltsy*, the permanent infantry corps equipped with handguns founded in 1550, decided in 1630 to form 'new order' military units, officered mainly by foreigners. Ten such regiments, totalling about 17,000 men, amounted to half the Russian army in the War of Smolensk with Poland (1632–34).

However, these changes were not decisive. Smolensk had been well fortified by the Russians before being lost to Poland during the Time of Troubles (1604–13), caused by a disputed succession. The Russian Siege of Smolensk (1632–34) was unsuccessful, and the Polish army under Wladyslaw IV inflicted a heavy defeat, with the Russians losing all but 8,000 of their 35,000 men. At the end of the war, the new Russian units were demobilized and the foreign mercenaries ordered to leave. Despite improvements to the Polish army, their few thousand infantry, dragoons, and artillery proved inadequate against a renewed Swedish invasion by Charles X, who seized Warsaw and Cracow. After their defeats at Zarnów and Wojinicz in 1655 (*map 1*), the Poles avoided battle with large Swedish formations, relying instead upon surprise attacks and raids.

POLISH TACTICAL ALTERNATIVES

The Poles and Russians had not only to fight 'western' style armies like the Swedes, but to resist the still powerful Turks

The Siege of Smolensk, 1609. Sigismund III sought to exploit the Russian Time of Troubles in order to gain control of the country. Smolensk, on the route to Moscow, withstood a siege from 19 September 1609 until it was stormed on the night of 2–3 June 1611. The fortifications comprised a 4-mile (6-km) circuit of walls, 38 towers, deep foundations, and a system of revetted listening galleries that thwarted the Polish attempts to dig mines under the Russian defences. Russian countermines blocked Polish mines in early 1610, and the Poles only succeeded after the garrison's strength had been reduced by the long siege.

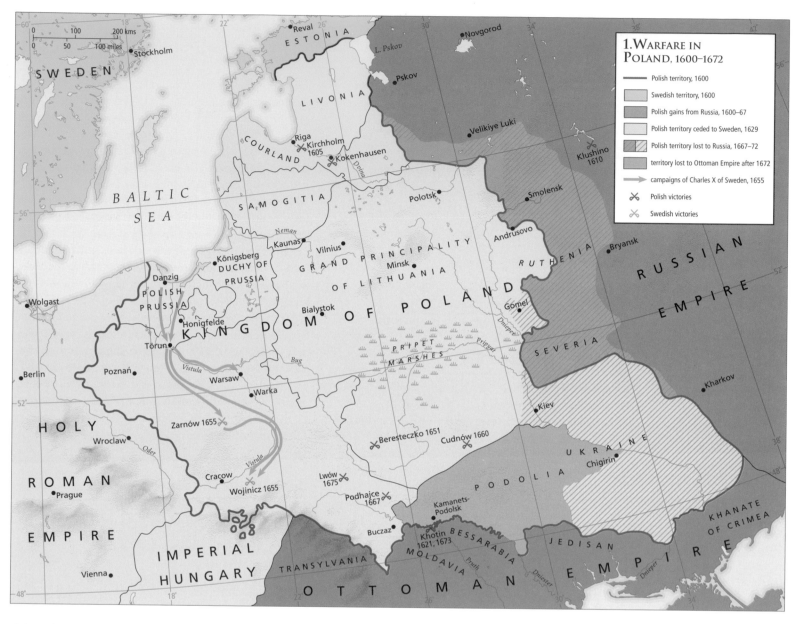

MAP 1

The great distances of Poland and its relatively low density of population led to a greater emphasis on cavalry than in western Europe. The Poles had to confront opponents with very different tactics and did so with some success. Although Warsaw fell to the Swedes in August 1655 and to the Transylvanians in 1657, the Poles were able to regain the city, not least because of their invaders' difficulties in controlling the countryside and supply routes.

and their Tatar allies. The Poles won cavalry victories over the Swedes at Kokenhausen (1601), Kirchholm (1605), and over a much larger Russo-Swedish army at Klushino (1610), though at Klushino the firepower of the Polish infantry and artillery also played a major role. The mobility and power of the Polish cavalry, which relied on shock charges, nullified its opponents' numerical superiority, and the Poles were able to destroy the Swedish cavalry before turning on their infantry. The Polish cavalry were deployed in shallower formations than hitherto. Just as the Dutch did not sweep to victory over Spain after the adoption of the Nassau reforms, so Gustavus was unable to defeat the Polish general Stanislaw Koniecpolski in his campaigns in Polish Prussia of 1626–29, where the two armies were roughly equal in quality. In view of the strength of the Polish cavalry, Gustavus was unwilling to meet the Poles in the open without the protection of fieldworks, while Polish cavalry attacks on supply lines and small units impeded Swedish operations. After defeating Christian IV of Denmark at Wolgast in September 1628, the Emperor Ferdinand II sent

12,000 men to the aid of his brother-in-law, Sigismund III of Poland, and the joint army advanced down the Vistula in 1629, pressing Gustavus hard at Honigfelde in June. In 1656, Stefan Czarniecki successfully used similar tactics of harassment, obliging the Swedes, who were not able to maintain their supplies, to withdraw: a Swedish force under Margrave Frederick of Baden was then destroyed by Polish cavalry at Warka, and Charles X was forced to abandon Warsaw and fell back on Polish Prussia. The Swedes had to admit failure.

Although the infantry techniques of countermarching and volley fire were not without relevance in eastern Europe, the small number of engagements fought between linear formations and settled by firepower is a reminder that these innovations were not all-powerful. Cavalry tactics remained especially important here, not least because the strategy of raiding could be employed to undermine an opponent's logistics. Sieges also played only a relatively minor role, although control of bases such as Riga, Smolensk, and Danzig (Gdansk) was of great importance.

THE FRANCO-HABSBURG WARS (II), 1628-1659

FRENCH EFFORTS to profit from Spanish Habsburg entanglement in the Thirty Years' War led to a gruelling struggle in which decisive victory eluded both sides. Neither France nor Spain succeeded in fielding armies large enough for the bold strategies necessary, and supply difficulties and desertion restricted campaigning to areas in which forces could support themselves by foraging.

A SERIES OF DEFEATS

French involvement in the Thirty Years' War was precluded for more than ten years by a fierce military and political struggle within France itself, between Catholics and the Protestant Huguenot community. However, after the fall in 1628 of the Huguenot stronghold of La Rochelle (map 1), Louis XIII and his leading minister Richelieu were free to turn their attention to France's most formidable neighbour, Spain, and to Spain's ally, Austria.

After a limited war in northern Italy in 1628–31, in which the Spanish failure to take besieged Casale led to a compromise peace, major military action began in 1635. The French sought a single decisive campaign and launched a number of attacks, but they were unsuccessful. The Duke of Rohan took the Valtelline Pass between Austria and Spanish-ruled Lombardy (map 1), but swiftly found himself without sufficient food, fodder, or pay for his troops. The French invasion of the Spanish Netherlands in 1635 collapsed, with supply failures leading to large-scale desertion. In 1636, Rohan invaded Lombardy itself, but his officers were unwilling to abandon their booty from Valtelline, and his troops were sick and mutinous. Without cannon,

ROCROI 19 MAY 1643

The Battle of Rocroi resulted from an attempt to end a siege. The Spanish Army of Flanders under Francisco de Melo, besieging the fortress of Rocroi in the Ardennes while advancing into France, was challenged by the 22-year-old Louis de Condé, Duc d'Enghien. Enghien deployed the superior French force in two lines, with cavalry on the wings. The French right, under his personal command, defeated the opposing cavalry under the Duke of Albuquerque (1), but the Spanish cavalry under the experienced Isembourg won the cavalry battle on the other flank, driving L'Hôpital and the French left from the field. Isembourg turned on the French centre, and was held off only by the commitment of every available French reserve (2). Enghien took the dramatic option of leading his cavalry behind the Spanish centre to rout Isembourg (3), and then attacked the Spanish infantry, which held off the French cavalry until weakened by French cannon and infantry fire. The Spanish infantry *tercios* under Fontaine, Velada, and Visconti were virtually destroyed; a sixth *tercio* under the German Beck failed to arrive in time to save the Spanish army. The battle had a great impact on contemporary observers and subsequent historians because of the high reputation of the Army of Flanders. It also established Enghien, with his resilience and rapid responsiveness in action, as one of the leading generals of the age. The French lost 4,000 dead and wounded out of an army of 23,000, but most of the Spanish infantry was wiped out. The consequences of the battle have, however, been exaggerated, for the Spaniards rapidly regrouped.

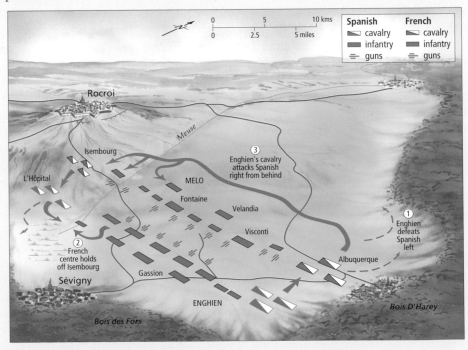

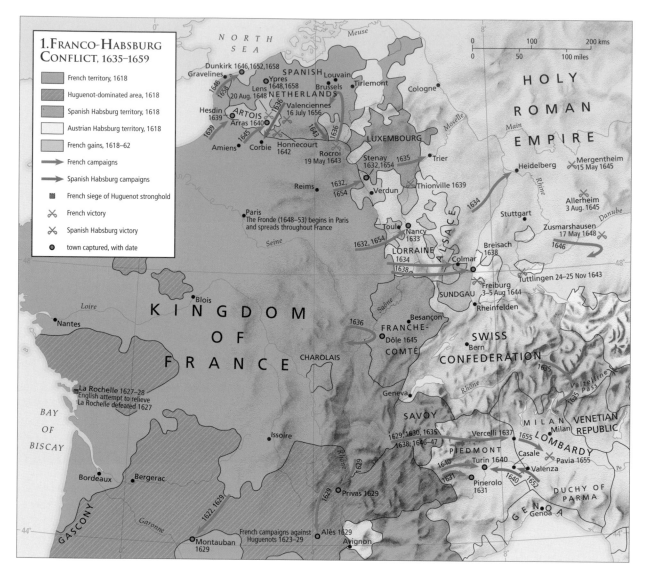

MAP 1
The Franco-Habsburg struggle was wide-ranging and fought on a number of fronts. Although France was the most populous state in western Europe and had a well-developed agricultural base, it proved unable to crush the Habsburgs, despite enjoying the alliance of the Dutch, the Swedes, and the German Protestants. The French lacked a system of effective military administration and sound finances, and the strains of the war revealed the inadequacies of their reliance on expedients. Logistical failures led to massive desertion and to campaigns in which the search for supplies played a major role. The French failed to conquer the Spanish Netherlands and Lombardy, but had more success in moving into the Rhineland where resistance was weaker.

munitions, or money, Rohan dared not move into the Lombard plain, and in the following year he had to abandon his Valtelline fortresses.

A Spanish counter-invasion of France in 1636 failed to overthrow Richelieu, but caused great anxiety in Paris, with Spanish forces advancing as far as Amiens and Corbie. This invasion emphasized the vulnerability of France to attack from the Spanish Netherlands: the centre of French power was nearby and there were no major natural obstacles.

After Corbie, the French launched offensives into the Spanish Netherlands, conquering Hesdin (1639), and Arras (1640). An invasion of Catalonia in 1637 (map 2) was unsuccessful, but the army of Bernard of Saxe-Weimar, incorporated into the French army, consolidated the French position in Alsace, crossed the Rhine, defeated the Austrians at Rheinfelden (1638), and captured Breisach (1638), cutting Spanish routes between northern Italy and the Netherlands and opening the way into Germany. A renewed French invasion of northern Italy (map 1) was unsuccessful in the face of the same problems of supply and desertion which had dogged Rohan.

From the mid-1630s, the war is often presented in terms of French victories, especially Rocroi (1643) and Lens

(1648) over the Army of Flanders. In fact, these were offset by continuing logistical problems, and a series of French defeats: a French invasion of the Basque country in 1638 was thwarted at Fuenterrabia (map 2), when a besieging army under Enghien was defeated by the Spanish; the Austrian Habsburg allies of the Spanish were victorious over a French army at Thionville (map 1) in the following year; and the Army of Flanders defeated the French at Honnecourt in 1642. The consequences of the French victory at Rocroi itself have been exaggerated, for the Spanish forces in fact speedily regrouped. In 1643, at Tuttlingen, the French army in Germany was defeated by the pro-Habsburg Bavarians and forced into a winter retreat to the Rhine, abandoning its baggage and losing most of its men. There were further French defeats at the hands of the Bavarians at Freiburg (1644) and Mergentheim (1645). Only in Catalonia, where France profited from an anti-Spanish rebellion in 1640 and Perpignan fell in 1642, was French success significant.

A COMPROMISE PEACE

After the mid-1640s, it was less a question of French defeats than of a failure to make much progress, certainly progress commensurate with the need to defeat Spain before debt

MAP 2

The French made a number of efforts to drive the Spaniards from Italy. They also sought to exploit the revolt of the Catalans. Spain faced a major crisis in 1638–43, but successfully overcame it and further displayed its resilience by beating off French challenges in Italy and by regaining Catalonia.

2. FRANCO-HABSBURG CONFLICT IN THE MEDITERRANEAN, 1618–1662

- French territory, 1618
- Spanish Habsburg territory, 1618
- French gains, 1638–62
- Spanish Habsburg territories in revolt
- → French campaigns
- → Spanish Habsburg campaigns
- ✂ Spanish Habsburg victory
- ● town captured, with date
- ▦ siege

Porto Longone (*below*), with Piombino and Orbitello, was one of the *presidios*, important Spanish bases on the Tuscan coast that controlled naval movements. Porto Longone, on the island of Elba, was captured by the French in 1646, at the same time that they gained Piombino. The Spaniards regained Piombino and Porto Longone in 1650.

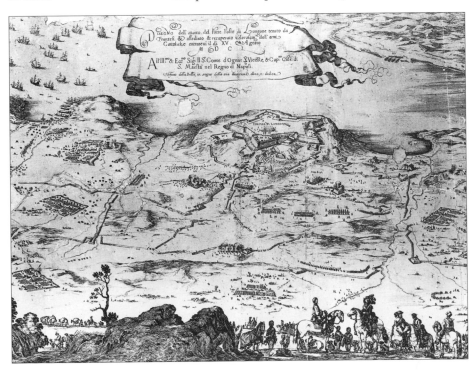

overwhelmed France's finances. Despite major efforts in the mid-1640s, decisive victory continued to elude the French. In Italy, a French army failed to take Genoa, Finale, and Orbitello and thus cut links between Spain and Italy, and attempts to exploit anti-Spanish rebellions in Palermo and Naples in 1647 met with equally little success (*map 2*). In the same year in Spain, Enghien abandoned the Siege of Lérida in the face of Spanish reinforcements.

Spain's North Sea naval base, Dunkirk, fell to Enghien in 1646 after a short siege, but it and other French gains, such as Ypres and Gravelines, were lost when Spain took advantage of the *Fronde*, the French civil wars of 1648–53. During this period the Spanish also regained Catalonia, with Barcelona falling in 1652 after a 14-month blockade had reduced the population to starvation. The fortress of Casale was captured in 1652, while Porto Longone and Piombino, lost in 1646, were regained in 1650. However, Spain's attempt to intervene directly in the *Fronde* by invading Gascony to help Mazarin's opponents in Bordeaux failed.

The end of the *Fronde* brought little improvement in French prospects, although a Spanish attempt to regain Arras in 1654 was unsuccessful. The Spanish captured Rocroi in 1654. Further defeats at Pavia (1655) and Valenciennes (1656) led France to offer reasonable peace terms, only for Philip IV to reject them. Valenciennes, where Spanish forces were commanded by the *frondeur* Enghien, was a spectacular victory, in which the French baggage train and supplies were captured. Pavia, where Spanish troops were commanded by the Marquis of Caraçena, was followed by the overrunning of the Duchy of Modena, whose Duke had abandoned Spain and encouraged Richelieu's successor Mazarin to invade Lombardy. In the following year, Spain won two more victories in Lombardy, showing how fruitless were Mazarin's Italian hopes.

Far from causing a collapse of the Spanish Empire, the war ended in the compromise Peace of the Pyrenees (1659). This came only after the intervention of fresh English forces on the side of France had tipped the balance in Flanders. Cromwell's Ironsides helped Turenne to defeat the Army of Flanders at the Battle of the Dunes (1658), as the Spanish tried to relieve the siege of Dunkirk. The Spanish army was outnumbered, its artillery had not arrived, the terrain prevented it from taking advantage of its superiority in cavalry, and its flank was bombarded by English warships. Having captured Dunkirk, Gravelines, Menin, and Ypres, Turenne could threaten an advance on Brussels. In the peace, England was rewarded with Dunkirk, only to see the recently restored Charles II sell it in 1662 to Louis XIV.

THE ENGLISH CIVIL WARS, 1638-1652

THE MOST SUSTAINED *serious civil conflict in seventeenth-century Europe occurred in mid-century Britain. A hard-fought war in England was eventually won by Parliament's forces thanks to their superior resources, generalship, and fighting qualities. These forces then conquered Ireland and Scotland and established a military dictatorship under Oliver Cromwell.*

THE ROAD TO WAR

The outbreak of civil war in England was a result of a political crisis in 1641–42, stemming from risings in Scotland (1638) and Ireland (1641). In Scotland, the absentee Charles I's support for episcopacy and liturgical change, and his tactless and autocratic handling of Scottish interests and patronage, led to a Presbyterian and national response which produced a National Covenant (1638). This was opposed to all ecclesiastical innovations. Episcopacy was abolished in Scotland, and Charles' military response in the Bishops' Wars (1639–40) was unsuccessful. The First Bishops' War was essentially a matter of inconsequential border manoeuvres. The Covenanters under Alexander Leslie, who had served under Gustavus Adolphus at Lützen (*page 69*), captured Aberdeen and Edinburgh Castle without loss in 1639, and went on to deploy a large army to block an advancing force under Charles I, which encamped near Berwick.

Neither side wanted a confrontation, and a treaty was signed in June 1639.

As with the last British military commitment, the wars with Spain and France of the 1620s, the new conflict weakened Charles by undermining both his finances and his political position. The war also altered the relationship between the English Crown and Parliament. Charles' 'Personal Rule' was no longer viable: rulers of England lacked the resources to fight unless they turned to Parliament. The Short Parliament (April–May 1640) refused to vote funds, and operations resumed. The Scots then invaded Northumberland and Durham in the Second Bishops' War. Leslie encountered no resistance until he forced the passage of the Tyne at Newburn (28 August). Newcastle fell two days later and Leslie remained there for a year. The Treaty of Ripon in October 1640 brought peace, but at the cost of a daily payment which forced Charles to summon the Long Parliament.

Charles' inability to retain control of the situation led him to attempt a coup, forcibly entering Parliament on 4 January 1642 to seize his most virulent opponents. They had already fled to the City of London. As both sides prepared for war, Charles left London in order to raise funds. This was a crucial move, as the history of civil conflict up to and including the Jacobite rising of 1745 was to demonstrate the importance of controlling the capital's resources and institutions. In 1642, most supporters of both sides sought peace, and local neutrality pacts were negotiated, but determined minorities polarized the nation.

MARSTON MOOR 2 JULY 1644

The siege of York by Parliamentary and Scottish forces led the Royalists to mount a relief effort under Prince Rupert. He approached York from the west with an army of about 18,000 men and, on 1 July, relieved the city. The next day, he confronted the larger allied army (about 27,000 men). Both armies deployed cavalry on the flanks and infantry in the centre. The allies launched a surprise attack at about 7pm. On the allied left, Cromwell and Leslie drove their opponents' cavalry from the field (1). On the opposite flank the Royalist cavalry was successful, and an infantry struggle in the centre ended when Cromwell's cavalry joined the assault on the Royalist infantry (2). The allies lost about 1,500 men, the Royalists 3,000 and their artillery, but more seriously their cohesion was broken and the Royalist cause in the north fatally defeated.

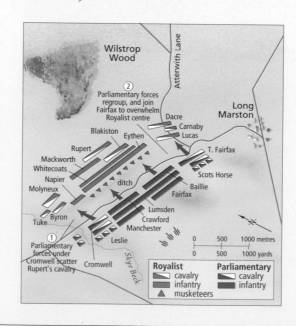

Charles raised his standard at Nottingham in the following month (map 1). He advanced on London, narrowly winning the Battle of Edgehill (23 October), but was checked at Turnham Green to the west of London (13 November). Charles failed to press home an advantage in what were difficult circumstances, and retreated to establish his headquarters at Oxford. His best chance of winning the war had passed.

In 1643, the Royalists made gains in much of England, particularly in the West Country where Bristol fell (26 July) to assault after a brief siege. But Charles' truce with the Irish rebels, freeing the royal forces in Ireland, was more than counteracted by the Solemn League and Covenant between the Scots and Parliament. However, the Royalist sieges of Glouceser and Hull were both unsuccessful, and the principal battle in the vital Thames valley and surrounding area, the first Battle of Newbury (20 September) was inconclusive. The Royalist cavalry outfought their opponents, but their infantry were less successful.

The Scots, under Leslie, now First Earl of Leven, accordingly entered England in the following January and, at Marston Moor near York on 2 July, they and a Parliamentary army under Sir Thomas Fairfax and Oliver Cromwell crushed the Royalists under Prince Rupert and the Duke of Newcastle (map 2). For Charles I the north had been lost. York surrendered on 16 July and Newcastle was stormed by the Scots on 19 October. In 1644, in the Midlands the Royalists were beaten at Nantwich (25 January), but relieved at Newark (22 March), and held off Parliamentary attack at Cropredy Bridge (29 June). Further south, the Earl of Essex advanced into Cornwall only to be cut off by Charles I and defeated at Lostwithiel (2 September). Charles fought off a larger Parliamentary army at the inconclusive second Battle of Newbury (27 October).

In 1645, the Parliamentary forces were reorganized as the New Model Army, with a unified national command under Fairfax, Cromwell as commander of the cavalry, and chaplains who were mostly religious radicals. This force defeated the Royalist field armies, most notably at Naseby (page 80). The principal Royalist army in the west was defeated at Langport (10 July 1645). Sherborne Castle fell on 15 August, Bristol was successfully stormed on 10-11 September. The Royalists were also defeated at Rowton Heath near Chester (24 September). By the end of the year the Royalists were reduced to isolated strongholds; Chester surrendered on 3 February 1646, Torrington was stormed on 16 February, Exeter surrendered on 13 April, Newark on 6 May, and Oxford on 24 June. In May 1646, Charles gave himself up to the Scots.

Amongst other reasons, Parliament's victory was due to the support of the wealthiest parts of the country, of the Scots, of London, of the major ports, of the navy, and also to its followers' religious zeal. On the other hand, the Parliamentarians suffered from lacklustre and unsuccessful commanders like Essex, Manchester, and Waller, aroused hostility by high taxation, and initially had far less effective cavalry than the Royalists. As with the collapse of royal

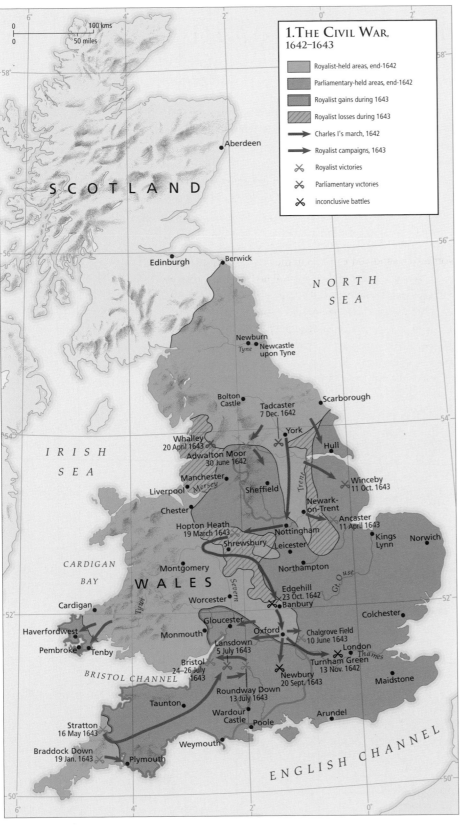

MAP 1

In the early stages of the war, operations in different regions were only loosely co-ordinated and neither side was able to gain a decisive advantage.

THE FIRST CIVIL WAR

Although crude socio-economic or geographical determinism should be avoided, Parliamentary support was strongest in the south and east, and in large towns and industrial areas, especially London and Bristol, while support for Charles I was strongest in the north and west and in Wales. Fighting began at Manchester in July 1642, and

NASEBY 14 JUNE 1645

The Battle of Marston Moor lost the North for the Royalists – York surrendered on 16 July – but elsewhere the King's forces fought on with great success. The principal Parliamentary army under the Earl of Essex unwisely advanced into Cornwall, a Royalist heartland, and, outnumbered, was then cut off and defeated at Lostwithiel (2 September 1644). At the second Battle of Newbury (27 October), the Parliamentarians failed to prevent Charles' return to his capital at Oxford.

In response to these failures, Parliament reorganized its army and in the summer of 1645 contested the Royalist control of the Midlands. Prince Rupert stormed Leicester for the King on 30 May, and the two sides met at Naseby, 11 miles (16km) north-west of

Northampton, on 14 June. The Parliamentary victory in three hours was especially decisive.

Charles I had only 3,600 cavalry and 4,000 foot; Fairfax 14,000 men. Rupert swept the cavalry on the Parliamentary left from the field (1), but was then unable to prevent his troop from attacking the Parliamentary baggage train (2). Cromwell, on the right, defeated the Royalist cavalry opposite (3) and then turned on the veteran but heavily outnumbered Royalist infantry in the centre, which succumbed to an overwhelming attack (4). Nearly 5,000 Royalists were captured, and the King's army ceased to exist. The superior discipline of the Parliamentary cavalry was thus decisive in the most important battle of the war.

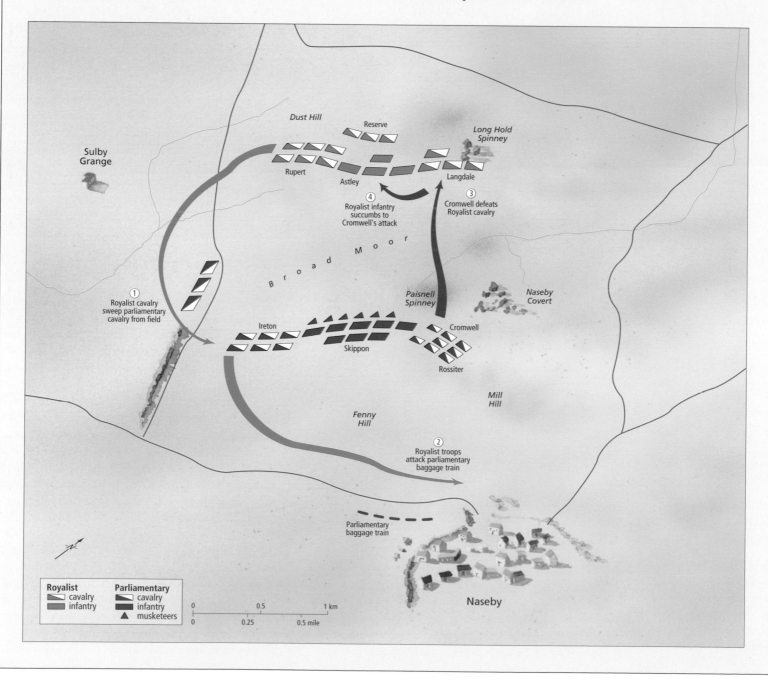

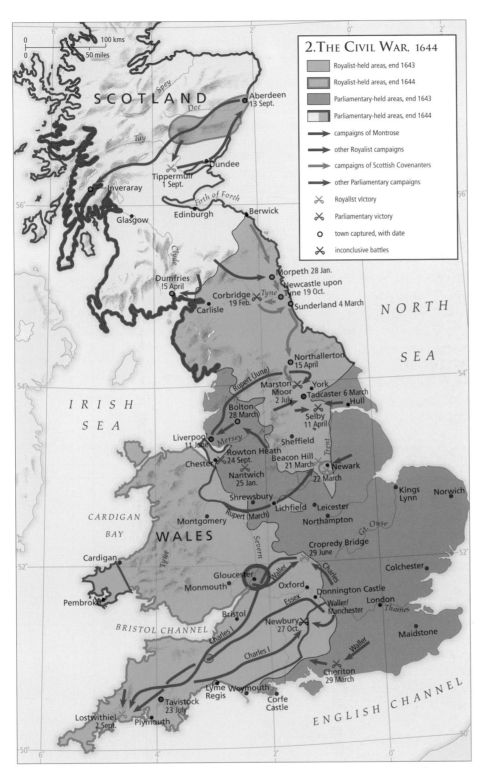

MAP 2

The Parliamentarians failed to achieve victory in the south and were defeated at Lostwithiel, but victory at Marston Moor gave them the north of England. Montrose revived the Royalist cause in Scotland.

power in 1638–40, the defeat of Charles I owed much to the Scots. The Union of the Crowns (1603) had ensured that the political fates of England and Scotland could not be separated, and the effect was destabilizing on both countries. The Cromwellian conquests of Scotland and Ireland (map 5) were attempts to restore stability and prefigured the Restoration in 1660 of Stuart monarchy throughout the British Isles. The war was a major struggle; more than half the total number of battles ever fought on English soil involving more than 5,000 men were fought in 1642–51. Out of an English male population of about 1.5 million, over

80,000 died in combat and another 100,000 of other causes arising from the war, principally disease. Bitter civil conflict was not new and more men may have fought at Towton (1461) in the Wars of the Roses than in any of the battles of the Civil War, but the sustained level of hostilities, the Britain-wide scale of the conflict, and the vicious politicization of popular attitudes were unprecedented. After the Battle of Hopton Heath (19 March 1643), for example, Sir John Gell, the Parliamentary Governor of Derby, paraded the naked corpse of the Earl of Northampton round the city. In addition, the war followed a long period in which most of England, especially the more prosperous south, had been peaceful; town walls had fallen into disrepair, castles into disuse.

Though sieges played a major role in the conflict, it was the battles that were decisive. As well as the major battles, there were also many small-scale actions that were successful locally, for the war was both a national conflict and a series of local wars. At Winceby (11 October 1643), for example, a minor cavalry engagement won by Oliver Cromwell was important to the course of the war in Lincolnshire. Such local engagements reflected and affected the geography of the conflict. Derbyshire was a linchpin of the Parliamentary cause in the Midlands, and therefore the goal of Royalist attacks from Yorkshire and the Midlands. Control of Derbyshire, especially the crossings over the river Trent, would have linked these areas and helped the Royalists to apply greater pressure on the East Anglian-based Parliamentary Eastern Association. Royalist failure lessened the co-ordination of their field armies, and led to longer lines of communication. Thus local struggles interacted with the national.

THE WAR IN WALES

The Royalist cause was also defeated in Wales and Scotland. When the Civil War broke out, the vast majority of the Welsh were loyal to the King; support for Parliament was strongest in Pembrokeshire. The gentry were overwhelmingly Royalist and there were no large cities within which support for Parliament and Puritanism could develop. Wales produced large numbers of men and much money for Charles, and Welsh troops played a major role in both distant and nearby operations, for example at Gloucester, which was besieged unsuccessfully in 1643.

Initially, fighting within Wales was confined to the southwest. Tenby and Haverfordwest fell to the Royalists in 1643 (map 1), but Pembroke was reinforced by a Parliamentary fleet in 1644 and much of the county was retaken. Parliamentary forces then advanced to capture Cardiganshire and Carmarthen, from which they were driven in the summer of 1644 (map 2). Fighting ebbed and flowed until, in late 1645, the impact of Parliamentary success elsewhere led to final victory in south-west Wales.

In November 1643, much of north Wales had been overrun by the Parliamentary forces, but they were driven back by troops from Ireland and it was not until the summer of 1644 that the Parliamentarians made a major impact again in north-east Wales. The fall of nearby English Royalist bases at Shrewsbury, Bristol, and Chester (1645–46) was crucial. Royalist confidence in Wales was undermined, as was the Welsh economy, and in the autumn of 1645 the Royalist position in south Wales finally collapsed, with mass defections. The castles remained in Royalist hands but one by one they fell to the remorseless pressure of superior Parliamentary forces, and Harlech finally surrendered in March 1647.

THE WAR IN SCOTLAND

After the Scots entered England in January 1644 (map 2), Charles sent James Graham, Marquess of Montrose, to invade Scotland. He did so with a poorly-prepared small army in April 1644 but, having captured Dumfries, he had to retreat in the face of more numerous opposition. Invading again in August, he routed Lord Elcho's larger army at Tippermuir on 1 September: Montrose's forces won a firefight and then charged an already beaten opponent. On 13 September, Montrose won another victory outside Aberdeen. At Inverlochy (2 February 1645), his men delayed firing on Argyll's Highlanders until the last moment and then followed up their devastating volley with a successful charge (map 3). As with the other Scottish battles, the bulk of the fighting was borne by Irish or Lowland infantry, and the Highlanders were then used to rout an already weakened enemy. More casualties were inflicted in the pursuit than in the battle.

Montrose took Elgin (19 February) and Dundee (4 April), and then retreated before an outnumbering force. At the Battle of Auldearn (9 May), Montrose's ability to respond decisively to the unpredictable won the day, as it did for Louis de Condé, Duc d'Enghien, at Rocroi (page 75) and for Cromwell at Naseby. A successful counter-attack brought him victory over a larger force. At Alford (2 July), victory in the opening cavalry battle left the opposing infantry exposed to attack in flank and rear; and at Kilsyth (15 August), the main government army in Scotland under General William Baillie was defeated in a confused battle, Montrose's cavalry again playing a decisive role. Glasgow and Edinburgh were then briefly occupied, but Montrose's army shrank as the Highlanders returned home. The Scottish army in England under General David Leslie marched north and at Philiphaugh (13 September), Montrose's outnumbered army was taken by surprise and defeated. Montrose fled back to the Highlands, his prestige shattered. After guerrilla action during the winter, Montrose failed to take Inverness, although another Royalist, the Marquis of Huntly, stormed Aberdeen on 14 May 1646. Both then dispersed their troops when Charles I, having surrendered to the Scots army in England, ordered them to lay down their arms.

Montrose was often at fault for neglecting to arrange effective reconnaissance, and he failed to gain control of an area of any size for long enough to establish himself and recruit substantial numbers of men – he lacked sufficient regular troops. Montrose was a brilliant tactician, a master of flank victory – putting his best troops on his flanks and

seeking to defeat the enemy flanks before his weaker centre engaged, and subsequently destroying the opponent's centre. As a commander, he was very successful in welding together both militia and regulars.

THE SECOND CIVIL WAR

The Parliamentary victory in England led almost immediately to renewed division within Parliament itself, within the army and in Scotland, and the imprisoned Charles I sought to exploit the situation (map 5). Royalist and discontented Parliamentarian risings in 1648 were important,

MAP 3

After a series of victories, Montrose was finally defeated at Philiphaugh. In England, the Royalist field armies were defeated, most notably at Naseby.

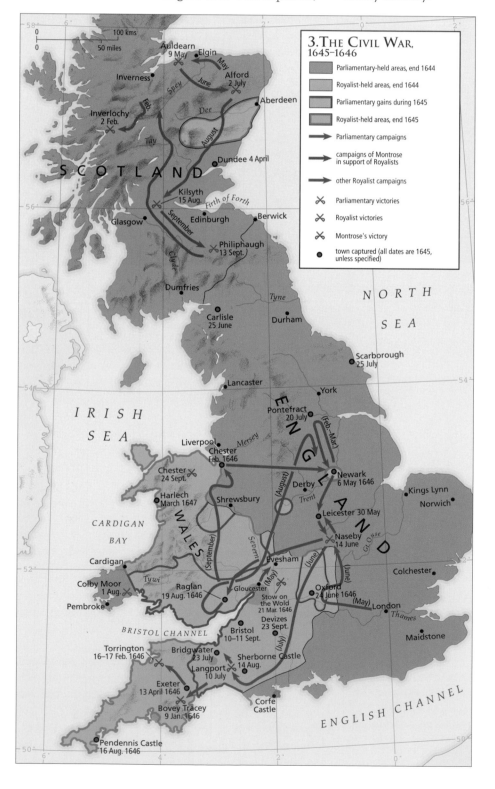

The Siege of Oxford by Jan Wyck. Oxford, the Royalist capital during the First English Civil War, was the goal of Parliamentary pressure throughout the conflict, but it was protected by outlying garrisons, such as Banbury, Wallingord, and Donnington Castle, by natural barriers such as the Chilterns, and by the principal Royalist army. The last, however, was defeated at Naseby in 1645 and Parliamentary pressure increased. On 13 May 1646 the Parliamentarians, under Sir Thomas Fairfax, finished a fort on nearby Headington Hill, from which artillery duels took place until a cease-fire was agreed at the end of the month, the prelude to the Royalist surrender in June.

but a Scottish invasion on behalf of Charles, who had agreed in return to recognize Scots Presbyterianism, was crucial. The risings were crushed: Cromwell advanced into south Wales and overcame the opposition at St Fagan's; Fairfax did the same in Kent. The Royalists then concentrated at Colchester, resisted assaults by Fairfax, and waited for news of the Scots.

The Scots entered Cumberland under the command of the Duke of Hamilton on 8 July and pushed south. Having taken the surrender of Pembroke (11 July 1648), Cromwell then pushed north, advancing into Yorkshire, where he sought to attack the flank of his opponent's advance at Preston. Hamilton ignored the warnings of the Royalist Sir Marmaduke Langdale, and his overstretched, unco-ordinated forces were pushed aside when Cromwell captured Preston on 17 August. The Scottish cavalry played no part in the battle. News of the Scots' defeat prompted a Royalist surrender at Colchester.

The formal trial and execution of Charles I took place on 30 January 1649. England was declared a republic and the House of Lords was abolished. However, the republican regime was faced with very different governments in Scotland and Ireland, and could not feel safe until these had been overthrown. In a tremendous display of military power which contrasted with the indecisiveness of much conflict on the Continent, the republican forces conquered both Scotland, a success which had eluded English monarchs throughout history, and Ireland, as well as the remaining English Royalist bases in the Channel Islands, the Isles of Scilly, and the Isle of Man.

IRELAND 1641–1652

In 1641, the Irish had risen in revolt and slaughtered many of the Anglo-Scottish settlers (map 6). Their leader Rory O'More defeated government forces at Julianstown (29 November), and then formed an alliance with many of the Royalist Anglo-Irish landowners of The Pale. Ulster was overrun by the rebels. The Scots sent an army to reimpose Protestant rule and it landed at Carrickfergus in April 1642. There followed a three-way struggle between Royalists, Scots/Parliamentarians, and the Catholic Confederacy of Kilkenny (the Irish rebels), who controlled most of the country, although part of Ulster was dominated by the Scots and The Pale by the Royalists.

The rebels, under Sir Phelim O'Neill, were defeated at Kilrush in 1642 and driven from Carlingford and Newry. They were poorly armed and disciplined and had a weak supply system which made lengthy sieges difficult. Instead, the rebels relied on avoiding battle, and on ambushes and raids. Their rivals, distracted by the war in England, were unable to sustain operations, and in 1643 the Royalists had to abandon the siege of Ross and to limit operations to the Dublin region. The Scots in Ulster also lacked sufficient force to overrun much of Ireland. In 1642, Owen Roe O'Neill, Thomas Preston, and 1,000 Irish veterans returned from Flanders and brought new energy to the rebel cause, organizing effective armies that pushed their opponents back in Ulster and Leinster. A truce between the Royalists and Irish rebels in September 1643 led the latter to turn against the Scots, but poor supplies and weather led to the failure of operations in Ulster in 1644. However, in

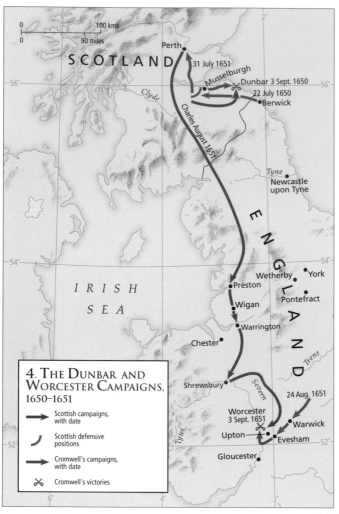

4. THE DUNBAR AND WORCESTER CAMPAIGNS, 1650–1651

→ Scottish campaigns, with date

〰 Scottish defensive positions

→ Cromwell's campaigns, with date

✗ Cromwell's victories

MAP 4

Greatly helped by the battle-hardened nature of his army, Cromwell revealed his ability in both offence and defence in the Dunbar and Worcester campaigns.

MAP 5

The Second Civil War was rapidly over, reflecting the strength, flexibility, and determination of the New Model Army, and the quality of its leaders. Cromwell's capture of Preston on 17 August revealed serious deficiencies in the Scottish army.

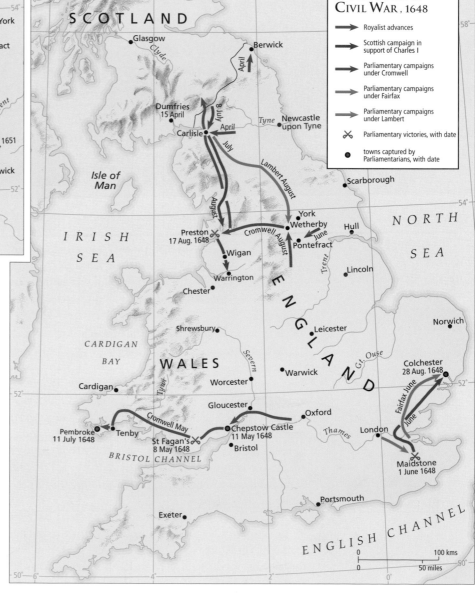

5. THE SECOND CIVIL WAR, 1648

→ Royalist advances

→ Scottish campaign in support of Charles I

→ Parliamentary campaigns under Cromwell

→ Parliamentary campaigns under Fairfax

→ Parliamentary campaigns under Lambert

✗ Parliamentary victories, with date

● towns captured by Parliamentarians, with date

1646, a new advance under O'Neill exploited Scottish over-confidence and the Scots army was crushed at Benburb (5 June 1646). Preston took Roscommon.

In 1647, with Charles I imprisoned, the Royalist commander, the Earl of Ormonde, surrendered Dublin to Michael Jones, a Parliamentary colonel. His position there was challenged by Preston, but at Dungan Hill (8 August), Preston's flanks were smashed by Jones' cavalry and the Parliamentary infantry defeated the Irish centre, inflicting heavy casualties. The military balance in Leinster had changed greatly. Later in the year, Jones took Athboy. Another Parliamentary army under the Earl of Inchiquin, operating in the south-west in 1647, captured Dungarvan, sacked Cashel and, with superior cavalry, defeated the Confederate Army of Munster at Knocknanuss (13 November). The Parliamentary cause deteriorated in 1648 when the Second Civil War led Ormonde to return from Scotland, while Inchiquin changed sides. In 1649, Ormonde took Drogheda and Dundalk, and in June besieged Jones in Dublin. The Irish were helped by Royalist warships under Prince Rupert. Jones defeated Ormonde at Baggarath/Rathmines (2 August), and Cromwell landed at Dublin thirteen days later with 12,000 New Model Army veterans.

Cromwell's campaign, especially the storming of Drogheda (10 September) and Wexford (11 October), has

since become proverbial in Irish consciousness for its cruelty. In fact, the conflict in the 1640s was as much an Irish civil war as an English invasion, and the struggle had begun with a Catholic uprising in 1641 in which Protestants were massacred. At neither Drogheda nor Wexford were there attacks on women and children, though at Drogheda, where

Cromwell's siege artillery achieved a firing rate of 200 cannonballs per day, the garrison of about 2,500 was slaughtered, the few who received quarter being sent to work on the sugar plantations in Barbados. Cromwell's forces were well-supplied with reinforcements, money, and supplies, enabling them to operate most of the year round. Well-equipped with carts, wagons and draft-horses, they retained the initiative and were were also supported by the Commonwealth's navy which blockaded Rupert's squadron and protected Cromwell's supply routes.

After Wexford, his forces captured Ross, Carrick, Clonmel, and Kilkenny, and on 26 May 1650 he left for England en route for Scotland. His successor, his son-in-law Henry Ireton, defeated the Irish at Scarrifhollis (21 June), thus ending Irish resistance in the north and captured Waterford (August), and Limerick (27 October 1651); Galway fell in April 1652. Largely as a result of subsequent famine, plague, and emigration, the conquest led to the loss of about 40 per cent of the Irish population, and was followed by widespread expropriation of Catholic land as the Anglo-Irish Catholics lost power and status.

THE CONQUEST OF SCOTLAND

Scottish quiescence was crucial to the early stages of the conquest of Ireland, but in 1650 Charles I's eldest son, Charles II, came to terms with the Scots. In response,

Cromwell invaded Scotland on 22 July 1650 (map 4). Unable to breach the Scottish fortified positions around Edinburgh and outmanoeuvred by David Leslie, he retreated to Dunbar. Cromwell, cut off from retreat to England by a force twice the size of his own, launched a surprise attack which defeated the Scottish cavalry, while much of the infantry surrendered (3 September). Edinburgh was then captured.

In the following summer, Cromwell used his command of the sea to outflank the Scots at Stirling and occupied Perth, but Charles then marched south into England, hoping to ignite a Royalist rebellion (map 4). He reached Wigan on 15 August, but, short of recruits, decided to head for the Welsh Borders rather than march directly on London. Shrewsbury, however, resisted the Royalist advance, and when Charles reached Worcester on 22 August he had recruited few additional men. His opponents concentrated on Warwick on 24 August and then advanced on Worcester, winning a crossing over the Severn at Upton. The Parliamentarians under Cromwell, who numbered about 30,000 men, drove at Worcester on 3 September from several directions. The Royalists, with about 12,000, launched an initially successful frontal attack on Cromwell's position, but numbers told and the Royalist army was overwhelmed. Hiding in an oak tree and supporters' houses en route, Charles II fled to France, leaving the Royalist cause crushed. By the summer of 1652, all Scotland had fallen.

MAP 6

The war in Ireland involved a number of parties and lacked a central focus. Political and personal differences, limited resources, and a failure to take Dublin weakened the Irish rebels, and although they often put up firm resistance, as at Waterford, Cromwell's superior resources and generalship brought a relatively rapid end to the conflict.

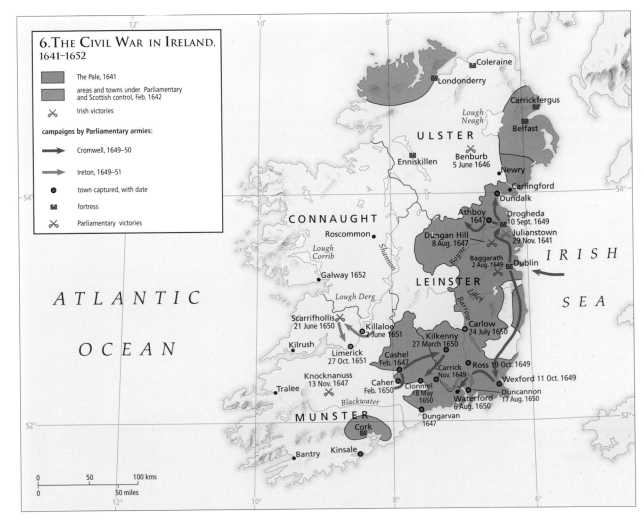

EUROPEAN NAVAL CONFLICT

ENGLAND and the Netherlands fought three inconclusive naval wars between 1652 and 1674 over trade and control of the southern North Sea. In the first of these, more major naval battles were fought than had taken place in the Atlantic for one hundred and fifty years. By the end of the century, the English navy was the most powerful in the world.

THE FIRST ANGLO-DUTCH WAR, 1652–54

The first Anglo-Dutch War revealed the extent to which English naval power had been developed by the republican 'Rump' Parliamentary government, which had toppled Charles I. Between 1649 and 1660 (*pages 78–85*), some 216 vessels were added to the fleet, many of which were prizes, but half were the fruits of a shipbuilding programme. The former dependence on large merchantmen ended with the establishment of a substantial state navy, which in 1653 employed almost 20,000 men.

In 1652, the English won battles off Dover and the Kentish Knock (*map 1*), but were badly defeated by a larger Dutch fleet off Dungeness. In February 1653, the English won a battle fought from Portland to Calais (Three Days Battle), and at the Texel, at which the Dutch Admiral Tromp was killed. The only major Dutch victory in 1653 was the destruction of an English squadron off the Mediterranean port of Leghorn (Livorno). But because the English warships were larger than the Dutch, they were unable to mount a close blockade of the Dutch ports.

Having replaced the Rump Parliament, Cromwell was happy to negotiate peace, but the war had demonstrated English naval power. Robert Blake, the leading admiral of the period, destroyed a Barbary pirate squadron with minimal losses at Porto Farina on the Tunisian Coast (1655), and sank a Spanish treasure fleet at Tenerife (1657).

THE SECOND WAR, 1665–67

The English were handicapped by French support for the Dutch, while the Dutch were strengthened by a shipbuilding programme in the 1650s and 1660s: in 1664–67 they constructed sixty ships-of-the-line. The size of their warships now began to match the English: in 20 years their total displacement tonnage grew from 30,000 to over 100,000.

Although war was not officially declared until 1665, hostilities began a year earlier off West Africa and in North America, where the English occupied New Netherland (*page 44*). In the first major battle, in Sole Bay off Southwold (June 1665), the English under the Lord High Admiral James Duke of York (later James II), defeated Jacob van Wassenaer-Obdam, whose flagship was destroyed by an explosion. Obdam's leadership was poor, but the English were unable to exploit the victory. In 1666, in the June Four Days Battle between the Downs and Dunkirk, the more numerous Dutch won after taking heavy losses in broadside exchanges: the English under George Monck had engaged rather than wait for a supporting squadron under Prince Rupert. In July, the two commanders attacked and defeated the Dutch under Michiel De Ruyter at the Two Days Battle (St James's Day Fight), and in August an English force destroyed several Dutch merchantmen in the islands of Terschelling and Vlie. In turn, Dutch privateers devastated English trade.

The financial burden of the war forced the English to lay up their larger ships in 1667, instead relying on commercial raiding and coastal fortification. The Dutch used

This painting by Van de Velde the Younger depicts the Battle of Texel (11–21 August 1673), which was a Dutch success in that, although the battle was largely indecisive, the Dutch fleet of sixty ships of the line and fifteen frigates fought off an Anglo-French fleet that was at least one-third stronger. The Dutch achieved superiority over a portion of the opposing line and forced it to retreat to the English coast.

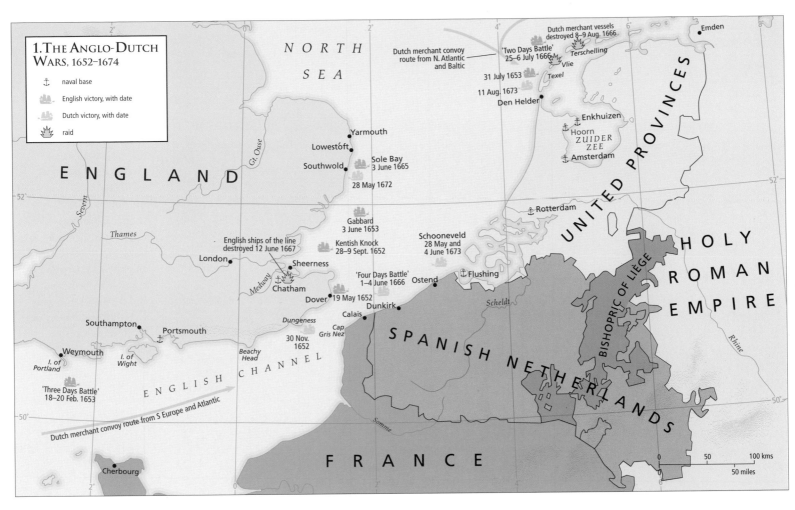

The map shows "1. The Anglo-Dutch Wars, 1652–1674" with a legend indicating:
- naval base
- English victory, with date
- Dutch victory, with date
- raid

MAP 1

Three conflicts between the English and Dutch, two of the leading naval powers in Europe, reflected and furthered the development of fleet naval power, and were characterized by battles fought with heavy guns. Attempts to preserve or cut trade links, crucial to the financial and military viability of the two powers, played a major role in the struggles. This was a war of fleet actions in European waters, commerce raiding and colonial strikes. Both sides realized the advantage of having a large permanent navy and greatly increased their naval strength with the construction of new and larger ships.

the opportunity to attack the major English base at Chatham: a raiding force captured the magazines at Sheerness, broke the protective boom across the Medway, and burnt six deserted ships of the line before towing away Monck's flagship, the Royal Charles. Another Dutch squadron captured Surinam on the coast of South America. The Treaty of Breda (July 1667) confirmed English possession of the former Dutch colony of New York, but the Chatham debacle left an impression of English weakness.

THE THIRD WAR, 1672–74

In the next conflict the Dutch faced a more difficult situation, as Charles II had formed an alliance with Louis XIV of France. Consequently, Dutch strategy was to maintain a fleet 'in being' to deter English attacks; important defensive actions like Schooneveld and the Texel (1673) achieved this aim. The English and French, by contrast, sought to destroy De Ruyter's fleet in order to assist a French invasion of the United Provinces from the east. In May 1672, De Ruyter surprised James' force in Southwold Bay, inflicting much damage and delaying a planned attack on the Dutch coast, and in the following year he skilfully fought off a superior Anglo-French fleet. The Dutch continued to attack English and French shipping in the Caribbean and off North America, recapturing New York. The city was returned by the Peace of Westminster (February 1674), in which Charles abandoned his alliance with France.

ADVANCES IN NAVAL WARFARE

The development of line-ahead tactics for warships was one of the most significant military changes of the seventeenth century. Admiral Maarten Harpertszoon Tromp used line-ahead tactics at Dunkirk in 1639. In 1653, the English fleet was ordered to adopt a line-ahead formation.

The importance of heavily-gunned ships-of-the-line greatly increased, and in the 1660s large two-deckers – ships displacing 1,100–1,600 tons (1,1117–1,625 tonnes) armed with 24-pounders (11kg) – were constructed in great numbers. The Dano-Swedish war of 1675–79 was the last in European waters in which armed merchantmen were much used in the main battle fleets: with only 12-pounders (5.4kg), the Swedish were outclassed. Firepower was enhanced by the replacement of bronze cannon, as advances in cast-iron produced cheaper and more dependable heavy guns. The number of cannon in the French navy rose from 760 in 1661 to almost 9,000 in 1700, while English broadside firepower increased with the development of improved tackles using the gun's recoil to speed reloading inboard.

THE GROWTH OF NAVIES

The Dutch, English, and French substantially increased their fleets between 1650 and 1690. New naval bases were created (by the Swedes at Karlskrona, by the French at Brest, Lorient, and Rochefort) and existing ones were enlarged (Dunkirk and Toulon). Shipbuilding techniques and new

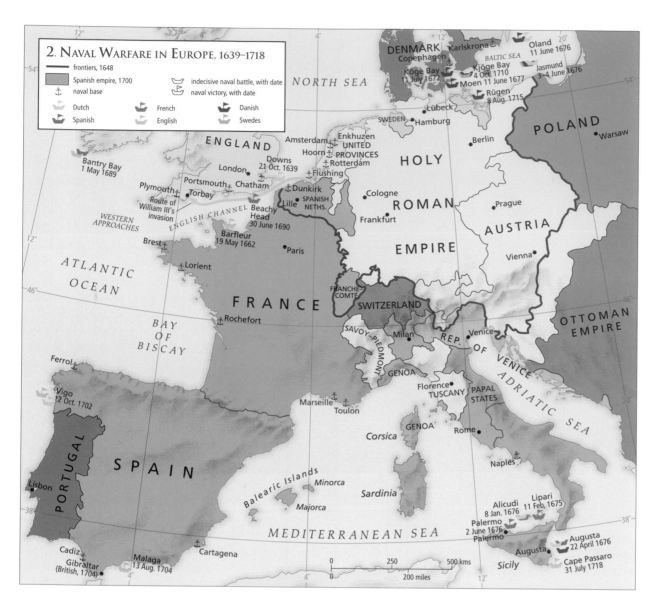

2. NAVAL WARFARE IN EUROPE, 1639–1718

frontiers, 1648
Spanish empire, 1700
naval base
Dutch
Spanish
French
English
indecisive naval battle, with date
naval victory, with date
Danish
Swedes

MAP 2

Naval engagements were generally near the coast and often arose from attacks on anchorages. The Baltic was a major area of conflict as Sweden and Denmark each sought to cut the other's maritime links. Once the Swedes had established themselves in Germany and the eastern Baltic, they became dependant on maintaining maritime links. The importance of amphibious operations, for example in Sicily, Spain, and the British Isles, was such that fleet actions were fought to ensure or prevent invasion attempts.

ship types were developed, including the two-masted bomb-ketch equipped with a heavy mortar for attacking positions on land. A professional naval officer corps was instituted, and under an Ordnance calling for more powerful ships, France launched ten in 1691, all of at least eighty-eight guns. Sweden built heavily in the 1680s and 1690s, to compensate for losses in the war with Denmark in 1675–79, especially the defeat at Köge Bay in 1677 (map 2).

After an Act of Parliament in 1691, England maintained a clear lead in launchings over both the United Provinces and France. English logistical backup also improved: expansion of Portsmouth and the creation of an entirely new front-line yard at Plymouth provided more effective projection into the Channel and Western Approaches. Revictualling at sea was first employed in 1705 to support an English fleet maintaining watch on Brest.

THE ENGLISH SAIL SOUTHWARDS

The decline of Dutch naval strength allowed a greater role for the English in the wars with France from 1689 onwards. A large English fleet was dispatched to the Mediterranean in 1694 and wintered at Cadiz. This projection of naval power was more important in the War of the Spanish Succession (1702–13). During that conflict, the strength of the English fleet enabled it to play a major role in Iberia, capturing positions, particularly Gibraltar in 1704 (map 2), and supporting English forces operating in the peninsula. Fear of English naval attack prompted Portugal to abandon France in 1703. The English took Minorca in 1708, and ten years later a decisive victory off Cape Passaro in Sicily thwarted Spain's plans to regain an Italian empire.

While there were indecisive engagements in the struggle between the English and French navies, for example the Battle of Bantry Bay (1689), some battles were decisive: the French, who were victorious at Beachy Head (1690), failed to exploit their victory. The English were the victors at Barfleur (1692), an engagement which ended the threat of French invasion, and at Malaga (1704), which enabled the English to consolidate their position at Gibraltar. Although no ships were sunk in the battle, casualties were heavy on both sides, and the French were also deterred by running low on ammunition. After Malaga, the French navy did not again challenge the English until 1744: the age of English naval hegemony had clearly begun.

LOUIS XIV'S WARS (I), 1672-1679

A POPULATION GREATER than that of Spain and England combined, a buoyant agrarian economy, and the defeat of the politico-military threat of the Huguenots (French Protestants) gave France the greatest military potential in western Europe. Under Louis XIV, who ruled in person from 1661 until 1715, France realized this potential and shattered Spain's European empire.

THE WAR OF DEVOLUTION

Greater French domestic stability after the Fronde was translated directly into military power under Louis XIV, who considerably increased the size of his army. There had been an earlier increase under Richelieu, to 125,000 men in 1636; but under Louis there were peaks of 253,000 during the Dutch War (1672), 340,000 for the Nine Years' War (1688–97), and 255,000 in 1710, when France was in a desperate situation during the latter stages of the War of the Spanish Succession.

Louis' first war was a relatively modest affair (map 1), the War of Devolution (1667–68). Motivated by an opportunistic claim to part of the succession of Philip IV of Spain, his late father-in-law, Louis was helped by the diplomatic isolation of Spain. Already at war with Portugal, whose 1640 rebellion it had failed to suppress, the Spanish government found England and the Dutch at war with each other, while the Emperor Leopold I, a fellow Habsburg,

was unable and unwilling to provide support. The French rapidly captured a number of fortresses in the Spanish Netherlands, including strategic Lille (1667), and invaded the Franche-Comté. The Spanish were not able to offer effective resistance, and were defeated at Bruges by a larger French force under Créqui. Alarmed at France's success, England, the Dutch, and Sweden formed the Triple Alliance (April 1668), and Louis negotiated the Treaty of Aix-la-Chapelle with Spain (May 1668), whereby he returned the Franche-Comté, but kept Lille and other nearby gains.

THE DUTCH WAR

The Dutch War (1672–79) was more protracted (map 2). It arose from Louis' anger at the Dutch role in the Triple Alliance. He was influenced by the prospect of easy alliances and quick victories held out by Turenne, one of his leading generals, but had little sense of how the war would develop diplomatically or militarily. Rather than planning to take Amsterdam, Louis hoped that Spain would come to the aid of the Dutch and that he could therefore resume the conquest of the Spanish Netherlands.

Having overrun hostile Lorraine and gained the alliance of Charles II of England in the secret Treaty of Dover (1670) and of most of the important German princes, Louis attacked in 1672. His army moved rapidly into the allied Electorate of Cologne, outflanking the Dutch, then crossed the Rhine and advanced into the United Provinces from the east. It seized Utrecht, but was stopped by flood water when the Dutch opened the dykes. In the following year, the war broadened out as Emperor Leopold I organized German

MAP 1

The French success in the War of Devolution contrasted with the failure of much of their campaigning in the Spanish Netherlands in 1635–59, indicating a major shift in the balance of military capability.

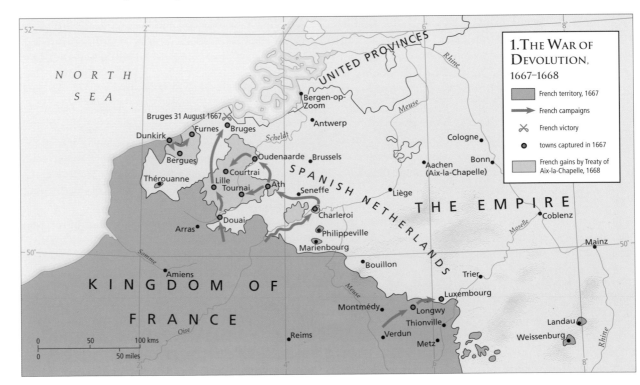

resistance. Louis besieged and captured Dutch-held Maastricht in order to improve his strategic position in the Rhineland.

However, 1673 also saw the fall of French-garrisoned Bonn, capital of France's ally, Elector Max Heinrich of Cologne. The Austrian general Count Montecuccoli had outmanoeuvred Turenne and forced him to retreat from east of the Rhine. In 1673, Louis abandoned his position in the United Provinces in order to protect the frontier, and as the pressure increased on the French they were obliged to defend Alsace. In a pre-emptive attack, Turenne defeated Duke Charles IV of Lorraine and the Austrian general Count Aeneas Caprara at Sinsheim (June 1674). He then seized Strasbourg (September) and defeated Bournonville at Enzheim (October). During a surprise winter campaign, fresh victories for Turenne at Mulhouse (December) and Turckheim (January 1675) cleared Alsace.

Campaigning against Montecuccoli in 1675, Turenne was killed by a cannonball at Sasbach in July. Montecuccoli then advanced deep into Alsace, while Charles IV of Lorraine captured Trier in August. Montecuccoli, however, was driven back across the Rhine by Enghien in October, after which campaign both generals retired. In 1676–78 Créqui and Charles V of Lorraine campaigned in the Rhineland with mixed results. Charles successfully besieged Philipps-burg (1676) but was then defeated at Kochersberg (1677), Rheinfelden and Gengenbach (1678). German forces crossed the Rhine and invaded Alsace.

The entry of Spain into the war in 1673 allowed France to conquer the Franche-Comté, to advance in the Spanish Netherlands, and to invade Catalonia. In 1675, Charles XI of Sweden entered the war on the French side, only to be defeated at Fehrbellin by the Great Elector of Brandenburg and in the Baltic by the Danish navy. However, a Danish invasion of Sweden was defeated at Lund in 1676. In the later stages of the war, French pressure increased both in the Rhineland, where Freiburg fell in 1677 and Kehl in 1678, and in the Spanish Netherlands, where William III was defeated by Enghien at Seneffe (1674), by Philip of Orléans at Mont Cassel (1677), and by Luxembourg at St-Denis (1678). The French also took a large number of fortresses in the Spanish Netherlands, including Dinant, Huy, and Limburg in 1675, Condé, Bouchain, and Aire in 1676, Valenciennes, Cambrai, and St-Omer in 1677, and Ghent and Ypres in 1678. In the Treaty of Nijmegen of 1678, France gained the Franche-Comté, Freiburg, Bouillon, and more of the Spanish Netherlands.

Louis' gains were part of a strategy designed to break Habsburg encirclement and made little attempt to reach the 'natural frontiers' of the Rhine, Alps, and Pyrenees. He does not appear to have thought in these terms, and in any event wanted to acquire positions beyond these lines like Freiburg and Casale. Unable to rely on allies, as he discovered with Sweden and the United Provinces in 1648 and with England in 1674, Louis was in a vulnerable position if his ene-mies united: defence was as important as opportunism. Nijmegen gave France a more defensible frontier with the Spanish Netherlands: Maubeuge improved French

defences on the Sambre, one of the possible invasion routes; Charlemont strengthened the French position on another route, the Meuse. Bouillon and Longwy secured the area opposite the Duchy of Luxembourg, and the Spanish loss of the Franche-Comté improved French links with Alsace.

FORTIFICATION AND SIEGECRAFT

Sieges were not inconsequential alternatives to battles. Fortresses were tangible manifestations of regional control which secured lines of supply and communication. In the late seventeenth century, governments were able to fund massive new programmes of fortification, developing the use of bastions, layering in depth, the enfilading of fire, and defensive artillery.

Louis XIV saw fortification both as a means of securing his domestic position and as an aspect of foreign policy, and he embarked on a systematic building programme. A double line of fortress supply bases was to defend and extend France's northern frontier. Sébastien Le Prestre de Vauban was appointed in 1678 to supervise construction and renovation of thirty-three fortresses, including Arras, Ath, Lille, New Breisach, Belfort, Besançon, Landau, Montmédy, Strasbourg, and Tournai. The costs were for-midable: New Breisach, at an important Rhine crossing,

MAP 2

The Dutch War rapidly spread to encompass much of western Europe. Louis could not recreate the suc-cess of his opening moves in the campaign of 1672.

cost nearly three million livres. Vauban, a master of positional warfare, showed in the successful siege of Maastricht (1673) how trenches could more safely be advanced close to fortifications under artillery cover by parallel and zigzag approaches. The garrison capitulated after less than a month, as did those at Valenciennes (1677), Ypres (1678), and Mons (1691). Vauban also demonstrated the effectiveness at Luxembourg of mortars (1684), and at Ath of ricochet cannon fire (1697).

Louis' opponents responded similarly. Menno van Coehoorn (1641–1704), a skilful Dutch engineer who specialized in successive zones of flanking fire, refortified Namur and Bergen-op-Zoom, a major fortress protecting the United Provinces from the south which the French were to take in 1747 only after great difficulties. Despite failures – Namur fell to the French in 1692 and Lille to the English in 1708 – this heavy investment in fortifications altered the nature of warfare by making siegecraft increasingly important. Coehoorn successfully besieged a number of fortresses: Kaiserswerth (1689), Namur (1695), Venlo (1702), Bonn, and Huy (1703). He also invented the small, highly effective 'cohorn mortar'.

In northern Italy, too, many new fortifications were built, for example by the Austrians at Mantua. Elsewhere, several campaigns in 1680–1740 revolved around important fortifications: Russia, Austria, and the Ottomans struggled over the fortifications of Azov, Ochakov, Vienna, Buda, Temesvar, Belgrade, and Orsova; while Kamenets-Podolsk was crucial in the Polish-Turkish struggle for control of Podolia and the western Ukraine (pages 113–115).

THE FRENCH ARMY

During Louis XIV's reign, the French army was greatly strengthened. It proved difficult to sustain change, however, and the essential precondition was better relations with the nobility. Whereas under Richelieu and Mazarin, control over army units had been weak, Louis and his ministers successfully re-established a state-controlled, state-funded military. Helped by rising tax revenues and better-regulated administration, the government sought to avoid reliance on military entrepreneurs. The payment of troops was regulated; progress was made in the standardization of drill, training, and equipment; and in 1670 distinctive uniforms chosen by Louis were introduced, asserting royal control and making desertion more difficult. The name of Martinet, Commander of the Régiment du Roi and, from 1667, Inspector-General of the Infantry, entered the language as a term for a strict disciplinarian. The conduct of French troops towards their compatriots became considerably better, and pillaging was punished. The command structure was also revised, and a table of rank established in 1672, although social hierarchy continued to conflict with military seniority.

The French developed the most effective logistical system in western Europe although, understandably, it was unable to cope in the lengthy wars in 1688–97 and 1701–14. The supply systems of men, money, munitions, and provisions were greatly improved, as was the supporting system of *Étapes* – supply depots along marching routes. Similarly, a network of magazines from which campaigns could be supplied was established near France's frontiers and used with considerable success in launching the War of Devolution and the Dutch War. Thanks to these, the French could seize the initiative by beginning campaigns early.

These achievements owed much to two successive Secretaries of War, Michel Le Tellier and his son Louvois, who between them held office from 1643 to 1691, and who presided over a well-organized War Office. Thus supported, the army was employed to great effect under the inspired leadership of Enghien, Turenne, and Luxembourg, and French innovations subsequently had a great influence on military developments in the rest of western Europe.

French artillery illustrated in Manesson-Mallet's Travaux de Mars, *1696.*

IV

WARFARE IN EUROPE, 1680-1740

In 1685–86, the English envoy in Constantinople, Lord Chandos, sent a number of reports explaining why the Ottoman Turks were doing so badly against the Austrians in their crucial struggle for Hungary. He claimed that 'they had no military discipline', nor were they numerous enough, whereas in the past 'their prodigious vast multitudes of men that by the weight of flesh bore down all their enemies before them' showed greater spirit in battle. Chandos's reports did not anticipate the Ottoman revival of 1689–91 on land, nor the modernization of their fleet begun in the 1680s, but they did offer a guide to what was believed important for warfare on land: discipline, numbers, and morale. Numbers became a major factor as states such as Austria, France, Russia, and Britain deployed several armies simultaneously on different fronts during the conflicts of the period. The percentage of the European male population under arms rose during this period: although there were post-war demobilizations, most states nevertheless had both the need and the ability to retain larger standing military and naval forces than they had prior to 1660. By 1678 the French army was the largest seen in Christian Europe since that of Imperial Rome. The armies of the period were capable of achieving decisive victories, such as the Austrians over the Turks at Zenta in 1697, the Russians over the Swedes at Poltava in 1709, and the Spaniards over the Austrians at Bitonto in 1734, all of which altered the territorial configuration of Europe. Naval warfare could also be decisive, as with the British defeat of the Spanish off Cape Passaro in 1718. The vast sums spent on warfare and on military preparedness placed a major strain on governmental resources, while systems of compulsory recruitment led to a partial militarization of society in some states, such as Russia.

THE OTTOMAN DEFEAT, 1683-1717

BETWEEN 1683 AND 1717 the Ottomans faced a Holy Alliance of Christian powers abroad and upheavals at home. A series of defeats at the hands of the Austrians steadily pushed them back from south-eastern Europe and culminated in the fall of Belgrade in 1717.

RETREAT FROM HUNGARY AND THE BALKANS

Suleiman the Magnificent's failure at Vienna in 1529 had been a check, but not a disaster. However, Kara Mustafa's crushing defeat at Vienna in 1683 (*page 95*) led to the loss of Hungary, and marked a fundamental change in the balance of power in Europe. The victory of King Jan Sobieski of Poland was followed up on 1 November when a Turkish attempt to make a stand was foiled and the Austrians captured Gran. In the following March, Sobieski, Leopold I, Pope Innocent XI, and Venice formed a Holy League. Challenged on several fronts and suffering from domestic discontent, the Ottomans were in a poor position to resist the Austrian advance.

In 1684, Charles of Lorraine besieged Buda, the most important point between Vienna and Belgrade and the key to Hungary, but the fortress was a strong one with powerful cannon, and disease and supply difficulties hampered the four-month siege, which was eventually abandoned. In 1685, however, Neuhäusel (Ersek Ujvár), a lesser fort which allowed the Turks to threaten Moravia, was successfully stormed on 18 August, and Thököly's pro-Turkish revolt in upper Hungary collapsed. The Ottoman Empire sued for peace, but would not accept the Austrian terms which required their withdrawal from Hungary.

In 1686, Buda was again attacked (*map 1*). A shell landed on the main powder magazine on 22 July, blowing open a breach in the walls, and repeated assaults then led to the fall of the city on 3 September after a brave defence by the Turks under Abdurrahman Pasha. In subsequent advances the Austrians captured much of Hungary, including Szegedin (1688). The Ottomans still refused the Austrian terms, and on 12 August 1687, Charles of Lorraine defeated the Grand Vizier, Suleiman Pasha, at Berg Harsan (Harkány). Esseg then fell, while the cumulative pressure of defeat led to a rebellion which drove Mehmet IV from his throne. Charles then advanced into Transylvania and took control of its major forts. In 1688, the Transylvanian Diet designated Leopold 'hereditary King of Hungary' and in September the Imperial army, under the command of Max Emmanuel of Bavaria, one of the leading German princes, captured the major fortress of Belgrade. The collapse of the Ottoman

position in the Balkans and an Austrian advance into the Greek Orthodox world appeared imminent.

The Austrians developed links with rebellious elements among the Bulgarians and Serbs and began negotiations with the Prince of Wallachia, an Ottoman client-ruler. In 1689, Ludwig Wilhelm of Baden had only 24,000 men to face the Ottomans, but he defeated their main force south of Belgrade and advanced to Nish, despite orders to remain on the defensive. The Austrians pressed on to seize Vidin, Pristina, and Skopje, and to reach Bucharest. The collapse of the Ottoman position appeared to be total. In April 1690, Leopold issued an appeal for the support of all Balkan peoples against the Ottoman Empire and promised them liberty, under his rule as King of Hungary.

OTTOMAN RESILIENCE

The late 1680s may have offered the best opportunity of driving the Ottomans from all or most of the Balkans until the nineteenth century, but from 1688 the Austrians were distracted by the outbreak of war with Louis XIV of France. Also, the Ottomans proved resilient: in 1688 the new Sultan, Suleiman II (1687–91), crushed rebellion in Constantinople; and an able new Grand Vizier from the Köprülü family, Fazil Mustafa (1689–91), restored order to the army and the government, as earlier members of the family had done in the middle of the century. Meanwhile, the Orthodox populations of areas now open to Catholicization by the Austrians were becoming restless.

In 1690, there was a revolt in Transylvania, and most Austrian troops had to be withdrawn to face France. In July 1690, Fazil Mustafa mounted a counter-offensive. He retook Nish, Semendria and, after only a six-day siege, Belgrade: treachery by a French engineer, timorous command by the Duke of Croy and Count Aspremont, and explosions in the

The Venetian fleet under Doge Francesco Morosini pursues the Turks, 1689. Morosini used his command of the sea to mount expeditions against the coast of the Morea. Venetian naval capability was increased by the capture of Nauplia, which became a forward naval base, in 1686. In the 1680s and 1690s, the Venetians largely altered their fleet from galleys to sailing vessels: 35 ships-of-the-line were launched in 1681–1700, built to a standardized design. The Turkish fleet was similarly transformed.

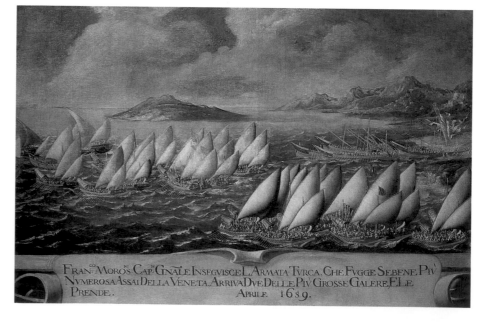

FRAN.CO MORO'S CAP. GN.ALE INSEGVISCE L'ARMATA TVRCA, CHE FVGGE SEBENE PIV' NVMEROSA ASSAI DELLA VENETA, ARRIVA DVE DELLE PIV' GROSSE GALERE, E LE PRENDE. APRILE 1689.

THE SIEGE OF VIENNA, 1683

A revolt in those parts of Hungary ruled by the Habsburgs had encouraged Kara Mustafa in 1681–82 to negotiate peace with Russia, to begin aiding the rebels, and to recognize their leader, Count Imre Thököly, as 'Prince of Middle Hungary'. Worried by the prospect of French attack on the Rhine, the Habsburgs were reluctant to fight the Ottomans, but French agents encouraged Kara Mustafa to march on Vienna by promising that France would not aid Austria.

In response, Leopold I sought general support, while Pope Innocent XI pressed all Catholics to unite in a crusade. King Jan (John) Sobieski of Poland and a number of German rulers prepared to assist as the Ottoman forces advanced. Such assistance was vital, as by 1682 Leopold had only 36,000 men under arms, and most of the Habsburg field units were in the Rhineland facing France. The Ottomans used the winter of 1682–83 to assemble their forces, and the main contingent left Adrianople on 31 March, reaching Belgrade on 3 May. About 100,000 strong, the Ottoman army advanced rapidly through occupied Hungary in June. Kara Mustafa appeared before the Austrian fortress of Györ on 2 July to find the Austrians, only about 33,000 strong and under the command of Charles V of Lorraine, determined to remain on the defensive. Charles left Györ and retreated towards Vienna. The Grand Vizier was determined to march directly on Vienna rather than to spend valuable time besieging fortresses near the frontier.

Leaving a force of 12,000 to blockade Györ, the Ottoman troops crossed the Raab and, as panic mounted, Leopold and his court left Vienna on 7 July, retreating to Passau. Meanwhile, Ottoman raiders devastated the surrounding countryside. The Austrians had intended to defend the line of the river Leitha, but the rapid Turkish advance led Charles to fall back.

The defence of Vienna was left to Count Ernst Rüdiger von Starhemberg, who had the suburbs burnt to deny the Ottoman troops cover. Their army surrounded the city on 16 July. While the relief force gathered, the Ottomans began building siegeworks and mounting assaults. The latter were increasingly successful and the garrison suffered heavy casualties as well as losses from dysentery. The Ottomans suffered similarly, but during August the city's outer defences steadily succumbed, although the Ottomans were heavily outgunned by the defenders. They lacked heavy-calibre cannon, and depended on undermining the defences, which they did with some success. There was bitter fighting in the breaches, and on 4 September the Ottomans broke through, prompting Starhemberg to fire distress rockets to urge the relief army to action.

A relief army had gradually built up, as Bavaria and Saxony added substantial forces to those under Charles of Lorraine. On 31 August, Sobieski had arrived with 30,000 troops and assumed overall command. By 6 September, the allied forces were moving into the Tulln basin, west of the hills that surround Vienna, and on

9 September they advanced through the Vienna woods. Kara Mustafa was aware of this deployment, but made little preparation for its attack.

On 12 September, the relieving army descended from the hills, with the German forces on the left and the Polish on the right. Operating independently, they broke the Ottoman battle line, whose troops were generally stronger in attack than in defence, and on this occasion were unable to turn their siege artillery on the relieving force. By the end of the day Kara Mustafa was in retreat towards Györ. He was punished for his failure by strangulation, while Christian Europe celebrated the relief of its most prominent bulwark.

The Siege of Vienna in 1683.

THE VENETIAN WAR

As a member of the Holy League, Venice attacked the Ottomans in Bosnia, Dalmatia, Greece, and the Aegean. An invasion of Bosnia was routed in April 1685 and landings on the Dalmatian coast, for example at Cattaro, were repelled in 1685–87, although they were subsequently more successful, leading to Venetian gains in Dalmatia. An anti-Ottoman revolt in the Morea was exploited by Venetian amphibious forces in 1685–86: Koron, Kalamata, Navarino, Modon, and Nauplia all fell to the Venetians, who in 1687 moved north to capture Athens, Patras, and Lepanto. At Athens, the Turkish magazine in the Parthenon was blown up by a mortar shell. Although the Venetians were unsuccessful on Euboea in 1689 and failed in Crete in 1692, they captured Chios in 1694; the unpopularity of their rule led to an uprising and their expulsion in the following year. At the Peace of Karlowitz (1699), Venice gave up Lepanto but retained the Morea and its Dalmatian gains.

War resumed in December 1714 in response to Venetian encouragement of an uprising in Montenegro. The Morea was reconquered in the face of weak resistance in 1715, and held against a Venetian counter-thrust in 1717, although the Venetians held the fortress of Corfu against Ottoman attack in 1717 and captured Prevesa with an amphibious landing. The Peace of Passarowitz (1718) left both sides with their gains.

View of the port of Chios in the seventeenth century.

powder magazine have all been blamed. In the following year, however, Fazil Mustafa's hopes of recapturing Hungary were dashed by Ludwig Wilhelm at Zalánkemén, a long, hard-fought battle which left a third of the Imperial army killed or wounded, but the Ottomans routed and Fazil Mustafa dead.

STALEMATE

Conflict over the next few years was indecisive and difficult due to the unwillingness of either power to offer acceptable terms and to Austrian commitments against Louis XIV in northern Italy and the Rhineland. In the battlezone, fortifications were improved, while local sources of supply were depleted and fighting in marshy, fever-ridden lowlands was difficult. The Austrians recaptured Grosswardein in 1692, but in 1693 were forced to raise the siege of Belgrade. Matters came to a climax, however, as a result of the accession of the energetic Mustafa II in February 1695 and the end of the war in Italy in 1696, which enabled Leopold to transfer more troops and his rising general, Eugene of Savoy, to Hungary.

Mustafa had some success: in 1695 he stormed Lippa, defeated Count Friedrich Veterani and relieved Temesvár; in 1696 he outmanoeuvred the new Imperial Commander, Augustus, Elector of Saxony, and engaged him in an inconclusive battle.

However, in 1697 Eugene moved rapidly and attacked Mustafa at Zenta as his army was crossing the river Tisza. The Ottomans, caught unprepared and divided by the river, were massacred with the loss of perhaps 30,000 casualties to only 300 in Eugene's army. The Ottoman infantry was completely destroyed and Mustafa fled, forced to abandon his supplies and artillery, including 6,000 camels, 5,000 oxen, and 9,000 baggage carts. The victory made Eugene's reputation. Eugene's men then went on to raid Bosnia, sacking Sarajevo, but it was too late in the year to attack Temesvár or Belgrade.

In the following year, the Ottoman forces refused to engage, while Eugene's army was troubled by a mutiny caused by lack of funds. With Leopold keen on peace in order to concentrate on the Spanish Succession, terms were negotiated at Karlowitz (1699) under which Austria kept Transylvania and most of Hungary, while the Ottoman Empire kept the Banat of Temesvár.

THE FALL OF BELGRADE

War resumed in 1716 when the Austrians became concerned at Ottoman pressure on Venice. The Ottomans refused to withdraw from their gains in the Morea, instead hoping to reconquer Hungary. In August, they besieged Eugene in a fortified camp at Peterwardein (Petrovaradin). Eugene sallied out on 5 August with 70,000 men and beat his 120,000-strong opponents: the Turkish janissaries had some success against the Austrian infantry, but the Austrian cavalry drove their opponents from the field leaving the exposed janissaries to be decimated. Possibly up to 30,000 Turks, including the Grand Vizier, Silahdar Ali Pasha, the Sultan's son-in law, were killed. Eugene then marched on

MAP 1

The war in the Balkans marked a major shift in the European balance of power. The Ottoman Turks were driven back and the Austrian Habsburgs became a great Danubian power.

1. THE OTTOMAN DEFEAT, 1683–1718

Ottoman empire, 1683

route of King Jan Sobieski's march to relieve Vienna, 1683

Austrian advances

○ towns captured by Austrians, with date

territory ceded to Austrians, 1699

territory ceded to Austrians, 1718

Venetian attacks, with date

Venetian territory, 1683

territory ceded to Venice, 1699

● towns captured by Venetians, with date

Ottoman counter-offensive, 1690

✕ Ottoman defeats, with date

Temesvár, which had defied the Austrians during the previous war, and which controlled or threatened much of eastern Hungary. Well-fortified and protected by river and marshes, Temesvár nevertheless surrendered on 23 October after heavy bombardment. In 1717, Eugene advanced to attack Belgrade, crossing the Danube to the east of the city on 15 June. The city had a large garrison of 30,000 men under Mustafa Pasha, and in August the main field army, 150,000 strong under the Grand Vizier, Halil Pasha, arrived to relieve the city, bombarding the Austrians from higher ground. In a difficult position, Eugene resolved on a surprise attack, and on the morning of 16 August, 60,000 Austrians advanced through the fog to crush Halil's army. This led to the surrender of Belgrade six days later and to the Peace of Passarowitz (21 July, 1718) which left Austria with the Banat of Temesvár, Little (western) Wallachia, and northern Serbia.

The Austrians did not push on to make fresh conquests in the Balkans. They had to consider challenges to their position, especially those mounted by the Bourbons who ruled France and, from 1700, the threat of Spanish expansion in the Mediterranean. Spain, under the rule of Philip V, who sought to reverse the Austrian gains from Spain in the War of the Spanish Succession, captured Sardinia in 1717 and attacked Sicily in 1718.

As so often, it is thus necessary to look at the wider international context in order to explain military decisions. The Ottomans had to consider their commitments on a number of fronts: the threat from Persia precluded them from taking advantage of favourable circumstances in Europe, for example in the 1620s, when Austrian strength was weakened by the challenge of rebellion in Bohemia and war in Germany. In the early 1740s, the Austrian Habsburgs were threatened by a renewed crisis in the early stages of the War of the Austrian Succession (*pages* 118–122), and the Turks had recently regained the military initiative, forcing the Austrians to return Belgrade in 1739. The Turks were nevertheless unable to exploit these Austrian difficulties because they were themselves at war with Nadir Shah of Persia (*pages* 142–143).

CONFLICT IN BRITAIN, 1685-1746

THE ACCESSION in 1685 of the Catholic James II to the English throne led to a period of intermittent civil war which lasted until 1746, when Charles Edward Stuart, 'Bonnie Prince Charlie', the son of the Jacobite claimant to the throne which had been taken in 1688 by William of Orange, was defeated at Culloden.

MONMOUTH'S RISING

The first challenge to James II was mounted in 1685. James Duke of Monmouth, the illegitimate Protestant son of James II's elder brother and predecessor Charles II, sailed from the United Provinces and landed with 82 companions and a supply of arms at Lyme Regis on 11 June (map 1). The landing was unopposed, and although Monmouth failed to overwhelm the Dorset force at Bridport, recruits joined rapidly, and a force of militia being assembled at Axminster to oppose Monmouth collapsed. Monmouth was proclaimed King at Taunton on 19 June, and by the time he marched on Bristol (21 June), he had 8,000 men. However, he failed to press home his advantage at Bristol, and instead attempted a night attack at Sedgemoor (6 July). But surprise was lost and the poorly organized rebel army was defeated by their experienced opponents' superior firepower.

Monmouth's rising was assisted in Scotland by Archibald Campbell, Ninth Earl of Argyll, who also returned from the United Provinces and rapidly recruited support. However, Argyll's operations were hampered by divided counsel and the speed of the governmental response, including the appearance of two frigates which took Argyll's ships and handicapped his operations around the Clyde estuary. Argyll advanced with about 2,000 men to confront a royal army near Dumbarton, but his demand to fight was overruled and the troops retreated. During the retreat the cohesion of Argyll's force was lost and its numbers fell as clansmen disappeared back to their homes. Like Monmouth after Sedgemoor, Argyll was captured and executed.

WILLIAM'S INVASION

The next attack on James II came with William of Orange's attempted invasions in 1688 (map 1). His first attempt in mid-October was defeated by the weather, with the loss of many supplies including over a thousand horses, which were crucial to the mobility of any invasion force. But his second attempt was more successful, and England was invaded despite its possession of an undefeated navy and a substantial army. A strong north-easterly wind prevented the English from leaving their anchorage off Harwich, and when the Earl of Dartmouth, the commander of James' fleet, finally sailed, the Dutch fleet had gained a crucial lead. William landed at Brixham on 5 November but was out-numbered by James II, who blocked the route to London on Salisbury Plain. However, indecision, ill-health, and the desertion of his daughter Anne, led James to abandon his army, weakening his troops' morale. William seized the initiative and marched on London, while James escaped to France as his army disintegrated.

Scotland and Ireland did not fall so easily. A Jacobite force of Scottish Highlanders won the Battle of Killiecrankie (July 1689) over a far larger force under Hugh Mackay of Scourie

MAP 1

Although only one invasion of southern England was successful, there were a number of serious attempts to invade.

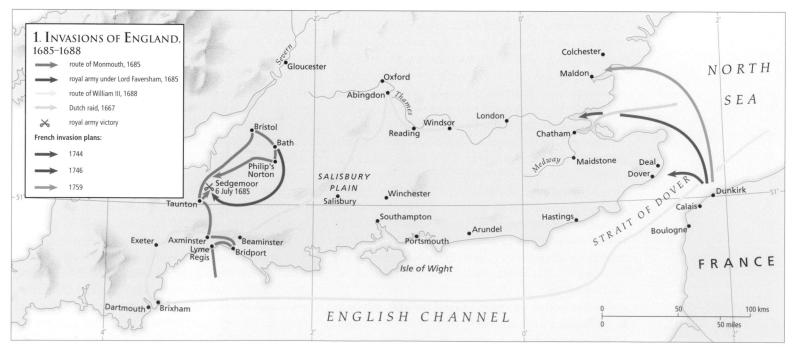

1. INVASIONS OF ENGLAND, 1685–1688

- ➤ route of Monmouth, 1685
- ➤ royal army under Lord Faversham, 1685
- ➤ route of William III, 1688
- ➤ Dutch raid, 1667
- ✗ royal army victory

French invasion plans:
- ➤ 1744
- ➤ 1746
- ➤ 1759

ENGLISH CHANNEL

MAP 2

The Williamite conquest of Ireland in 1690–91 revealed how a numerous and armed population could be reduced by a far smaller alien force.

by charging with their broadswords against static musketeers. However, the death in the battle of their commander John Graham of Claverhouse, Viscount Dundee, was followed by poor leadership, an unsuccessful attack on the fortified position of Dunkeld, and the collapse of the Jacobite position in Scotland in 1690–91.

IRELAND

The decisive battles were fought in Ireland, which was more accessible than Scotland to the major French naval base of Brest. In 1689, James' supporters controlled most of Ireland, although Derry, fearing massacre by the Catholics, resisted a siege and was relieved by the English fleet on 28 July, after the boom blocking the harbour had been broken. Naval power thus offered William military flexibility and denied James overall control.

On 13 August 1689, 10,000 of William's troops, many Huguenots (French Protestants) and Dutch, landed near Bangor, County Down. They were under the command of the Duke of Schomberg, a Protestant who had left the service of Louis XIV when that king revoked the Edict of Nantes in 1685. Schomberg sent some troops to occupy Belfast, leading most of his army on a successful advance on Carrickfergus (map 2), which surrendered on 27 August, after a two-day bombardment by warships and shore batteries. This gave William's forces control of another important port. Schomberg then marched south to Dundalk where he assembled his army in a good defensive position. The Jacobite forces under James II moved north, but Schomberg refused to march out to fight them, and both armies then retired to winter quarters. Schomberg lost up to half of his troops that winter due to disease. Critical of Schomberg for having failed to force a battle, William decided that he would have to take command in the 1690 campaign.

The campaigning season in early 1690 was taken up by Schomberg's siege of Charlemont, on the Armagh-Tyrone border, which began on 22 April. It surrendered on 14 May. Meanwhile, William had been building up his forces in Ireland. He hired 7,000 Danish troops and fresh Huguenot units and brought over another 6,000 English recruits. The new forces were well-armed, with firelock muskets, and the Dutch and Danes had bayonets as well. The French also sent reinforcements to James, but they were fewer than those joining their opponents.

William landed near Carrickfergus on 14 June and marched south. The Jacobites in turn marched north to Dundalk: James ignored French advice that he should abandon Dublin and retreat to western Ireland. After a skirmish at Moyry Pass, between Dundalk and Newry, the outnumbered James withdrew to take up a defensive position behind the river Boyne. Having launched a diversion that outflanked the Jacobite left, William crossed the river and his forces, thanks in part to their bayonets, fought off Irish infantry and, particularly, cavalry attacks for two hours. Finally the Irish cavalry were attacked on their right flank by Williamite cavalry that had crossed further downstream. Under heavy pressure and concerned about the dangers of

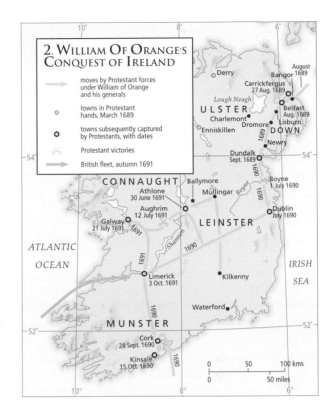

being surrounded, the Jacobites retreated. The retreat rapidly deteriorated into a confused flight with only the French infantry successfully delaying the pursuit. A demoralized James fled to France, never to return. Yet his army had only lost about 1,000 men (WIlliam lost about 500) and, although Dublin was abandoned, the Jacobites were able to regroup at Limerick.

Having entered Dublin on 6 July, William advanced on Athlone, a major bridging point over the Shannon, but was thwarted when the bridge was broken. William then turned on Limerick, though his siege train was badly damaged en route. The fortifications were still largely intact when William unsuccessfully failed to storm Limerick on 27 August, suffering over 2,000 casualties.

A separate expedition, under John Churchill, Earl of Marlborough, was more successful. Cork surrendered on 28 September after its fortifications were breached by a bombardment from higher ground, and the Jacobite outworks were overrun. James Fort and Charles Fort, which dominated the harbour at Kinsale, followed in October. These successes improved British naval capability and made French reinforcement of the Irish more difficult.

In 1691, the British forces were commanded by the Dutch general Godard van Reede de Ginkel. Athlone fell on 30 June, after hard fighting and a very heavy bombardment, with more than 12,000 cannonballs fired. On 12 July, the two armies met at Aughrim. After a bitter struggle in which the Irish made good use of field boundaries as breastworks, their commander was killed by a chance cannon shot and the demoralized cavalry on the Irish left retreated. The leaderless Irish centre then came under intense pressure and much of the infantry was killed in the retreat. The Irish lost possibly 7,000 killed, to about 2,000 of their opponents dead and wounded. Aughrim was far more decisive than the Boyne. The Irish army was broken. Galway surrendered on 21 July, and with the surrender of Limerick on 3 October the war in Ireland was brought to a close.

The Irish campaigns were far from static. Bold generalship and success in battle were far more important than the holding of fortified positions. Though Derry, Athlone, and Limerick had successfully resisted attack, at least initially, the Boyne had given William a number of Jacobite strongholds, and Aughrim was followed by the fall of Galway. Both of the major engagements had been won by the attacking force, and in each case tactical considerations relating to the terrain and to the ability to take advantage of developments had been crucial; the vulnerability of defending armies to flanking attacks by opponents that retained the initiative had been clearly demonstrated. William III also saw more clearly than Louis XIV the importance of Ireland as a source of supplies.

THE '08

The French planned an invasion of Scotland in support of the Jacobites in 1708. A squadron under Forbin carrying James II's son, 'James III', and 5,000 troops, evaded the British fleet blockading Dunkirk in the mist, and reached the Firth of Forth on 12 March. However, the initial landfall, as a result of error, had been too far north and when Forbin was ready to land the troops he was deterred by the proximity of the pursuing British fleet. Forbin succeeded in evading the larger British squadron and returned safely to Dunkirk.

THE '15

In 1715, the Jacobites planned three risings independent of foreign assistance. 'James III' was to copy William III by landing in the south-west of England, where the main rebellion was to be followed by a march on London. There were also to be rebellions in the Highlands and Border counties. The rising in the south-west was promptly nipped in the bud in September 1715 thanks to Jacobite indecision and government intelligence.

However, on 6 September John Erskine, Earl of Mar, raised the Stuart standard at Braemar (map 3). Perth was seized, and the royal forces under the Duke of Argyll were outnumbered, but then delay on Mar's part lost valuable campaigning time. He should have attacked Argyll quickly so that Scotland could become the base for risings in the Borders and the north of England. Instead he delayed marching on Edinburgh until November, confronting Argyll at Sheriffmuir north of Stirling on 13 November. Unaware of the other's dispositions, each general drew up his forces so that his right wing overlapped the other's left. The left wings of both armies were defeated, but Mar failed to exploit his superiority. The indecisive battle was more to Argyll's advantage, as Mar needed a victory to keep his army united and to maintain the momentum of success.

In October, the Jacobites had risen in Northumberland and the Scottish Borders. An attempt to seize Newcastle was

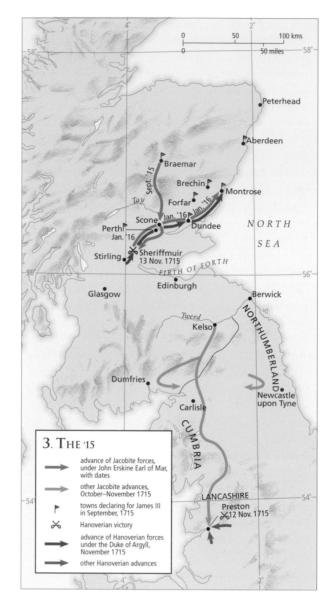

3. THE '15

→ advance of Jacobite forces, under John Erskine Earl of Mar, with dates

→ other Jacobite advances, October–November 1715

⚑ towns declaring for James III in September, 1715

✕ Hanoverian victory

→ advance of Hanoverian forces under the Duke of Argyll, November 1715

→ other Hanoverian advances

MAP 3
The Scots who rose for the Stuarts in 1715 were more numerous that those who had served under Montrose, and in 1689 under Dundee. In 1715 many Lowlanders rose as well as Highlanders. The Northumbrian Jacobites were far less formidable as a military force, but this was consistent with their role as the light forces for the Jacobite army, designed to prepare the ground for more heavily-armed French and Scottish forces. The Jacobites were clearly not without resources in 1715, but they suffered from poor leadership, in both Scotland and England, and from an absence of foreign support.

unsuccessful and the Jacobites concentrated at Kelso. Instead of marching north to help Mar against Argyll, the Jacobites decided, against the wishes of the Scots, to invade Lancashire, an area with many Catholics whom they hoped to recruit. The army, less than 3,000 men, crossed the border on 1 November. Carlisle was judged too strong to attack, as Dumfries had earlier been, but the march south was initially successful. The Cumbrian militia offered no resistance, and on 9 November the Jacobites entered Preston; this was to prove as unfortunate for them as it had been for the invading Scots in August 1648. Thomas Forster failed to defend the line of the river Ribble in Lancashire against the government troops under generals Carpenter and Wills, though a government assault on the town, which had been hastily fortified with barricades, failed on 12 November. However, instead of attacking the besiegers or trying to fight their way out, the Jacobites allowed their enemies to surround the town, and the weak Forster unconditionally surrendered on 14 November.

On 22 December 1715, 'James III' arrived at Peterhead, and on 8 January 1716 at Scone, where his coronation was planned. However, freed of concern about England where the Battle of Preston marked the end of the Jacobite rising, Argyll had now been provided with a far larger army, including 5,000 Dutch troops. Despite the bitterness of the winter and a Jacobite scorched earth policy, Argyll marched on Perth on 21 January. The Jacobites suffered badly from low morale and desertion, and James abandoned Perth, throwing his artillery into the Tay. The army retreated to Montrose, but rather than defending it, James and Mar sailed for France and their troops dispersed.

ORMONDE'S EXPEDITION

After the '15, the next Jacobite military action came in 1719, when Britain and Spain were at war. The leading Spanish minister wanted an invasion: 'to attack England is to attack the heart'. An expeditionary force under James, Duke of Ormonde, sailed from Cadiz on 7 March 1719, but a violent storm off Cape Finisterre at the end of the month damaged and dispersed the fleet.

Two separate frigates reached Stornoway carrying a diversionary force of 300 Spanish troops under George Keith, the Earl Marischal, intended to tie down British troops in Scotland. This small force moved to the mainland, but its main magazine was destroyed by British frigates. The Earl Marischal advanced on Inverness, but the failure of Ormonde's expedition discouraged much of the Highlands from supporting him.

The Jacobites, about 1,850 strong, met 1,100 government troops under Major-General Wightman in Glenshiel on 10 June 1719. The Jacobites did not charge, remaining instead in a good defensive position. However, their morale was low and Wightman, assisted by mortar fire, took the initiative and successfully attacked the Jacobite flanks. The Jacobite army disintegrated, the Highlanders retiring to their homes and the Spanish surrendering.

THE '45

In 1744, the year when Britain and France next went to war, the French planned an invasion of southern England on behalf of the Jacobites. The French plan was to send the Brest fleet to cruise off the Isle of Wight in order to prevent the British from leaving Spithead, or, if they did, to engage them in the western Channel. Five of the Brest ships were to sail to Dunkirk and to escort Maurice of Saxe's invasion force to the Thames, but the plan was then delayed by storms.

In the following year, the landing of James III's son, Charles Edward Stuart (Bonnie Prince Charlie) at Glenfinnan was followed by a rising in Scotland (map 4). On 21 September 1745, his army attacked a British force under Sir John Cope to the east of Edinburgh at Prestonpans. The first Highland charge, whose formation was unbroken by the fire of Cope's infantry, quickly caused Cope's men to flee in panic: they fired only one round before the Highlanders were upon them with their broadswords.

After Prestonpans, the Jacobites consolidated their position around Edinburgh. Their opponents assembled an army under Field-Marshal Wade at Newcastle, but the Jacobites avoided it by invading via Carlisle, which fell after a short siege (10–15 November). Wade's slow attempt to relieve Carlisle was hampered by winter weather, and the Jacobites advanced towards London unopposed through Lancaster, Preston, and Manchester. Cumberland's army had been out-manoeuvred, misled by deliberately circulated reports that the Jacobites intended to advance on Chester and North Wales, and was exhausted by its marches in the west Midlands. Nevertheless, despite this failure of opposition, the Highland chiefs were discouraged by a lack of English support and by the absence of a French landing in southern England, and they forced Charles Edward to turn back at Derby (6 December).

The Battle of Sheriffmuir by John Wootton (c. 1678-1765). Sheriffmuir was decisive in stemming the tide of Jacobite success in Scotland during the '15. Wootton was primarily an animal- and landscape-painter but he also produced a series of works which glorified the Hanoverians, including a portrait of the Duke of Cumberland, which showed the Battle of Culloden in the background.

Royal troops sought to block their retreat, but were unsuccessful. Once back in Scotland, a Highland charge was again decisive in giving the Jacobites victory at Falkirk (17 January 1746), where the royal troops were hindered by fighting uphill, by growing darkness, and by the heavy rain wetting their powder. Brigadier-General James Cholmondeley made it clear that a lack of fighting spirit had also been decisive: 'they [the cavalry] began the attack with spirit which did not last long…our foot gave a faint fire and then faced to the right about, as regularly as if they had had the word of command, and could not be rallied, 'till they got a considerable distance, although I do not think that they were pursued by two hundred men'. The Hanoverian artillery was also ineffective.

But Falkirk was to be the last Jacobite victory: at Culloden (16 April), royal forces under the Duke of Cumberland finally shattered the rebel army (page 103). Cumberland's aide-de-camp at Culloden, Joseph Yorke, noted of the Jacobites, 'the broad-swords succeeding so ill, the rebels turned their backs, and in flying were so well received by the cavalry under Hawley and Bland, who had broke down two dry stone walls, and unperceiv'd had gained their rear, that a general rout and slaughter ensued'. Following the defeat, Charles Edward fled into exile.

COULD THE JACOBITES HAVE WON?

The '45 took place against the background of a wider European conflict, the War of the Austrian Succession. The classic image of that conflict is the apparently parade-ground Battle of Fontenoy in 1745 (page 119), and the battles of the '45 seem very different. The Jacobites placed an emphasis on both the attack and on cold steel that appears distinctive, if not anachronistic. Strategically, the '45 has an 'all-or-nothing' character that appears out of keeping with a form of warfare that is commonly presented as limited, if not indecisive. This is misleading. The Jacobites were indeed essentially a force of attacking infantry relying on shock power, rather than on any initial disruption by infantry and artillery fire. Yet other armies relied on the attack; Marshal Saxe, the leading French general of the mid-1740s, and Frederick the Great were also exponents of the strategic offensive and close-quarter tactics.

Until Derby, the Jacobites had the advantage over their opponents: the campaign hitherto had revealed that the Jacobites could expect little resistance except from regulars and that these could be out-manoeuvred in turn. The sole battle, Prestonpans, had suggested that the firepower of the regulars was of little value, unless the Jacobites fought on their terms, as they were to do at Culloden. The following January, the Battle of Falkirk was to reveal the vulnerability of cavalry to Highland infantry.

If the Jacobites had marched on from Derby they would have found capturing London a formidable task. They lacked heavy artillery, and might have made as little impact on the Tower of London as they did on Edinburgh Castle. Yet, despite these difficulties, London could have been stormed, and the fall of the towns of Carlisle and Edinburgh could

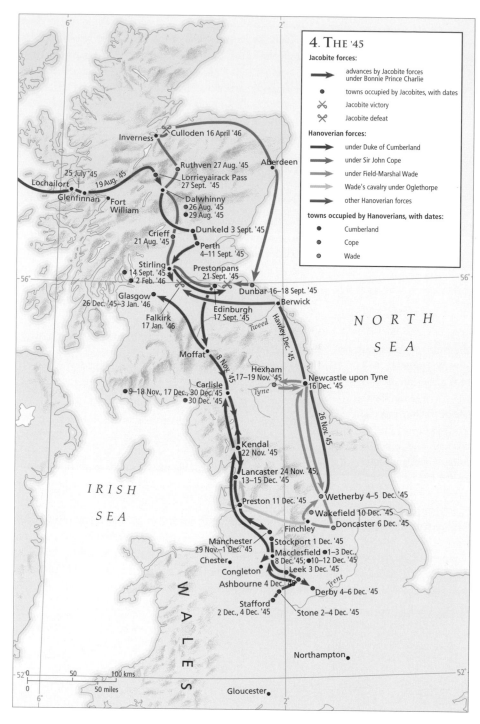

scarcely have been an encouraging omen for the defenders of London. If London had fallen, the chances of a successful resistance to French invasion would also have been lessened. The French could offer the Jacobites all the advantages they lacked: siege artillery, regular infantry able to stand up to Brtitish regulars in a firefight, financial and military resources, a secure logistical base, and supporting naval strength. If the French had landed in England in the winter of 1745–46, they would have been capable of defeating whatever forces the local authorities could have mustered and would also have considerably outnumbered the regular troops in and around London. Especially considered in combination with France, the Jacobites presented a formidable military challenge.

MAP 4

When the Jacobites entered Derby on 4 December 1745, they held the strategic initiative. Wade's army had not left Newcastle until 26 November and were still only in Yorkshire. Cumberland's army had been out-manoeuvred. On Finchley Common the government was assembling a new army to protect London.

CULLODEN 16 APRIL 1746

At Culloden, in contrast to Falkirk, the terrain suited the Duke of Cumberland's defensive position. Cumberland also outnumbered his opponent 9,000 to 5,000, and the Jacobites were outgunned. Cumberland's artillery and infantry so thinned the numbers of the advancing clansmen that those who reached the royal troops were driven back by bayonet. The general rate of fire was increased by the absence of any disruptive fire from the Jacobites, while the flanking position of the royal units forward from the left of the front line made Culloden even more of a killing field. James Wolfe's regiment of foot was moved forward so that it was at right angles to the left of the front line, and this new axis was extended by the Argyll men and the dragoons. Many factors led to confusion amongst the Jacobites: the slant of the Jacobite line, the nature of the terrain, which was partly waterlogged, the difficulty of seeing what was happening in the smoke produced by the guns, and the independent nature of each unit's advance. Nevertheless, despite these difficulties, they were able to reach the left of Cumberland's front line.

Cumberland's report emphasized the importance of his infantry's firepower – 'the Royals and Pulteney's hardly took their fire-locks from their shoulders' – and the role of their bayonets when pressed: 'Barrel's regiment and the left of Monroe's fairly beat them with their bayonets…in their [Jacobites'] rage that they could not make any impression upon the battalions, they threw stones at them for at least a minute or two, before their total rout began'. Jacobitism as a military force was finished.

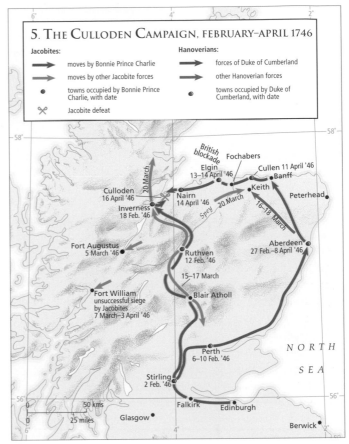

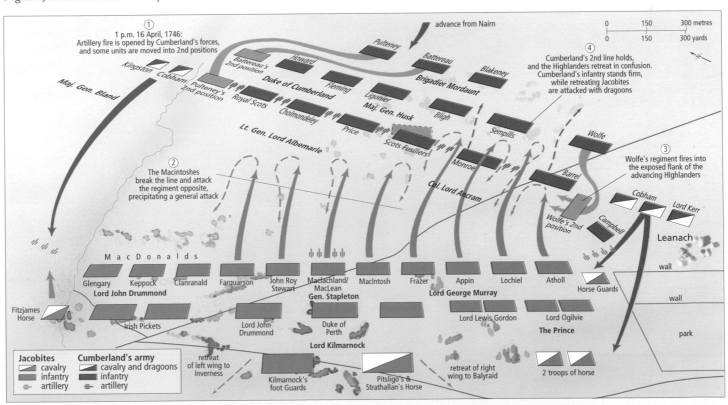

LOUIS XIV'S WARS (II), 1688-1714

LOUIS XIV sought further to expand French power in Europe in two wars, neither of which was decisive and which together resulted in a weakening of France's position. Louis' attempts to build on his earlier successes proved an expensive failure. A coalition centring on the Austrians, British, and the Dutch defeated France in Germany, Italy, and the Low Countries.

THE NINE YEARS' WAR, 1688-97

In 1688, French forces advanced into the Empire in order to press Louis XIV's claims in the Rhineland. The conflict rapidly widened, and by the summer of 1689 Louis was at war with Austria, Bavaria, Britain, the Low Countries, and Spain; in 1690, Victor Amadeus II of Savoy-Piedmont joined the alliance. Louis' isolation was a significant diplomatic defeat and influenced the course of the conflict: in contrast to the Dutch (1672–78), Spanish (1701–14), Polish (1733–35) and Austrian (1741–48) Wars of Succession, and the Seven Years' War (1756–63), in all of which France had allies, French operations in the Nine Years' War were more confined to the border regions of France itself (map 1), although colonial conflicts raged from Hudson's Bay to India.

The diversion of much of the Anglo-Dutch military effort to Ireland in 1689–90 (page 99) gave Louis an opportunity. The aggressive François, Duke of Luxembourg, invaded the Spanish Nertherlands in 1690 and defeated George Frederick of Waldeck's army at Fleurus by turning its left flank while mounting a frontal assault. Waldeck was forced to create a new front with his reserves, second line, and his infantry and, attacked from two directions, had to make a fighting retreat. The French retained the initiative in 1691, successfully besieging Mons and defeating Waldeck at Leuze by a surprise attack. Luxembourg captured Namur and defeated William III at Steenkirk (1692), and after a hard struggle at Neerwinden (1693). But the commitment of Anglo-Dutch strength denied Louis decisive victory, and the loss of Namur in 1695 shook French prestige.

The anti-French alliance collapsed in 1696 with the defection of Victor Amadeus, while the French capture of Barcelona in 1697 led Spain to sue for peace. By the Treaty of Rijswijk (1697), Louis achieved recognition of his acquisition of Alsace, but lost Luxembourg, Philippsburg, Breisach, Freiburg, and Kehl.

THE WAR OF THE SPANISH SUCCESSION

The death of the childless Charles II of Spain in 1700 and his will in favour of Philip, Duke of Anjou, brought Louis XIV's grandson to the Spanish throne, but he was challenged by a rival claimant, Leopold I's second son Charles. War broke out in 1701 and in the following year Britain and the Dutch joined Leopold's side.

In Germany, the Archbishopric of Cologne, allied to France, was overrun in 1702–03, but the combination of French and Bavarian troops in southern Germany threatened the collapse of Austria. Leopold was saved in 1704 in

MAP 1

Although facing a formidable coalition, Louis XIV's forces made important inroads in the Low Countries, in part thanks to the excellent generalship of the Duke of Luxembourg, nearby supply sources, and a large army. William III proved a stubborn but less successful opponent.

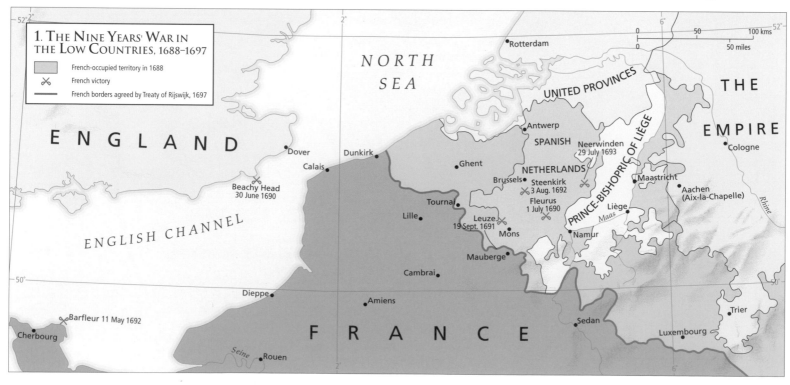

1. THE NINE YEARS' WAR IN THE LOW COUNTRIES, 1688-1697

- French-occupied territory in 1688
- French victory
- French borders agreed by Treaty of Rijswijk, 1697

NORTH SEA

ENGLAND

ENGLISH CHANNEL

Rotterdam

UNITED PROVINCES

THE EMPIRE

Antwerp

SPANISH

Neerwinden 29 July 1693

Dover

Dunkirk

Ghent

NETHERLANDS

Brussels

Steenkirk 3 Aug. 1692

Maastricht

Calais

Tournai

Fleurus 1 July 1690

Liège

Aachen (Aix-la-Chapelle)

Beachy Head 30 June 1690

Lille

Leuze 19 Sept. 1691

Mons

PRINCE-BISHOPRIC OF LIÈGE

Maas

Namur

Rhine

Mauberge

Cambrai

Dieppe

Amiens

Sedan

Trier

Barfleur 11 May 1692

FRANCE

Luxembourg

Cherbourg

Seine Rouen

BLENHEIM 13 AUGUST 1704

In 1703–04 the combination of France, Bavaria, and the Hungarian rebels appeared about to extinguish Habsburg power, and thus to destroy the basis of Britain's alliance strategy – the use of Austrian strength to resist French expansion. The crisis was averted by Marlborough's bold march at the head of an Anglo-German army from Koblenz to the Danube, and by his subsequent victory, in co-operation with Prince Eugene, at Blenheim. This was the most decisive British military move on the Continent until the twentieth century. Marlborough was skilful in holding the anti-French coalition together, and was expert in conducting mobile warfare. The advance was a formidable logistical challenge: depots of supplies were established along the route, providing the troops with fresh boots as well as food. The campaign was a great triumph for mobility and planning, both in strategy and on the battlefield. .

Blenheim was hard-fought, with over 30,000 casualties out of the 108,000 combatants. Victory was largely due to Marlborough's tactical flexibility; in particular, to his ability to retain control and manoeuvrability. The decisive factors were mastery of the terrain, the retention and management of reserves, and the timing of the heavy strike. Having pinned down much of the French infantry in defensive engagements, Marlborough launched the substantial force he had kept unengaged in the centre and broke the French lines with an intense forty-gun bombardment followed by an infantry assault and a shock cavalry charge.

The battle was followed by the conquest of southern Germany, the major fortresses of Ulm

and Ingolstadt falling before the end of the year, while Marlborough captured Trarben-Tarbach and Trier. After Blenheim and the retreat to the Rhine, most of the Franco-Bavarian army was no longer effective. Austria had been saved and French forces were not to campaign so far east again until 1741. Marlborough had destroyed the image of French military superiority.

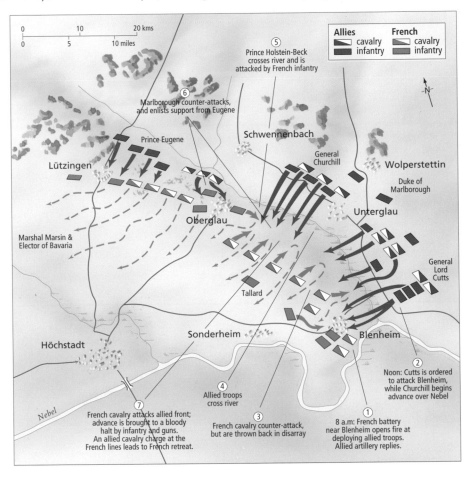

the Blenheim campaign (map 2). The French were also driven from Italy. Their army besieging Turin was defeated by Eugene and Victor Amadeus at the Battle of Turin (1706), and the French withdrew from Italy. The Spanish lost Naples to the Austrians in 1707.

The Grand Alliance had less success in conquering Spain and invading France. Despite the intervention of the English and their naval power, and despite the support of Catalonia and Valencia and of German and Portuguese troops, the attempt to establish Archduke Charles as Charles III failed. Amphibious forces captured Gibraltar in 1704 (map 3), Barcelona in 1705, and Minorca in 1708, and Madrid was occupied briefly in 1706 and 1710, but Castilian loyalty to Philip V and Louis XIV's support for his neighbouring grandson proved too strong. Philip's cause became iden-tified with national independence despite his military

reliance on French troops, who decisively defeated the Allies at Almanza (1707), forcing Charles back to Catalonia. In 1710, Charles defeated Philip at Almenara (July) and Saragossa (August) before occupying Madrid, but few Castilians rallied to him and his communications became hazardous. As a result he withdrew from Madrid and, at Brihuega (December), part of his retreating force was attacked by a superior army under Vendôme and forced to surrender. On the following day, another section of his retreating force fought off a French attack at Villaviciosa, but Charles had now lost Castile. His Catalan supporters resisted but were defeated in a series of sieges: Gerona fell in 1711, Barcelona in 1714 and Palma de Mallorca in 1715.

By the time major attacks were launched on France, exhaustion was beginning to affect the Grand Alliance. Marlborough's plan (page 108) to invade Lorraine up the

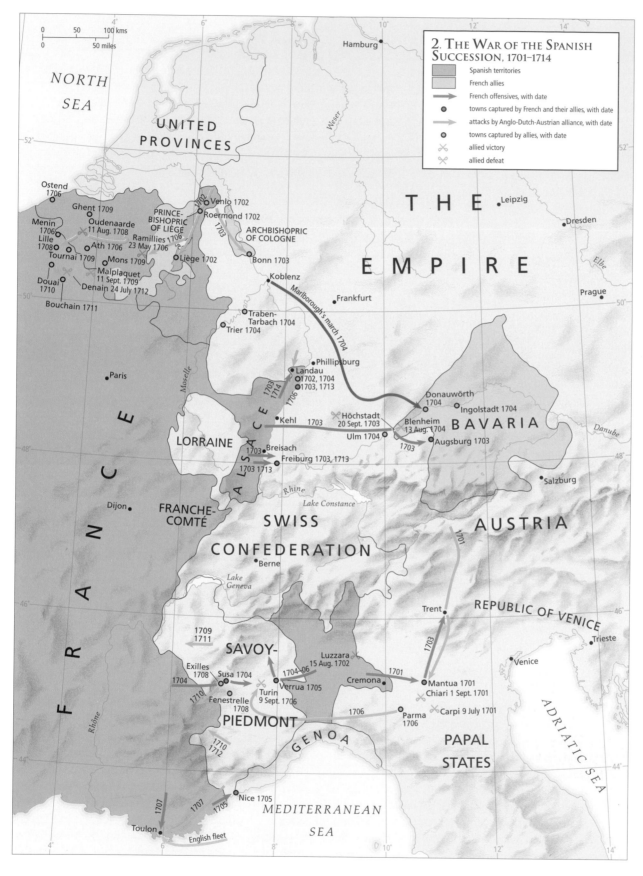

NORTH
SEA

UNITED
PROVINCES

THE

EMPIRE

Hamburg

Leipzig

Dresden

Prague

Frankfurt

Ostend 1706
Ghent 1709
Menin 1706
Oudenaarde 11 Aug. 1708
Lille 1708
Ath 1706
Tournai 1709
Mons 1709
Douai 1710
Malplaquet 11 Sept. 1709
Denain 24 July 1712
Bouchain 1711
PRINCE-BISHOPRIC OF LIÈGE
Venlo 1702
Roermond 1702
Ramillies 23 May 1706
Liège 1702
ARCHBISHOPRIC OF COLOGNE
Bonn 1703
Koblenz
Marlborough's march 1704

Traben-Tarbach 1704
Trier 1704

Paris

Phillipsburg
Landau 1702, 1704 — 1703, 1713
Kehl 1703
Höchstadt 20 Sept. 1703
Ulm 1704
Blenheim 13 Aug. 1704
Donauwörth 1704
Ingolstadt 1704
BAVARIA
Augsburg 1703

Danube

LORRAINE
ALSACE
Breisach
Freiburg 1703, 1713

Moselle

Rhine
Lake Constance

Salzburg

Dijon
FRANCHE-COMTÉ
SWISS
CONFEDERATION
Berne

AUSTRIA

Lake Geneva

F R A N C E

Rhône

1709 1711
SAVOY-
Exilles 1708
Susa 1704
Fenestrelle 1708
Turin 9 Sept. 1706
Verrua 1705
1704-06
Luzzara 15 Aug. 1702
Cremona
Mantua 1701
Chiari 1 Sept. 1701
Carpi 9 July 1701
Parma 1706
PIEDMONT
GENOA
PAPAL
STATES

Trent
REPUBLIC OF VENICE
Venice
Trieste
ADRIATIC SEA

1710 1712

1707 1707 1705
Nice 1705
MEDITERRANEAN
SEA
Toulon
English fleet

2. THE WAR OF THE SPANISH SUCCESSION, 1701–1714

- Spanish territories
- French allies
- French offensives, with date
- towns captured by French and their allies, with date
- attacks by Anglo-Dutch-Austrian alliance, with date
- towns captured by allies, with date
- allied victory
- allied defeat

MAP 2

Louis XIV's last war was conducted over a wide field of operation. Initially France took the initiative, but in 1704–06 she suffered a number of crucial blows in Germany, Italy, and the Low Countries and, thereafter, was largely forced onto the defensive, except for her activity in Spain.

Moselle in 1705 had to be abandoned due to lack of German support. Vauban's fortifications proved their value as Allied forces invaded France. Whereas most of the fortresses in the Spanish Netherlands had fallen rapidly to Allied attack, Lille held out for 120 days in 1708 before capitulating

on 9 December, too late for the Allies to make further advances before the onset of winter. A poorly-co-ordinated attack on defensive positions on 7 September had left nearly 3,000 attackers dead or wounded, and the Allies were only successful when they concentrated their artillery fire.

The Austrian invasions of Alsace in 1706 and the Franche-Comté in 1709, and a combined Anglo-Austrian-Sardinian attack on Toulon in 1707 were also unsuccessful (map 2). The last was intended to seize the French navy's Mediterranean base and to expose southern France to attack. The Austrian and Sardinian forces advanced overland while the British fleet under Sir Cloudesley Shovell provided naval support. Eugene, however, was unenthusiastic and failed to seize the initiative. The French were able to send reinforcements and the siege was acrimoniously abandoned.

The course of the War of the Spanish Succession reflected the respective strategic strengths of the combatants. France had a relatively secure home base protected by a large army and excellent fortifications, and was largely immune to British amphibious attack. French forces could take the offensive in the Low Countries, Germany, Italy, and Spain, and their ability to campaign simultaneously in these areas testified to France's military, fiscal, and administrative might.

But France's opponents were also effective: the British provided financial support, and Marlborough refuted France's claims to military superiority. The Dutch, Austrians, Savoy-Piedmont, Portuguese, and the lesser German princes, were also crucial to the anti-French effort, providing forces and maintaining a united front up to the Peace of Utrecht (1713), at which Louis was forced to accept terms and which marked the passing of French predominance.

The siege of Namur, 1692. Namur was a fortress in the Spanish Netherlands, and its capture was crucial to the French if they wanted to campaign down the river Meuse. Louis XIV besieged the city with a large army in May 1692. The siege was rapidly driven forward by Vauban, helped by a siege train of 151 cannon, and the fortress fell after five weeks.

NAMUR PRIS PAR SA MAJESTÉ
LE DERNIER JUIN 1692

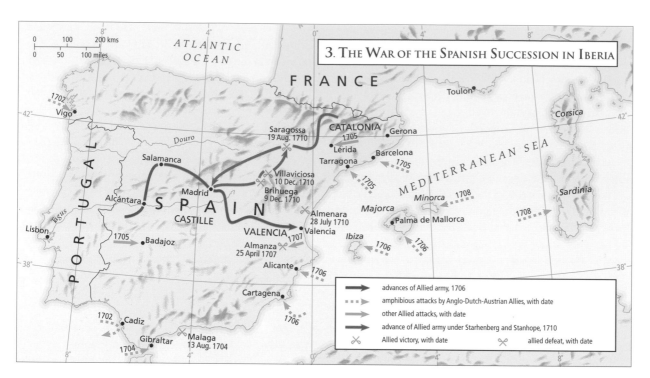

3. THE WAR OF THE SPANISH SUCCESSION IN IBERIA

advances of Allied army, 1706
amphibious attacks by Anglo-Dutch-Austrian Allies, with date
other Allied attacks, with date
advance of Allied army under Starhenberg and Stanhope, 1710
Allied victory, with date ✕
allied defeat, with date ✕

MAP 3

The war in Iberia was fluid and fast-moving: the Allies had the great advantage of command over the seas, especially after the French navy failed to win at the Battle of Malaga, and were helped by the support of Portugal and Catalonia. However, Castilian hostility to Archduke Charles and French military intervention proved crucial, and the Allies lost a number of important battles.

MARLBOROUGH

John Churchill, First Duke of Marlborough (1650–1722), was one of the greatest of British generals. He rose under the Stuarts, serving in the English garrison in Tangier (1668–70) and in an English regiment in French service during the Third Anglo-Dutch war. His desertion of James II in 1688 led William III to regard him with some uncertainty, but in 1701 he appointed him Captain-General of the English forces in the Netherlands, a post he held until dismissed by the pacific Tory ministry in 1711.

Having captured Venlo, Roermond, and Liège in 1702 and Bonn in 1703, Marlborough saved Austria by his victory at Blenheim (1704). After an inconclusive campaign in Flanders in 1705, Marlborough again won victory at Ramillies (1706) by breaking the French centre to support action on a flank; he went on to conquer the Spanish Netherlands. The French attempt to regain their position was thwarted at Oudenaarde (1708), where after several hours' fighting they were almost enveloped by Marlborough's cavalry. Marlborough was less successful in the following year at Malplaquet. His tactics had become stereotyped, allowing the French to devise a response. They held his attacks on their flanks and retained a substantial reserve to meet his final central push. The French eventually retreated, but their army had not been routed. The casualties were very heavy on both sides, including a quarter of the Anglo-Dutch force: the battle was the bloodiest in Europe before Borodino (1812). Malplaquet was followed by the capture of Mons and Ghent, but hopes of breaching the French frontier defences and marching on Paris were misplaced. In 1711, Marlborough captured Bouchain, but such achievements could no longer keep Britain in the conflict.

John Churchill, First Duke of Marlborough, by Sir Godfrey Kneller, c.1706.

THE GREAT NORTHERN WAR, 1700-1721

THE GREAT NORTHERN WAR illustrated the potentially decisive nature of warfare in this period. It began with the accession of Charles XII to the throne of Sweden in 1697, which encouraged hopes of Swedish weakness. It led to the collapse of the Swedish empire and ended with Russia acquiring a Baltic coastline and becoming the strongest power in northern Europe.

THE ANTI-SWEDISH ALLIANCE

The accession of the young Charles XII (1697–1718) of Sweden raised expectations among Sweden's neighbours of a possible end to Swedish hegemony in the Baltic. The conclusion of the Ottoman war released Russian forces, while the recent accession of Augustus, Elector of Saxony,

as King of Poland marked the arrival of a new, ambitious player in Baltic diplomacy.

The most active role in negotiating an anti-Swedish alliance was taken by Denmark. Danish attempts over the previous quarter-century to reconquer Scania and to dominate Holstein-Gottorp had suffered from the lack of any diversion of Swedish strength to the eastern Baltic. Augustus hoped to gain Livonia and to use it as the basis for establishing a hereditary Saxon dynasty in Poland. It was therefore agreed that in 1700 Peter the Great would invade Ingria, Augustus would invade Livonia, and Frederick IV of Denmark would invade first Holstein and then southern Sweden. It was assumed that these attacks would divide the Swedish forces and ensure speedy success.

Charles, however, responded rapidly. A landing on Zealand threatened Copenhagen and, by the Treaty of Travendal, Frederick IV abandoned the war, restoring the pro-Swedish Duke of Holstein-Gottorp (map 1). Swedish

MAP 1

Charles XII's boldness and military skill led to the initial defeat of the coalition that attacked him and to considerable success when the Swedes invaded Poland, but Charles' failure to crush or settle with Peter the Great proved decisive.

1. THE GREAT NORTHERN WAR, 1700–1721

- Swedish empire, 1660
- → campaigns of Charles XII of Sweden, with date
- ⚔ Swedish victory
- ⚔ Swedish defeat
- ▪▶ planned attacks on Sweden, 1700
- ▨ territory gained by Russia
- ▨ territory gained by Prussia
- ▨ territory gained by Hanover

forces were then sent to the eastern Baltic where the quiescence of most of the Livonian nobility and the strength of Riga's defences had ended the Saxon invasion. Charles was thus able to focus on the Russian army besieging Narva under Peter. In November 1700, 11,000 Swedes defeated 24,000 Russians through a combination of professionalism and the favourable direction of a snowstorm (*page 111*).

INVOLVEMENT IN POLAND

Charles then decided to replace Augustus with a more pliable ruler, leading to his embroilment for a number of years in the unsteady complexities of Polish politics, and thus to a delay in concentrating his military attention against Russia. In the summer of 1701, under cover of a smoke screen, Charles crossed the river Dvina near Riga in the face of Saxon-Russian opposition. After this well-co-ordinated operation the Swedish infantry under fire successfully advanced to engage in hand-to-hand conflict. Charles then occupied Mitau and overran Courland, before moving on

into Livonia. The Swedes encountered guerrilla opposition there, although they also won the support of the powerful Sapieha family of nobles.

Charles captured Warsaw (March 1702) and Thorn (1703) and defeated Polish-Saxon armies at Klisów (1702), Pultusk (1703), Punitz (1704), and Fraustadt/Wschowa (1706) (*map 1*). The victory at Klisów over a larger Saxon army was symptomatic of Charles' generalship. A silent march through difficult terrain secured the element of surprise, the Swedish cavalry attacked without firing, the artillery was quicker than the more numerous Saxon cannon, and the infantry advanced to attack with cold steel in the face of Saxon musket fire. Saxon losses in dead and wounded were at least twice those of the Swedes, and the Saxons also lost 2,000 prisoners and many cannon. At Fraustadt, a Swedish army under Rehnskjold defeated a Saxon force twice the size, the numerous Swedish cavalry enveloping both Saxon flanks while the relatively small Swedish infantry held off attacks in the centre.

Charles XII at the Battle of Narva (1700), which represented the final triumph of the bold generalship that had totally defeated the strategic plan of the coalition arrayed against him.

NARVA 20 NOVEMBER 1700

Peter the Great concentrated his efforts in 1700 on the fortress of Narva which protected the crossing point over the river Narova and guarded the eastern approaches of Estonia. The siege was opened in September but it was badly managed. The lines of defensive fortifications were far too long – 4 miles (6.5km) – and were dominated by higher ground outside. By October, Peter had a force of about 24,000 besieging the fortress, but in the following month he decamped when Charles XII of Sweden advanced to relieve the fortress.

The 11,000 Swedes advanced rapidly, giving the Russians no time to deploy their 177 cannon and mortars, and broke into the Russian entrenchments in two columns. The Swedes rapidly came to hand-to-hand conflict and proved adept with their bayonets. A snowstorm blew directly into the faces of the defenders, and the Russian position collapsed, the cavalry on the left fleeing first. The troops on the right flank also fled and tried to cross the Narova bridge, only to cause the bridge to collapse under their weight. The remaining units were forced to surrender. The Swedes lost 2,000 dead and wounded, the Russians 8–10,000 and all their artillery. As Vienna in 1683, Narva demonstrated the vulnerability of a poorly commanded and badly deployed siege army to a relief attempt.

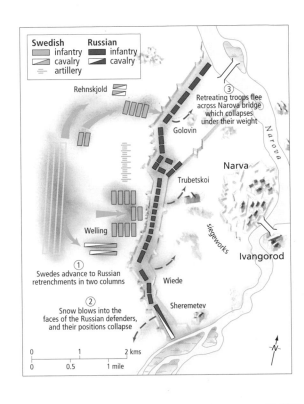

Swedish involvement in Poland allowed Peter to increase the size and improve the fighting capacity of his army. A Swedish expedition failed to take Archangel by surprise in the winter of 1700–01. In 1701–03, the Russians scored successes against the Swedes in the Baltic provinces in the battles of Eristfer (1701) and Hummelshof (1702), and in 1703 Peter founded St Petersburg. In 1702, the Swedish flotilla on Lake Ladoga was defeated by a far larger Russian squadron. While Charles was kept busy in Poland, to which Peter sent troops to aid Augustus, the Russians successfully besieged Narva and Dorpat in 1704. The Swedish forces that tried to relieve them were short of supplies and outnumbered. In that year Charles used his control of much of Poland to have Augustus dethroned, and his protégé, Stanislaus Leszczynski, crowned in 1705.

The war led to increased Swedish ambitions. By a treaty of 1705 with Poland, Charles promised to help conquer the lands ceded to Russia in 1667. In 1706, his invasion of Saxony led Augustus to recognize Stanislaus. However, Peter made it clear that he was unwilling to give up Ingria and his 'window on the west', despite the growing threats to Russia from the Cossacks and from the Ukraine.

THE SWEDES' RUSSIAN DISASTER

In 1708, Charles invaded Russia, successfully crossing the river lines that blocked his advance. A diversionary attack was instrumental in a successful crossing of the Beresina river in June. In the following month, at Holovzin,

Charles defeated a much larger Russian army that was trying to block the route to Smolensk and Moscow. The Swedes won an extended firefight and the Russians fled, opening the road to the Dnieper. But the Swedes had lost over 1,250 dead and wounded, losses they could ill afford. The Russians had fought better than at Narva. Furthermore, their scorched-earth policy of destroying crops and farms, which they used not only in Livonia and Poland but also within Russia itself, created grave problems for Charles.

Supply problems, the severity of the winter of 1708–9 and the hope that Mazepa, the *hetman* (elected leader) of the Ukraine, would raise his people against Peter, led Charles to turn southwards. This lent military backing to the diplomatic threat to destabilize Russia's western and southern borders. The possibility of developing Charles's alliance system to include the Tatars and the Ottoman Empire was entertained. However, Mazepa's inadequate preparation, combined with the swift brutality of Peter's military response and the savage cold of the winter, undermined Charles' move. His army lost many men during one of the coldest winters on record.

A Swedish supporting force under Lewenhaupt escorting a major supply train had been defeated by Peter at Lesnaja on 29 September 1708. In early 1709, Charles won the support of the Zaporozhian Cossacks, but the Don Cossacks, Tatars, and Ottomans refused to help. The gruelling Swedish campaign came to a disastrous end at the decisive Russian victory of Poltava (*page 112*).

Charles took refuge in the Ottoman Empire, where he stayed until 1714. In the meantime, the Swedish position around the eastern Baltic collapsed. Augustus regained the Polish throne, while Frederick IV invaded Sweden in November 1709.

RUSSIA EMERGES DOMINANT

The loyalty of Scania and a decisive Swedish victory by Magnus Stenbock at Hålsingborg in February 1710 forced Frederick to withdraw, and the Danish fleet was defeated at the Battle of Kjöge Bay in 1710. However, Peter had more success; in October 1709 he occupied Courland, and in 1710 he successfully besieged the cities of Viborg, Reval, Mitau, and Riga.

The Danes seized the Duchy of Bremen in 1712 and then all of Holstein, though at Gadebusch (1712), Stenbock and 13,800 men defeated a 16,600-strong Dano-Saxon army. The Swedish artillery achieved battlefield superiority thanks to Cronstedt's innovations which included a screw setting to control the elevation of the barrel and a better coupling-mechanism that enabled the gun to be pulled into firing position muzzle to the front, instead of the rear. Peter, however, took Helsingfors in 1713 and then all of Finland. In the same year, a Swedish army was defeated in Holstein at Tønning by Russian, Saxon, and Danish forces.

In 1714, the Russian fleet defeated the Swedes off Cape Hangö and Frederick William I of Prussia seized Stettin with Russian assistance. In July 1715, George I of Great Britain, as Elector of Hanover, declared war on Charles, and an indecisive Dano-Swedish naval battle off the island of Rügen was followed by a Dano-Prussian amphibious attack on Rügen which the vastly outnumbered Charles was unable to dislodge. After a hard-fought siege by Danes, Saxons, and Prussians, the Swedes lost Stralsund in December 1715. A large Prussian siege train containing eighty 24-pounders (10.8kg) and forty mortars played a major role in covering the successive assaults of the besiegers and they were also helped by the freezing-up of the defensive ditches. Wismar also fell to siege in April 1716.

A planned Russian invasion of Scania from Jutland did not materialize, but Charles failed to split the opposing alliance. Charles opened an offensive which was designed to enable him to invade Denmark and northern Germany, and to strengthen his negotiating hand with Russia, but in 1718 he was shot while besieging the Norwegian fortress of Fredrikshald, which he had earlier failed to take in 1716. Charles' death ended the siege and the Swedes retreated from Norway. The following year, Russian galley-born forces ravaged the eastern coast of Sweden. In 1719–20, the Swedes reached agreement with Hanover, Denmark, and Prussia, and yielded Bremen Verden, Stettin, and part of Pomerania. An alliance was then formed between the former rivals to try to force Peter the Great to surrender part of his gains, but when a settlement came, at Nystad in 1721, Peter was still left with Livonia, Estonia, Ingria, and Kexholm.

POLTAVA 27 JUNE 1709

Charles, hopeful that he would regain the initiative with a major victory, attacked the Russian army entrenched behind redoubts at Poltava. This was not, however, to be a second Narva. The Swedes did not use their artillery to try to weaken the Russian position, probably because Charles XII preferred to rely on a rapid infantry attack rather than the attrition of firepower. In contrast, Peter the Great, who was in command of the Russian forces at Poltava, placed great weight on artillery and had developed a formidable munitions industry. Whereas at Poltava the Swedes had only 4 cannon, the Russians had 102, 21 of them heavy pieces, and plentiful ammunition. Short of supplies, the Swedes decided to attack the powerful Russian position. The Russian redoubts were penetrated at heavy cost, but in the final engagement the Russians advanced from their camp with their entire force and their superior strength and firepower proved decisive. Their 102 cannon fired 1,471 shot and Charles lost about 10,000 men. The Russians lost 1,356 dead, the Swedes 6,900, as well as 2,800 prisoners and about 1,500 wounded who escaped, a high total ratio from an army of 19,700. The defeat turned into disaster when most of the withdrawing army surrendered to their Russian pursuers three days later.

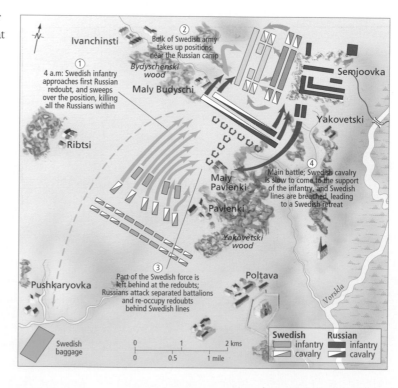

WAR IN EASTERN EUROPE (I), 1710-1739

PETER THE GREAT *was less successful against the Ottoman Empire than against the Swedes. His ambitious plans to roll back the frontiers of Islam were thwarted by stubborn Ottoman resistance. The Russians resumed the advance in 1735–39 and had greater success, but were let down by the failure of their Austrian ally.*

RUSSO-OTTOMAN CONFRONTATION

The Ottomans opposed the Russian dominance of Poland which appeared to be the consequence of Augustus' reinstatement after Poltava (*page 112*). Thanks in part to the influence of Devlet-Girei II, the Russophobe Khan of the Tatars, and to Turkish governmental fears about Russian intentions, the Ottoman Empire declared war in November 1710. Peter had sought to avoid war, as Ottoman neutrality was important for him in the Great Northern War (*pages 109–12*), but eventually he responded by reviving his hopes of the late 1690s. Like Leopold I in the 1680s, Peter also sought to give the war a religious interpretation. In conscious imitation of Constantine the Great, Peter had the cross inscribed on his Guards' standards with the phrase 'Under this sign we conquer'.

In March 1711, Peter issued appeals for assistance to 'the Montenegrin People' and to 'the Christian People under Turkish Rule'. In the following month, a treaty was signed with Demetrius Cantemir, Hospodar of Moldavia, providing for Russian protection over an independent Moldavia under his rule and Moldavian assistance against the Turks.

Peter's planned invasion was, however, a humiliating failure (*map 1*). The 54,000-strong Russian army advanced through Poland towards Moldavia, but were affected by shortages of food and water and by Tatar harassment. Though Peter received Moldavian support, the speedy advance of a large Ottoman army dissuaded Constantine Brancovan, the Hospodar of Wallachia, from sending his promised forces, and he instead blocked the march of Peter's Serbian reinforcements. The failure of the Moldavian harvest affected Russian logistics. Peter planned to reach the Danube before the Turks could cross it and was encouraged by inaccurate reports that the Turks were frightened of him. The Russians, however, had advanced too slowly and lost the initiative. Far larger Turkish forces were already across the Danube and moving north along the right bank of the Pruth. Peter was surprised and out-manoeuvred as he retreated. Tatars blocked the Russian retreat route towards Jassy. Based on the hills dominating the Russian position, the far larger Ottoman forces had moved faster than expected and surrounded the Russians, and their superior Turkish artillery bombarded the Russian camps. Ottoman attacks were repelled only with difficulty and, short of food, water, and forage, Peter was forced to sign a peace in July 1711 handing back Azov. Peter's supporters in the Balkans were abandoned. The Montenegrins, who had been conducting a guerrilla war since 1702, held out until 1714, while

MAP 1

Though the Russians maintained considerable pressure, they were unable to gain a Black Sea coastline until Catherine II's reign. The Austrians proved incapable of maintaining the impetus of their 1683–97 and 1716–18 wars with the Turks.

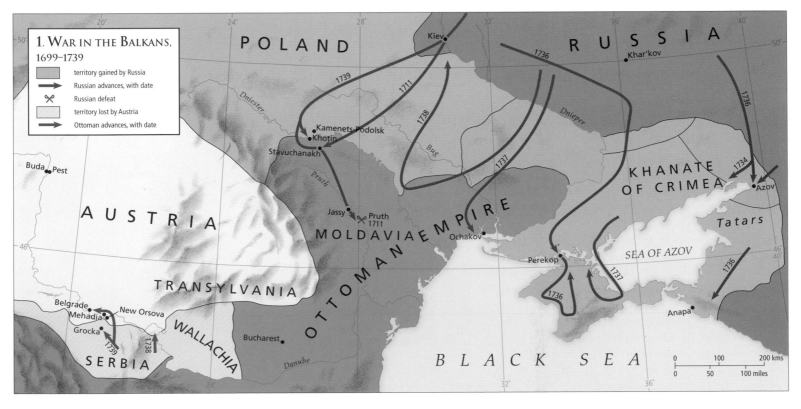

Cantemir and several thousand Moldavians followed Peter back into Russia.

Relations between Peter and the Turks remained poor after the conflict on the river Pruth, and Peter's reluctance to observe the peace terms agreed in July 1711 led to Turkish declarations of war in October 1711, November 1712, and April 1713. Eventually a twenty-five-year peace was concluded at Adrianople in June 1713. During the remaining years of the decade, both powers were more concerned with their other opponents, Austria and Sweden, but the collapse of the Safavid dynasty in Persia and Russian ambitions on the western shore of the Caspian were to lead to fresh problems. The Shah appealed for Turkish support against his Afghan assailants in 1720, but nothing was done. In 1722, Peter occupied Derbent, and in 1723 Shah Tahmasp ceded him the provinces to the west and south of the Caspian Sea. The Turks responded by occupying Tiflis (Tbilisi) in 1723, but war was avoided when Peter and the Turks agreed a delimitation of their interests in 1724. Relations became less troublesome as Turkey faced internal problems centring on a revolution in Constantinople in 1730, while the Russians were involved in a confrontation with Britain and her allies in 1725–31, and the War of the Polish Succession in 1733–35 (map 2). The Russians successfully invaded Poland in 1733, capturing Danzig and defeating a relieving French force in 1734. They went on to deploy an army in Germany in 1735.

THE RUSSIANS STRUGGLE TO ADVANCE

Russo-Ottoman differences over the Caucasus, however, led to renewed conflict in 1735. After an unsuccessful attempt on Azov, the Russians declared war in the following year, seizing the city when its main powder magazine blew up after being hit by a Russian mortar bomb. A Turkish attempt to regain the city in 1737 was repelled. Though exhausted by fighting France, Sardinia, and Spain in the War of the Polish Succession, the Austrians joined the war in 1737, fearing that if they did not act they would lose Russia, their only surviving major ally.

Russian ambitions had expanded. In 1736, General Burkhardt Christoph von Münnich, the German head of the Russian War College who had entered Russian service in 1721 and risen to the top under the Tsarina Anna, spoke of gaining Constantinople in three years. His troops stormed the earthworks which barred the isthmus of Perekop at the entrance to the Crimea; after a bombardment, Münnich ordered a night attack in columns against the western section of the lines. The troops climbed the wall and gained control with scanty losses. The fortress of Perekop surrendered soon after. However, though the Russians then invaded the Crimea, the Tatars avoided battle and the Russians, debilitated by disease and heat, retreated. Further invasions of the Crimea under Lacy in 1737 and 1738 were also unsuccessful. Field-Marshal Peter Lacy (1678–1751) was an Irishman who served at the age of thirteen in the defence of Limerick. He entered the service of Peter the Great in 1700, and fought at Poltava and at the siege of

Danzig. In 1737, Münnich advanced on the Ottoman fortress of Ochakov, supported by supplies brought by boat down the Dnieper and thence by 28,000 carts. The initial assault failed, but the fortress was taken, again after its powder magazine exploded. The survivors were massacred in the storming of the fortress.

Disease and logistical problems thwarted further Russian advance in 1737, and in 1738 the same difficulties ended Münnich's hopes of crossing the Dniester to invade the Balkans; Ochakov was abandoned in the face of a major outbreak of the plague which killed thousands of Russians. Tatar irregular cavalry was also a formidable challenge, employing a scorched-earth policy in which crops and forage were burnt and wells poisoned, as for example when the Russians invaded the Crimea in 1736. In 1737, the Tatars burnt the grass between the Bug and the Dniester, hindering Münnich's operations after he captured Ochakov.

In 1739, the Russians were to be more successful, marching across Polish territory, and avoiding the lands near the Black Sea. Münnich crossed the Dniester well upstream, drove the Ottoman army from its camp at Stavuchanakh and captured the major fortress of Khotin and the Moldavian capital of Jassy. The Moldavian nobility pledged loyalty to

Peter the Great (1672–1725), Tsar of Russia from 1682, although he did not acquire complete power until 1689. He was a vigorous ruler who defeated Charles XII of Sweden and campaigned successfully in Persia in 1722–23, but he was outmanoeuvred by the Turks in 1711. Peter sought to modernize Russia by initiating major governmental, ecclesiastical, military, and economic reforms, although many of these were only partially implemented.

MAP 2

In this wide-ranging conflict, the Russians successfully overran Poland, but their Austrian ally lost much of Austrian Italy to the attacking coalition of France, Spain, and Savoy-Piedmont (the kingdom of Sardinia). Fighting in the Rhineland was indecisive.

2. THE WAR OF THE POLISH SUCCESSION, 1733–1735

- France and her allies
- French advances, with dates
- feared French advance, 1734
- Austrian counter-attack, 1734
- unsuccessful French relief force, 1734
- towns besieged by French with year of fall
- French victory
- Spanish invasions of southern Italy
- towns captured by Spanish with year of fall
- Spanish victory
- Austria and her allies
- Russian invasion of Poland
- Russian march west, 1735
- town captured by Russians, with year of fall

the Empress Anna. But Russia was let down by the weakened Austrians, who made a unilateral peace with the Ottomans, ceding besieged Belgrade, Little Wallachia, and northern Serbia.

THE AUSTRO-TURKISH WAR OF 1737–39

Exhausted by the War of the Polish Succession (1733–35), Austria did not wish to fight the Turks but was concerned that if it did not, it might jeopardize its important Russian alliance and lose the ability to influence Russian expansion into the Balkans. Charles VI therefore went to war in 1737 (map 1). His troops, under Field-Marshal Seckendorf, advanced into Serbia in 1737, but were then driven back, though Turkish attempts to subvert the Habsburg position in Transylvania were unsuccessful. The Turks ravaged Habsburg Wallachia and Serbia in early 1738, and in June they besieged New Orsova. Under their new commander, Count Königsegg, the Austrians set out to relieve the fortress,

defeating the Turks nearby at Cornea (4 July). The Turks then lifted the siege but, in face of a second Turkish army and despite another victory near Mehadia, Königsegg retreated, abandoning both Mehadia and New Orsova. The Austrian army was decimated by disease. Command in 1739 was entrusted to Count Wallis, an Irishman in Habsburg service, but at Grocka/Kroszka, south-east of Belgrade, his advancing troops suffered heavy casualties when forcing their way through a defile in the face of the Turkish army. Although the Austrians won control of the battlefield, Wallis responded cautiously by withdrawing. Taking advantage of the situation, the Turks besieged Belgrade, refortified since its capture in 1717. The local Austrian commanders, their confidence gone, surrendered. Austrian prestige had suffered a heavy blow. The Russians had to make peace too: their gains in the southern steppe and retention of an unfortified Azov still left them without a Black Sea coastline.

V

WARFARE IN
EUROPE, 1740-1792

The historian Edward Gibbon, whose *Decline and Fall of the Roman Empire* appeared in 1776–88, was convinced that the specialization of warfare represented a marked improvement on the past. He wrote of tenth-century western Europe that government at that time was weak and 'the nobles of every province disobeyed their sovereign . . . and exercised perpetual hostilities against their equals and neighbours. Their private wars, which overturned the fabric of government, formed the martial spirit of the nation. In the system of modern Europe, the power of the sword is possessed, at least in fact, by five or six mighty potentates; their operations are conducted on a distant frontier by an order of men who devote their lives to the study and practice of the military art; the rest of the country and community enjoys in the midst of war the tranquillity of peace, and is only made sensible of the change by the aggravation or decrease of the public taxes.' The strong tendencies towards the professionalization of warfare which were already evident were strengthened in the decades of conflict and confrontation that began with Frederick the Great of Prussia's invasion of Silesia in 1740. Austria, Prussia, and Russia further developed their armies, while Britain became the strongest naval power in the world. France sought to be both a leading land and sea power and her failure to do so during the Seven Years' War (1756–63) led to a fatal decline in France's military reputation. This not only weakened France abroad, but also led to a serious decline in the prestige of the monarchy.

Instead of the ruler of France it was Catherine II, Tsarina of Russia (1762–96), who seemed the strongest ruler in Europe. The westward movement of Russian armies in 1735 and 1748 had already encouraged France to negotiate peace with Russia's ally, Austria. During the Seven Years' War, Russia proved a formidable and frightening foe for Frederick the Great, and after the first partition of Poland in 1772 the Russian frontier moved further west. Russian power also threatened both Sweden and the Ottoman empire, while the development of naval strength, not matched by Austria or Prussia, strengthened Russian as a Baltic power and led to the entry of a Russian fleet into the Mediterranean in 1769. There was no intimation that it would soon be France under Revolutionary and then Napoleonic rule that would threaten the stability of Europe.

THE WAR OF THE AUSTRIAN SUCCESSION

BEGUN *by a Prussian invasion of Austrian-ruled Silesia on 16 December 1740, the War of the Austrian Succession was an attempt to exploit the end of the Habsburg male line with the succession of Maria Theresa. France and Bavaria also sought gains at Austria's expense, while Britain moved to counter French expansionism. In Italy, Austria was pitted against a Bourbon alliance of France and Spain.*

AUSTRIAN REVERSES

Frederick's father, Frederick William I, had developed the Prussian army into a well-trained force and his son used it to devastating effect against the Austrians, who were weakened by their recent disastrous war against the Otto-

mans. The attack on Silesia (*map 1*) was unexpected and the wealthy province fell rapidly, with a Prussian victory at Mollwitz on 10 April 1741 (*page 119*). The Prussian cavalry was ridden down by the Austrians, causing Frederick to flee, but the well-trained Prussian infantry then operated in a parade-ground fashion and, despite sustaining heavier casualties, prevailed over their slower-firing opponents.

In the following year, Frederick invaded Bohemia and defeated Maria Theresa's brother-in-law, Prince Charles of Lorraine, at Chotusitz (17 May). The Austrian cavalry again defeated its Prussian counterpart, but the disciplined Prussian infantry forced the Austrians to withdraw. In 1742, Maria Theresa bought peace by ceding most of Silesia.

War resumed in August 1744 because of Frederick's concern at Austrian pressure on eastern France and the risk that the Austrians would then turn on Prussia. As in 1740–41, he exploited the element of surprise. He crossed Saxony,

MAP 1

The assault on Austria was a formidable challenge, but the Austrians were greatly helped by the poor co-ordination of their opponents' plans and by their failure to seize Vienna.

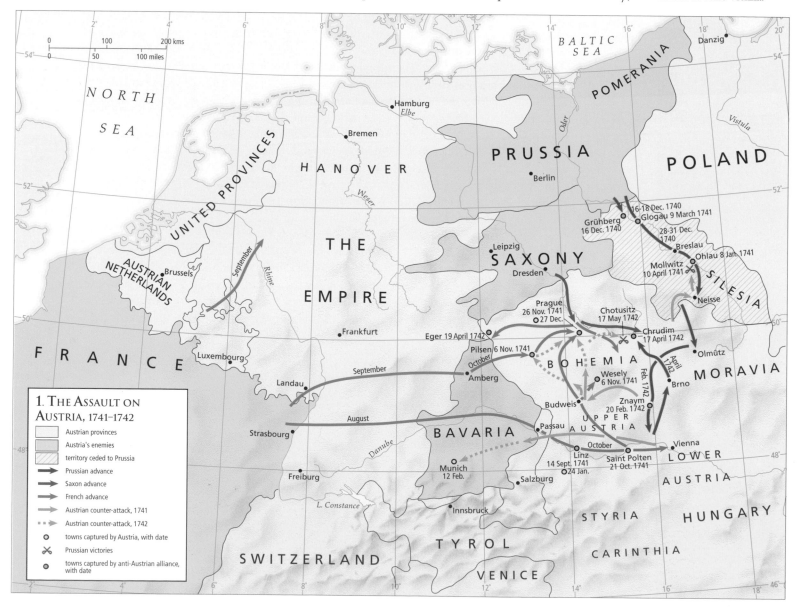

1. THE ASSAULT ON AUSTRIA, 1741–1742

- Austrian provinces
- Austria's enemies
- territory ceded to Prussia
- → Prussian advance
- → Saxon advance
- → French advance
- → Austrian counter-attack, 1741
- → Austrian counter-attack, 1742
- ○ towns captured by Austria, with date
- ✕ Prussian victories
- ○ towns captured by anti-Austrian alliance, with date

MOLLWITZ 10 APRIL 1741

The first battle of the War of the Austrian Succession was also the first battle involving Prussian forces for many years. Field-Marshal Neipperg led 19,000 Austrians, who advanced from Moravia in order to drive the Prussians back in Silesia. The Prussians, under Frederick the Great and the more experienced Field-Marshal Schwerin, had 21,600 men (1), and heavily outnumbered the Austrian infantry by 16,800 to 10,000. The Prussians advanced in two lines of battle across the snowy landscape (2), but on the Prussian right the superior Austrian cavalry under General Römer shattered their Prussian opponents (3). Schwerin advised Frederick to leave the battlefield in order to avoid possible capture. Frederick fled, but his infantry fought well, and were more effective than the outnumbered Austrian infantry, many of whom were raw recruits. When darkness fell, Neipperg withdrew from the battlefield. Prussian losses in killed, wounded, or missing – 4,800 men – were 300 greater than those of the Austrians, but the battle was seen as a Prussian victory.

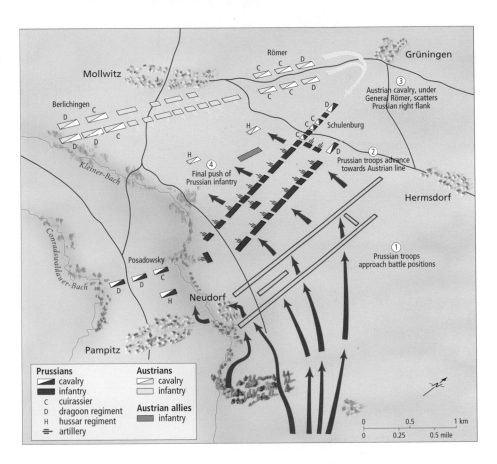

advanced on Prague meeting little resistance, and captured it after a short siege. However, Frederick failed to consolidate this success. He could not bring the Austrians to a decisive battle: their position near Beneschau (map 2) was too strong to attack, while Frederick's army was being harried by light forces from Austria's Balkan frontier raiding his supply lines, and foragers. At the end of the campaign, Frederick retreated, having suffered heavy losses.

In 1745 the Austrians, with Saxon support, determined to drive Frederick from Silesia, and took the offensive (map 2). At Hohenfriedberg (4 June), the advancing Prussian infantry were supported by more aggressive cavalry, and successfully surprised the Austrians, vindicating the Prussians' flexibility. Charles of Lorraine was again defeated by Frederick at Soor (30 September) and Hennersdorf (23 November), while Leopold of Anhalt-Dessau, a Prussian general, was victorious at Kesseldorf (15 December). At Hohenfriedberg and Soor, Frederick used an attack that has been called oblique, but can also be seen as a flanking movement. He devised several methods of strengthening one end of his line and using that end in the attack, while minimizing the exposure of his weaker end. This tactic depended on the speedy execution of complex manoeuvres for which well-drilled troops were essential.

Frederick's victories in 1745 forced the Austrians to confirm the Prussian acquisition of Silesia in the Peace of Dresden; they did not try to regain Silesia for over a decade, and then only with Russian support.

CONFLICT IN THE AUSTRIAN NETHERLANDS

The war also involved conflict in southern Germany, Italy, the Low Countries, India, and North America. In 1741, the opportunities presented by the succession of Maria Theresa prompted Charles Albert of Bavaria, with French support, to attack Austria. On 14 September, Linz fell. Eleven days later, the threat of a French attack led George II of Britain, who was also Elector of Hanover, to promise not to help Austria. In October, as French and Bavarian troops camped at Saint Polten (map 1), Vienna prepared for a siege, but Charles Albert decided to turn instead on Prague, which fell to a nocturnal storming on 26 November.

The French and the Bavarians were then abandoned by Saxony and Prussia, and the Austrians displayed unexpected resilience, recapturing Linz in January 1742, seizing Munich in February, and besieging Prague in July: by a daring winter retreat the French abandoned Prague in December.

In 1743, George II of Great Britain entered the war on the Austrian side, leading an Anglo-Austrian army into

FONTENOY 11 MAY 1745

In May 1745, during the French invasion of the Austrian Netherlands, William Duke of Cumberland, second son of George II and British Captain-General, attempted to relieve Tournai, which was under siege by Marshal Saxe. Cumberland's infantry assailed the hastily prepared French position at Fontenoy (1), displaying anew their discipline and fire-control, but the battle demonstrated the strength of a defensive force relying on firepower and supported by a strong cavalry reserve. A British participant recorded 'there were batteries constantly playing upon our front and both flanks'. After several frontal attacks (2), and in the presence of Louis XV and his son, Cumberland was forced to retreat (3) with casualties far heavier than his opponent's.

Though the British fought well, as they had done at Dettingen, the different results of the two battles reflected in part the better French generalship and also the degree to which British steadiness and firepower were more effective in defence. The battle signalled the failure of British attempts to prevent French gains in the Austrian Netherlands and was rapidly followed by major French gains. Tournai fell on 19 June. The battle also greatly raised Saxe's reputation. Though ill with dropsy, he controlled the French forces with great skill. Cardinal de Tencin noted that the victory was a close one and said 'that he was very glad that the king should have seen for himself how much princes risked in making war'. It was reported that Louis XV said to the Dauphin, 'Learn, my son, how dear and painful is victory'.

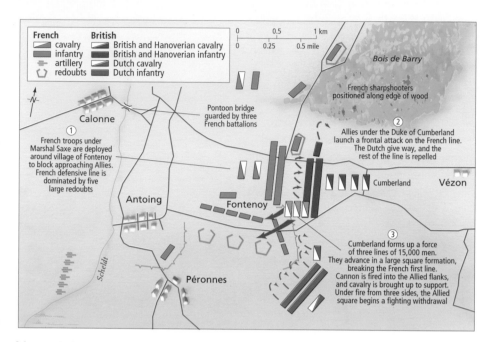

French
- cavalry
- infantry
- artillery
- redoubts

British
- British and Hanoverian cavalry
- British and Hanoverian infantry
- Dutch cavalry
- Dutch infantry

Bois de Barry

French sharpshooters positioned along edge of wood

Calonne

Pontoon bridge guarded by three French battalions

(1) French troops under Marshal Saxe are deployed around village of Fontenoy to block approaching Allies. French defensive line is dominated by five large redoubts

(2) Allies under the Duke of Cumberland launch a frontal attack on the French line. The Dutch give way, and the rest of the line is repelled

Antoing

Fontenoy

Cumberland

Vézon

Scheldt

Péronnes

(3) Cumberland forms up a force of three lines of 15,000 men. They advance in a large square formation, breaking the French first line. Cannon is fired into the Allied flanks, and cavalry is brought up to support. Under fire from three sides, the Allied square begins a fighting withdrawal

---

Germany and, thanks to superior British discipline, defeating the French at Dettingen. George was not, however, able to exploit the victory by making a major impact on France's frontier fortifications. In 1744, Prince Charles of Lorraine invaded Alsace, but was recalled when Frederick II invaded Bohemia. Louis XV then accompanied an army that crossed the Rhine and successfully besieged Freiburg, the major Austrian position in the Black Forest. However, though besieged in September, the fortress did not fall until 7 November and its fall was not followed by any significant French gains.

The French responded to Britain's entry into the war by invading the hitherto neutral Austrian Netherlands in 1744. After the French victory at Fontenoy (11 May 1745), Tournai, Ghent, Bruges, Ostend, and Nieuport followed. While the British forces were busy suppressing the Jacobite revolt, Marshal Saxe took Brussels and Antwerp in early 1746, continuing with Mons, Charleroi, and Namur. At Roucoux (11 October), Saxe defeated an Anglo-Dutch-German army under Charles of Lorraine. In 1747, Saxe overran Dutch Flanders, outmanoeuvred Cumberland when he sought to regain Antwerp, and defeated him at Lawfeldt (2 July). The French then besieged the crucial Dutch fortresses of Bergen-op-Zoom, the fortifications of which had been strengthened with casemented redoubts by Vauban's Dutch rival Menno van Coehoorn. The French were under the command of Saxe's protégé Count Ulric Lowendahl, a Danish royal bastard. They began the siege in mid-July, but progress was slow, and on 16 September the French resorted to the desperate expedient of storming the defences. The following year, Saxe threatened the allied lines, and his opponents massed at Maastricht which fell to siege by an army of over 100,000 men (7 May), fresh evidence both of French military dominance in western Europe and of the professionalism of French siegecraft.

THE FIGHT FOR ITALY

In Italy, the struggle was between Austria and the Bourbons: Philip V of Spain sought territorial gains for his son Charles of Naples, but the threat of the bombardment of Naples by a British fleet made Charles declare his neutrality (August 1742). British pressure on Maria Theresa to win over Charles Emmanuel III of Savoy-Piedmont, King of Sardinia, resulted in the promise to him of Piacenza and part of Lombardy in the Treaty of Worms (September 1743).

A month later, the Second Family Compact committed France to help conquer Lombardy, Parma, and Piacenza for Philip V's second son, Don Philip. Spanish forces occupied

The Siege of Prague by the Austrian army. Prague fell to Bavarian-French-Saxon attack in 1741, to the Austrians in 1742, and to the Prussians in 1744.

COMTE DE SAXE

Hermann Maurice, Comte de Saxe (1696–1750), was an illegitimate son of Augustus II of Saxony and later became a noted womanizer. Enrolled in the Saxon army, he fought at Malplaquet (1709) and then against the Swedes in Pomerania (1711–12), before serving against the Ottomans (1717–18) and narrowly avoiding death at the Battle of Belgrade.

Saxe entered French service in 1719, served against Eugene in the War of the Polish Succession, and played a major role in the War of the Austrian Succession. He stormed Prague in 1741 and commanded the main army in the Low Countries in 1744–48, achieving victories at Fontenoy (1745), Roucoux (1746), and Lawfeldt (1747).

He was a bold general with good battlefield control of large numbers in both attack and defence; he espoused manoeuvrability, maintaining the initiative, and high troop morale. Saxe was a man of the age, embodying the contradictions of the eighteenth century: forward-looking in his use of light troops and his motivation of soldiers; backward-looking in his support for the reintroduction of the ancient Roman legion and of armour.

Charles Emmanuel's Duchy of Savoy in 1743, holding it for the rest of the war, but Bourbon attempts to storm his Alpine defences failed. The French advanced in 1743, but were checked by the Piedmontese position near Casteldelfino in October 1743. The following October, a Franco-Spanish advance was checked when Cuneo was besieged unsuccessfully and in 1747 an attempt by the more northern route was blocked at the battle on the Colle-dell'Assietta (19 July). Winning the alliance of Genoa in April 1745, Bourbon forces under Marshal de Maillebois advanced along the Genoese coast and then marched towards Alessandria. They defeated Charles Emmanuel at Bassignano on 27 September, captured Asti, Casale, and Milan before the end of the year, and negotiated a secret armistice with

Sardinia in February 1746. However, their hopes of driving the Austrians from Italy were dashed when Charles Emmanuel returned to the anti-Bourbon fold in March 1746. Asti, Casale, and Milan were recaptured, and the Austro-Sardinian forces won a decisive victory at Piacenza.

An Austro-Sardinian invasion of Provence was a failure. Supported by the British navy, they crossed the border on 30 November 1746, but in January the French counter-attacked and forced them back. The Austrians were expelled from Genoa by a popular revolt in December 1746, and their longstanding efforts to regain the city and drive Charles from Naples were thwarted. The war ended with the Prussian gain of Silesia recognized. France and Bavaria did not benefit territorially from the war.

MAP 2

The War of the Austrian Succession lacks a single narrative thread because it was so wide-ranging and involved a large number of powers with very different objectives.

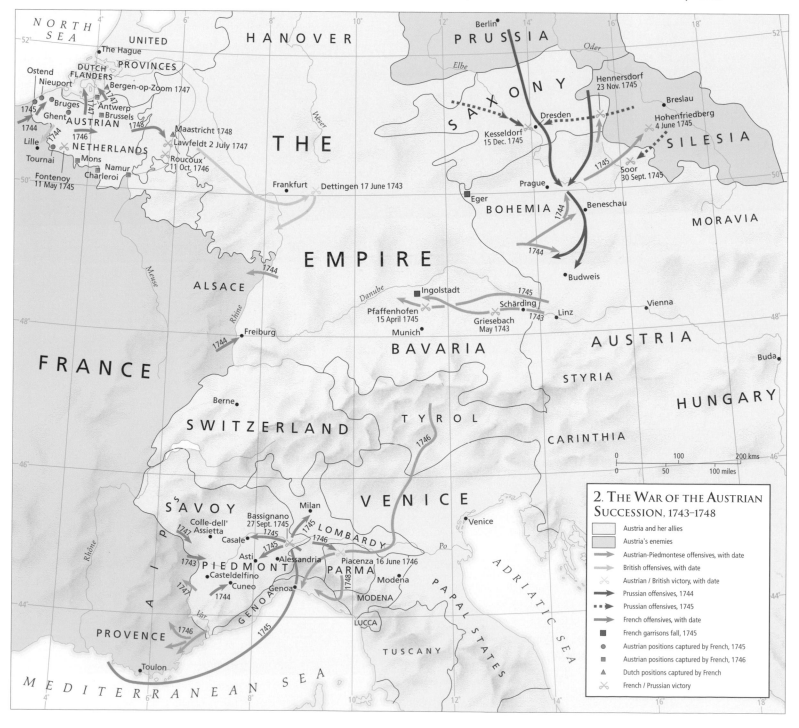

2. THE WAR OF THE AUSTRIAN SUCCESSION, 1743–1748

Austria and her allies
Austria's enemies
Austrian-Piedmontese offensives, with date
British offensives, with date
Austrian / British victory, with date
Prussian offensives, 1744
Prussian offensives, 1745
French offensives, with date
French garrisons fall, 1745
Austrian positions captured by French, 1745
Austrian positions captured by French, 1746
Dutch positions captured by French
French / Prussian victory

THE SEVEN YEARS' WAR IN EUROPE, 1756-1763

THE RISE OF PRUSSIA led to a determined effort on the part of both Austria and Russia from 1756 to 1763 to crush their dangerous neighbour. France, already at war with England, formed an alliance with the two eastern European powers which ensured that the Seven Years' War would involve most of Europe in conflict on land and sea.

PRUSSIA AT BAY

The end of the War of the Austrian Succession (pages 118–122) left Maria Theresa determined to regain Silesia, the loss of which she saw as a humiliating blow to Austria's power and prestige. Elizabeth of Russia regarded Frederick as the principal obstacle to Russian domination of eastern Europe. The Russians produced a plan for war in March 1756, but the Austrians persuaded Elizabeth to delay the attack until 1757. Frederick, fully aware of Austro-Russian military activity, decided to ignore British advice to adopt a defensive strategy and instead launched a pre-emptive strike with his well-prepared army. In order to deny a base to the coalition gathering against him and to gain more room for manoeuvre, Frederick invaded Austria's ally Saxony in August 1756.

This was a dangerous move. Louis XV of France felt obliged to succour his heir's father-in-law Augustus III of Saxony, and Frederick found himself in an increasingly desperate situation. In January 1757, Russia and Austria concluded an offensive alliance, and in May France followed suit, promising an army of 105,000 and a substantial subsidy to help effect a partition of Prussia. Sweden and most of the German rulers joined the alliance, although Frederick retained the powerful support of Britain, already at war with France, as well as of Hanover, Hesse-Cassel, and Brunswick. Frederick was conscious of his vulnerable position, comparing himself to Charles XII of Sweden in 1700, when three neighbouring powers had plotted his fall.

Frederick's survival, the so-called 'miracle of the House of Brandenburg', was the result both of good fortune and

---

LEUTHEN 5 DECEMBER 1757

Faced by Austrian successes in Silesia, Frederick advanced to attack the Austrians under Prince Charles of Lorraine. Frederick had a first-rate army of 35,000 men, Prince Charles of Lorraine 54,000 men. Frederick, crucially, took and retained the initiative, by using a fine example of the oblique order attack. Benefiting from the cover of a ridge, the Prussians turned the Austrian left flank (1), while a feint attack led the Austrians to send their reserves to bolster their right (2). The Prussians were helped greatly by mobile artillery. Charles wheeled his army, creating a new south-facing front stretching through the village of Leuthen (3). The second phase of the battle centred on repeated Prussian attacks on this new front, especially on Leuthen, which was finally carried after bitter fighting, but the Prussian infantry became exposed to the Austrian cavalry. An Austrian cavalry counter-attack under Lucchese (4) was prevented from reaching the open flank of the Prussian infantry by the prompt action of their cavalry, and the battered Austrian infantry finally fled.

The Prussians lost 6,380 killed and wounded, the Austrians 10,000 killed and wounded and 12,000 prisoners. After their defeat, the Austrians abandoned most of Silesia. Leuthen was a hard-fought victory by a well-honed army. It reflected Prussian firepower, Frederick's skilled exploitation of the terrain, the fighting quality of the Prussian cavalry, and the ability of Prussian commanders to take initiatives.

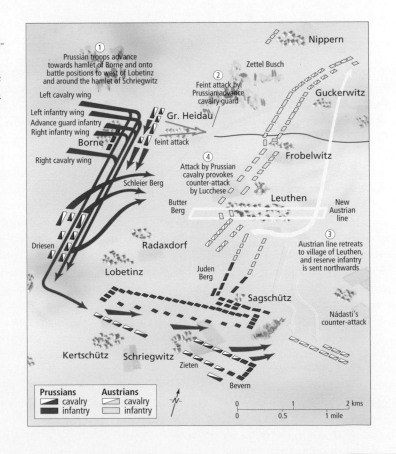

Prussian troops advance towards hamlet of Borne and onto battle positions to west of Lobetinz and around the hamlet of Schriegwitz ①

Feint attack by Prussian advance cavalry guard ②

Attack by Prussian cavalry provokes counter-attack by Lucchese ④

Austrian line retreats to village of Leuthen, and reserve infantry is sent northwards ③

Nádasti's counter-attack

Nippern
Zettel Busch
Guckerwitz
Gr. Heidau
Left cavalry wing
Left infantry wing
Advance guard infantry
Right infantry wing
Borne
feint attack
Right cavalry wing
Frobelwitz
Schleier Berg
Butter Berg
Leuthen
New Austrian line
Driesen
Radaxdorf
Juden Berg
Lobetinz
Sagschütz
Kertschütz
Schriegwitz
Zieten
Bevern

Prussians
cavalry
infantry

Austrians
cavalry
infantry

0   1   2 kms
0   0.5   1 mile

ROSSBACH 5 NOVEMBER 1757

An army of 30,000 French and 10,900 Germans of the army of the Empire advanced to attack 21,000 Prussians under Frederick, at Rossbach in Saxony in 1757. The Allies planned to turn the King's left flank, but they wrongly assumed that Frederick would not stand and fight, and consequently they took inadequate care with their battle dispositions.

Frederick responded vigorously, using the ridge of the Janus Hill to screen the move of his army to the north-east (1); he then swept south and west towards the allied columns. The Prussian cavalry under Major-General Seydlitz surprised the opposing horse and routed them (2), attacking them in front and with a double-flanking movement. The Allied cavalry was pushed back and dissolved into a confused mass. Seydlitz was an unusually impressive cavalry commander, able to keep control over his men. He then rallied the Prussian cavalry and turned them against the opposing infantry (3). The advancing columns of French infantry were rapidly brought low by salvoes of Prussian musket fire, supported by a battery of eighteen Prussian heavy cannon. Seydlitz's cavalry then attacked the French infantry, and was joined by the advancing Prussian infantry, firing as they moved. The French fled in confusion, covered by their light infantry. The Prussians lost fewer than 550 men, their opponents more than 10,000, many of them prisoners. Frederick's ability to grasp and retain the initiative, and the disciplined nature of the Prussians, both infantry and cavalry, were decisive.

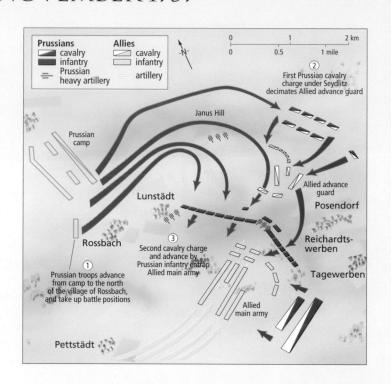

Rossbach secured Frederick's western flank, persuaded George II to resume fighting the French in Hanover, and seriously challenged the prestige of the French army and monarchy. Thereafter, the French were far more cautious about acting against Prussian forces.

military success, not only in stunning victories like Rossbach (1757) over the French, Leuthen (1757) and Torgau (1760) over the Austrians, and Zorndorf (1758) over the Russians, but also through fighting on interior lines against a strategically divided alliance (map 1). Russian interests centred on East Prussia, the Austrians were most concerned by Silesia while, after Rossbach, the French concentrated on Westphalia, where the British-financed and part-manned Army of Observation sought to protect the Electorate of Hanover, George II's German possession. Frederick's task was far harder than in the First (1740–42) and Second (1744–45) Silesian Wars, not only because of the number of his enemies (crucially including Russia), but also because Prussia was the chief target of the Austrians: Maria Theresa was no longer at war with Bavaria, France, and Spain, as she had been during the 1740s (page 118). Thus the opportunistic diplomacy which Frederick had earlier used with great skill was to be of little value during the period of the Seven Years' War.

Although Prussia survived the war, it was a hard-fought struggle. In 1757, Frederick had to confront a Russian attack on East Prussia, a Swedish invasion of Pomerania, the French conquest of Hanover, the raising of the Prussian siege of Prague, and the end of the Prussian invasion of Bohemia

after the Austrian victory at Kolin, as well as the Austrian capture of Berlin and most of Silesia. Frederick saved the situation at Rossbach, before using his tactic of the oblique attack to repeat the experience at Leuthen (page 123) at the expense of the Austrians. Leuthen helped to make the Austrians very cautious and paralyzed many of their initiatives later in the war.

In 1758, the Russians captured East Prussia, which they were able to retain for the rest of the war, but Frederick's victory at Zorndorf blocked their invasion of Brandenburg. In the following year, the Russians defeated Frederick at Kunersdorf, but failed to follow up the victory with concerted action with Austria. In 1760–61, the Austrians consolidated their position in both Saxony and Silesia, while the Russians temporarily seized Berlin in 1760 and over-ran Pomerania.

Frederick responded to Austrian and Russian strength with a number of innovations. He used artillery as a key to open deadlocked battlefronts, distributed cannon among the battalions of infantry, and made offensive use of the arching trajectory of the howitzers. At Burkersdorf (1762), Frederick employed fifty-five heavy guns wheel-to-wheel. These artillery-based tactics were not simply a response to the growing potential of a military arm benefiting from technical improvements and economic strength. They also reflected the military problem posed by the successful use of hilly positions by the Austrian Field-Marshal Daun. The defensive potential of the north Bohemian and Moravian hills revealed the defects of Prussian tactics – in particular of the oblique order. As at Kunersdorf, Austrian and Russian defensive positions failed to crumble before this tactic. Diversionary attacks were used to break up hilltop defensive concentrations. Frederick also used light infantry, though the Prussian command feared desertion and did not favour employing infantry out of sight of their officers.

Because Frederick restricted himself to gaining control of the battlefield, his great victories were less decisive than they might have been. He could not spare the time for a lengthy pursuit of any one enemy, and his well-disciplined troops could not be unleashed in headlong pursuit without the danger of the units losing coherence or even disintegrating through desertion. Frederick often lost more men than his enemies, even in his victories. Moreover, the Prussians also lacked competence in siegework and the troops lost momentum and advantage when confronted by

fortresses or fortress-cities; Frederick was unable, for example, to exploit the Battle of Prague by destroying Prince Charles of Lorraine's army which took refuge in the city.

PRUSSIA SURVIVES

Frederick's difficulties stemmed in part from recent reforms in the Austrian and Russian armies. The Russian Military Commission created in 1755 produced new regulations for the infantry, cavalry, and Cossacks. The infantry code published in that year stipulated Prussian-style tactics. In 1756, the artillery held a number of long exercises which built up its speed and accuracy, and in 1757 it displayed a clear superiority over the Prussians at Gross-Jägersdorf. A series of new cannon in the late 1750s gave the Russians greater firepower and their artillery a sound professional basis. Along with the fighting power of the Russian infantry at Zorndorf and the Austro-Russian success at Kunersdorf, this led Frederick to a permanent fear of the Russians; a fear which he attempted to assuage by making disparaging remarks about the Russians, but which conditioned his policies for the rest of his life.

MAP 1

Attacked by powerful forces from several directions, Frederick the Great faced a formidable challenge, but managed to prevent the destruction of Prussian power.

1. PRUSSIA AT BAY, 1756–1763

- Prussia
- Prussian allies
- Prussia's opponents
- ✗ victories of Prussia and her allies, with date
- ✗ defeats of Prussia and her allies, with date

The adoption of more flexible means of supply helped to reduce the cumbersome baggage train of the Russian field army. The daily rate of march increased – crucial for an army operating in such fragile alliances at great distances from its bases. The Russians also made progress in the use of field fortifications, the handling of battle formations, and the use of light troops. By the end of the war their army was the most powerful in Europe: it had succeeded in Germany against Prussian power, which had itself overcome west European superiority.

Political will was all-important. Frederick should have been beaten after Kolin, and especially after Kunersdorf, but neither defeat knocked Prussia out of the war. Equally, neither Leuthen nor even Rossbach led his enemies to abandon the struggle. Frederick was saved by the death in January 1762 of his most implacable foe, Elizabeth of Russia, and by the succession of her nephew as Peter III. Frederick was his hero, and he speedily ordered Russian forces to cease hostilities. In May, a Russo-Prussian peace restored Russian conquests, and was followed by a Prusso-Swedish peace. Peter's assassination in July and the succession of his wife as Catherine II (the Great) led to a cooling of Russo-Prussian relations, but Catherine had no wish to continue the war.

Austria was now isolated and driven from Silesia. The Battle of Burkersdorf broke Daun's will to continue, and Frederick's victory at Freiburg gained most of southern Saxony, putting the Austrians at an even greater negotiating disadvantage. On 15 February 1763 at Hubertusburg, they were obliged to make peace on the basis of a return to pre-war boundaries.

THE BRITISH IN EUROPE

The outbreak in 1754 of Anglo-French hostilities over their competing territorial claims in North America (*pages 150–53*) led to formal war in 1756, when the French landed on British-ruled Minorca in April. The war began humiliatingly for Britain with the failure of a relief force under Admiral John Byng to defeat the French fleet; he was subsequently shot for cowardice. The British troops on the island surrendered to Marshal Richelieu in June.

There were widespread fears that the French would then invade Britain itself. Britain's sole ally was Prussia, but in 1757 George II's son, the Duke of Cumberland, was defeated by the French as he led a German army defending Hanover and Prussia's western frontier. Cumberland agreed to disband his army, but pressure from George's ministers resulted in the British offer of further assistance to Prussia. Under an Anglo-Prussian treaty signed on 11 April 1758, both powers agreed not to continue separate negotiations, Britain paid a subsidy, and George, as King and Elector, promised to maintain an army of 55,000 in Hanover to protect Frederick's flank from French attack. An Anglo-German army in Westphalia under Ferdinand of Brunswick recovered the military position lost by Cumberland, while victories such as Minden, where British infantry overcame French cavalry, denied the French control of Hanover.

At the bloody Battle of Zorndorf, on 25 August 1758, Frederick lost one-third of his force, while the Russians lost 18,000 men. The Russian infantry displayed considerable fighting power, while Frederick found it difficult to control his troops once combat had begun. Nevertheless, the Russian invasion of Brandenburg was blocked.

THE AUSTRIAN ARMY

Defeats in the 1740s led to a programme of military, financial, and administrative reform which transformed Austrian capability. The army's training and equipment were improved, new drill regulations were issued in 1749, and Prince Liechtenstein reformed and improved the artillery. The system of military entrepreneurship (that is, private ownership of regiments) was gradually dismantled in favour of a military establishment financed by regular taxation and commanded by loyal professionals.

In an effort to improve the officer corps, the Wiener-Neustadt Academy was opened to the sons of serving officers (including commoners and minor nobles), while the Engineering Academy was opened to all ranks. Duelling in the army was suppressed, and promotion within the officer corps, previously largely controlled by regimental commanders, was gradually transferred to the government. After the victory over Prussia at Kolin in 1757, the Empress founded the Military Order of Maria Theresa, a graduated scheme of decorations awarded to officers regardless of birth, social rank, or religion.

The Austrian army fought well in the Seven Years' War. It had already grasped the principles of Prussian strategy and tactics, interior lines and the oblique order. Colonel Horace St Paul, the English aide de camp to Marshal Daun, argued correctly that Frederick was foolish to repeat his tactics: 'as he always launches his attack against one of the two wings of the army he attacks, it is necessary simply to plan a suitable response'. The use of dispersed columns was one such response which helped to bring the Austrians success in 1758–59.

The new emphasis on planning brought many benefits. A General Staff was established in 1758, maps were used as much as possible, and terrain was carefully studied, and operations were characterized by improved supplies and greater flexibility in the field. Austrian medium artillery, effectively balancing mobility and firepower, was to be copied by Frederick and by the French.

Austrian Privates by David Morier (c.1705-1770).

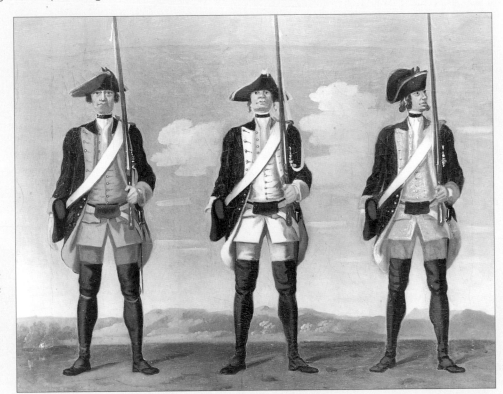

The thwarting of French invasion plans contrasted with the failure of British attacks on the French coast to divert forces away from the war with Frederick. Poor intelligence, inadequate co-operation between navy and army commanders, and indifferent generalship, led to a British failure to take Rochefort in 1757 (map 2). In 1758, Cherbourg was temporarily seized and its fortifications destroyed, but an attempt on St Malo had to re-embark with losses in the face of a superior French force. Belle-Isle, off the Breton coast, was captured in 1761 and held until the peace. However, whereas Britain could be threatened with invasion with serious strategic consequences, France was not so affected: Britain was more vulnerable to amphibious attack and had smaller armed forces, both regular and militia.

In 1762, Britain sent an expeditionary force to its ally Portugal, which appeared to France and Spain a vulnerable target negotiable in a general peace treaty for British gains elsewhere. Spanish successes in overrunning poorly defended Portuguese fortresses led to urgent Portuguese requests for British troops, and these helped to turn the tide. Also, the Spanish failed to march on Oporto and exploit their early gains. British generals complained about poor Portuguese communications and supplies, but the army operated effectively nevertheless, and Burgoyne successfully stormed the Spanish camp. Facing the onset of the winter rains, the imminence of peace, and the strength of the British presence, the French and the Spanish retreated.

NEW WEAPONS AND TACTICS

The experience of the Seven Years' War encouraged the major powers to search for greater effectiveness in weaponry and tactics. These changes, many made in the early decades

LAGOS AND QUIBERON BAY

As in 1744 and 1745–46 when invasions of Britain had been planned, the French in 1759 sought a knockout blow. Choiseul, the leading French minister, proposed a joint attack with Russian and Swedish forces transported by a Swedish fleet to Scotland. Neither power agreed, and instead the French planned landings of 100,000 troops in the Clyde and at Portsmouth, the latter subsequently being altered to Essex because of a Royal Navy blockade of the embarkation port of Le Havre. Choiseul's plan was unrealistic, in so far as it anticipated significant Jacobite support, and it is unlikely that the invading regular forces could have conquered Britain. Nevertheless, the landing of a regular force, several times greater than the Jacobite army which had invaded England from Scotland in 1745, would have still posed some serious problems.

The division of the French navy between Brest and Toulon made concentration of the necessary covering force difficult, and the blockading British squadrons sought to maintain the division. Though the Toulon fleet, under La Clue, managed to leave first the harbour and then the Mediterranean, it was defeated by Admiral Edward Boscawen near Lagos on the Portuguese coast on 18–19 August. Stubborn resistance by the rearmost French warship, the *Centaure*, held off the British while La Clue sailed the rest of his fleet into neutral waters, but on the following day Boscawen violated Portuguese neutrality and launched a successful attack. Mortally wounded, La Clue ran his vessel ashore and burnt it to prevent British capture, and the outnumbered French lost a total of five ships.

Bad weather forced Admiral Edward Hawke, the chief exponent of close blockade, to lift his blockade of Brest in November, but the Brest fleet under Conflans failed in its attempt to reach Scotland via the west coast of Ireland. Conflans was trapped by Hawke while still off the French coast, and took refuge in Quiberon Bay, counting on its shoaly waters and strong swell to deter Hawke's ships. The British had little knowledge of the Bay's rocks. On 20 November, Hawke made a bold attack; with topsails set despite the ferocity of the wind, which was blowing at nearly forty knots, his ships overhauled the French rear division and forced a general action, in which British gunnery and seamanship proved superior and seven French ships were captured, wrecked, or sunk. French casualties were heavy. The *Superbe* sank with the loss of its entire crew of 630 after two broadsides from Hawke's *Royal George*. All possibility of a French invasion of Britain was lost in these two decisive naval engagements. After Quiberon Bay there was 'nothing [in London] but bonfires and illuminations'.

The Battle of Quiberon Bay, 20 November 1759, by Richard Paton.

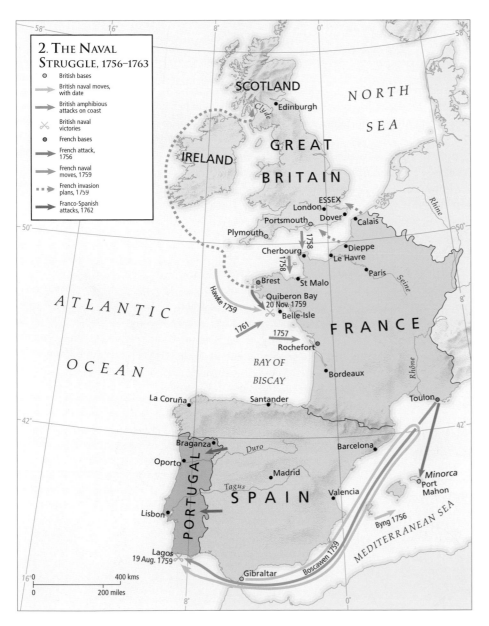

2. THE NAVAL STRUGGLE, 1756–1763

- ⊙ British bases
- → British naval moves, with date
- → British amphibious attacks on coast
- ✕ British naval victories
- ● French bases
- → French attack, 1756
- → French naval moves, 1759
- ‑‑‑ French invasion plans, 1759
- → Franco-Spanish attacks, 1762

MAP 2

The Anglo-French naval struggle was undoubtedly won by Britain, evidence of the possibility of decisive victory at sea. Yet the British navy also faced serious problems. The difficulty of wooden ships maintaining all-weather stations precluded effective blockades.

of the eighteenth century, developed the European military systems which had evolved in the fifteenth century. They were to be of considerable importance in the French Revolutionary Wars.

Towards the end of the seventeenth century, there came two important changes in European weaponry: the bayonet replaced the pike, while the flintlock replaced the matchlock. Together these ensured the dominance in the next century of exchanges of fire between close-packed infantry lines which formed formidable barriers to cavalry. Infantry, all armed with the same weapon, now had a greater tactical flexibility, exploited by Frederick the Great and later by the armies of Revolutionary and Napoleonic France.

The rapid change to the bayonet in the 1680s and 1690s was accelerated when the early plug type, which prevented firing, gave way to ring and socket fittings. In the flintlock, powder was ignited by sparks produced by a flint striking a steel plate. The new flintlocks were not generally issued until the end of the century and were more expensive than matchlocks, but the flintlock musket was lighter,

more reliable, easier to fire, and more rapid. The rate of fire, which was helped by pre-packaged paper cartridges, almost doubled. The Prussians introduced an iron ramrod and designed a funnel-shaped touch-hole which made priming easier. Without the hazard of the burning matches, musketeers could stand closer together, and their greater firing rate required fewer ranks; it became common to have three or four, with the first rank kneeling. Although at Rossbach (1757) the cavalry played a major role, battles generally became firefights between linear infantry formations, with flanking cavalry engaging virtually separately. Infantry did not usually advance against cavalry, though the British did so impressively against the French at Minden (1759).

Unrifled, smoothbore muskets without accurate sights firing irregular shot were not very effective in the noise and smoke of a battlefield. Also, the musket was heavy and unwieldy. Infantry tactics therefore demanded massed firepower, and most European economies could provide large quantities of weapons: between 1701 and mid-1704 the British Ordnance Office issued 56,000 muskets; the first Russian gun factory opened at Tula in 1632 and produced about 14,000 weapons per year between 1737 and 1778. Armament towns like Nuremberg, Sühl, Potsdam, Birmingham, Liège, and Toledo had collections of small assembly shops which contracted work out, with the inevitable problems of standardization.

On a global scale, Europe had a clear lead in arms production: in most of Africa, Australasia, and the Pacific there were no metallurgical or shipbuilding industries to compare with the Europeans', and in the Islamic world and India they were not of comparable quality, although the Indian artillery proved effective against the British in the Second Maratha War (1803). The Ottoman Empire concentrated on large cannon, which were of little use on the battlefield, rather than on smaller, more mobile weapons. European forces, with their concentrated firepower and linear tactics, were militarily more potent than Asian armies.

GRIBEAUVAL'S GUNS

Jean de Gribeauval (1715–89), who served during the Seven Years' War with the Austrian artillery, then the best in Europe, standardized the French artillery from 1765, being appointed Inspector-General of Artillery in 1776. He used standardized specifications: four-, eight-, and twelve-pounder cannon and six-inch howitzers in eight-gun batteries. Mobility was increased by stronger, larger wheels, the use of shorter barrels, and lighter-weight cannon, thanks to better casting methods. Accuracy was improved by better sights, the issue of gunnery tables, and the introduction of inclination-markers. The rate of fire rose thanks to the introduction of pre-packaged rounds. Horses were harnessed in pairs instead of in tandem, and this further increased the mobility and flexibility of the artillery. Thanks to these important changes in the decades after the Seven Years' War, Revolutionary France was to have the best artillery in Europe, and the most famous product of this development was to be Napoleon Bonaparte.

PRUSSIA AT WAR, 1778-1787

SUCCESS in the Seven Years' War had given Frederick the Great's army the highest reputation in Europe. Prussian military reviews were eagerly attended by observers from other countries, and Prussian drill was widely copied. However, Frederick's last foray, the War of the Bavarian Succession in 1778–79, failed to produce the expected victories.

THE AUSTRIANS PREPARE

The death in 1777 of the childless Elector of Bavaria, Max Joseph III, provided opportunities for Austria to pursue territorial schemes that threatened Frederick the Great's position in Germany. In contrast to the Seven Years' War, the Austrians in 1778 faced Frederick without help from either France or Russia. Nevertheless Field-Marshal Lacy was able to use massive concentrations of defensive forces in strong positions in the Bohemian hills to thwart Frederick's bold plan for the conquest of Bohemia. The war revealed serious weaknesses in the Prussian army: insufficient supplies, demoralized infantry, undisciplined cavalry, poor medical

services, and an inadequate artillery train. In some respects, the army Frederick had created was inferior to the one he had inherited from his father and used so successfully in the 1740s.

In 1778 Frederick planned the conquest of Bohemia by concerted advances from a number of directions (map 1). He hoped that diversionary attacks on Moravia and north-east Bohemia would leave the way clear for a march via Saxony on Prague by his brother Prince Henry. Frederick's diversionary move into north-east Bohemia was blocked by Austrian field works along the western bank of the upper Elbe. He wanted to breach the Austrian positions near Jaromiersch, but decided that their lines, composed of batteries, palisades, and *abatis* (ramparts constructed of felled trees) supported by Lacy's 100,000-strong Elbe Army, were too strong. In 1764, Lacy had argued that greater attention should be devoted to the idea of defending Bohemia along the line of the Upper Elbe. This led to the construction of the fortress of Königgratz, which provided the Austrians with a major base in 1778.

THE 1778 CAMPAIGN

Frederick therefore decided to abandon his original plan and to rely upon Henry's advance to provide a diversion.

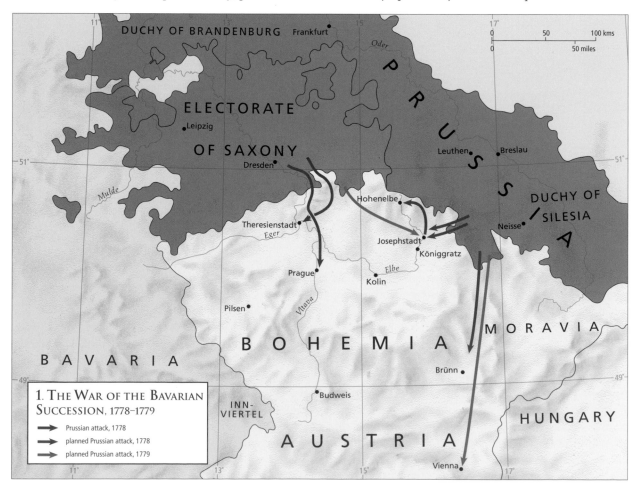

1. THE WAR OF THE BAVARIAN SUCCESSION, 1778-1779

➤ Prussian attack, 1778
➤ planned Prussian attack, 1778
➤ planned Prussian attack, 1779

MAP 1

Frederick's plans were thwarted by the strength of Austrian defensive positions and he found it impossible to repeat earlier successes.

'Old Fritz' reviewing his troops. Frederick the Great successfully combined military and political leadership. He led his army throughout his reign, not only winning spectacular battles, but also drilling his army and conducting major manoeuvres in peacetime. Frederick was a prudent general who believed in the need for detailed planning and cautious execution. He was bruised in 1760 when a canister ball hit him in the chest at the Battle of Torgau.

Henry negotiated a number of supposedly impassable passes, outflanking Loudon's force on the middle Elbe, but he then refused to pursue Loudon, instead moving to little purpose to the middle Elbe. Henry was affected by supply problems and by a crisis of confidence. Frederick, meanwhile, quickly crossed the river at Hohenelbe, where a rapid Austrian response blocked his advance. Frederick did not attack the Austrian positions, and his campaign ended; suffering badly from dysentery and desertion, his forces withdrew to Silesia.

THE 1779 CAMPAIGN

In 1779, the Prussian king proposed an advance on Vienna through Moravia, while the army from Saxony invaded north Bohemia and attacked the line of the upper Elbe from the rear (map 1). However, the Austrian army was now far larger than in 1778, and Frederick, whose military capac-

ity and energy were clearly diminished since the Seven Years' War, was happy to negotiate peace. Both Prussia and Austria had increased their artillery: heavy artillery slowed movement and made commanders reluctant to risk attack. By the Treaty of Teschen of 13 May 1779, the Austrians failed in their major goal of gaining much of Bavaria, but acquired a small and strategic area, the Innviertel. Catherine the Great's role, as co-mediator of the peace with France, represented Russia's growing status and significance in central European politics. The Austrians followed up the war by winning Russia's alliance and by building a series of fortifications to block possible Prussian invasion routes into Bohemia, especially Theresienstadt at the confluence of the Elbe and the Eger, and Josephstadt on the upper Elbe.

Frederick's cautious diplomacy kept Prussia at peace for the remainder of his reign. Although the war had revealed serious deficiencies in the Prussian military system, there had been no dramatic battle, no equivalent to Rossbach or Valmy, to register a shift in military prowess. Foreign commentators continued to attend Prussian military reviews and manoeuvres, and Louis-Alexandre Berthier, later Napoleon's Chief of Staff and Minister of War, was much impressed by the manoeuvres in Silesia in 1783, though two years later Cornwallis was critical of the lack of flexibility in Prussian tactics.

Frederick's successor and nephew, Frederick William II (1786–97), was more volatile, but the successful Prussian intervention in the Dutch crisis in 1787 (map 2), and the peaceful confrontation with Austria in 1790, and with Russia in 1791, did not lead to the major conflict that might have shattered the myth of Prussian military supremacy.

THE DUTCH CRISIS OF 1787

Prussian intervention in the Dutch Crisis of 1787 indicated the potential effectiveness of *ancien régime* armies and the weakness of a citizens' force on the very eve of the French Revolutionary wars. Frederick William II of Prussia (1786–97) intervened on behalf of William V of Orange, who was opposed by the 'Patriot' Movement based in the leading cities in Holland.

On 13 September, the Prussians, under the Duke of Brunswick, invaded and advanced to Nijmegen. The principal Patriot force, 7,000 strong under the Rhinegrave of Salm, abandoned Utrecht in panic on the night of the 15th. The Prussians entered Utrecht on the 16th, Gorcum after a short bombardment on the 17th, Dordrecht on the 18th and Delft on 19 September. The last Patriot stronghold, Amsterdam, held out for longer, but surrendered on 10 October 1787.

Although the Dutch Crisis clearly represented an unequal struggle, it is easy to appreciate why it was widely anticipated that Brunswick would have another swift success against Revolutionary France in 1792.

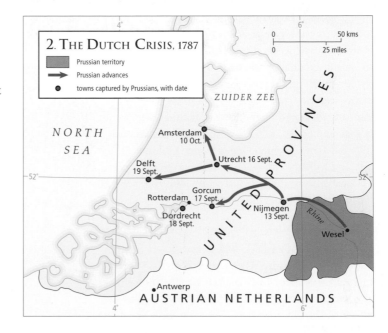

WAR IN EASTERN EUROPE (II), 1787-1792

OTTOMAN opposition to Russian influence in Poland led in 1768 to the outbreak of war. The Russians won significant concessions from the Ottomans in 1774. When the Ottomans declared war on Russia in 1787, there were conflicts between Austria and the Ottomans, Sweden and Russia, Sweden and Denmark, and Prussian preparations against Austria and Russia.

THE OTTOMANS FALL BACK

The Ottomans were concerned about the potential consequences of Russian control of Poland in any future war and, encouraged by France and by the Tatars, responded to Russian violations of Polish territory by declaring war in October 1768. In 1769, Prince Aleksander Golitsyn captured Kamenets Podol'sk, Khotin, and Jassy, and advanced to the upper Dniester.

Golitsyn was replaced by Count Petr Rumyantsev (1725–96), who had played a major role in the Seven Years' War. Greatly influenced by Frederick the Great, Rumyantsev was a firm believer in the offensive. In late 1769 he sent units forward into Wallachia and into Moldavia (map 1), where the Russians were supported by the local population. The Russians advanced as far as Bucharest; Azov and Taganrog were also secured. Rumyantsev's army wintered on Polish territory between the Dniester and the Bug. In 1770, while Prince Petr Panin overran Bender on the lower Dniester, Rumyantsev advanced down the Pruth, successively storming the main Ottoman positions at the Battles of Ryabaya Mogila, Larga, and Kagul.

In battle, Rumyantsev organized his infantry into columns able to advance independently while affording mutual support in concerted attacks. The columns included mobile artillery and relied on firepower to repel Ottoman assaults.

After his victories over larger forces on the river Pruth, Rumyantsev advanced to the lower Danube, where he rapidly captured Izmail, Kilia, Akkerman, and Braila; Bucharest also fell. The Ottoman Grand Vizier, Mehmet Emin Pasha, lacked military competence, had no effective plan, and was unable to arrange adequate supplies or pay for his army. The way to Constantinople seemed clear.

FURTHER RUSSIAN GAINS

Also in 1770, a Russian fleet, which had sailed from St Petersburg under Admiral Orlov, attacked the Turks at Chesmé near Chios. Poor Ottoman tactics and manoeuvring and the subsequent use of Russian fireships resulted in the destruction of the Ottoman fleet. The Russians were then able to blockade the Dardanelles, although their attempts to capture Lemnos, Euboea and Rhodes were unsuccessful.

Encouraged by Russian promises of assistance, the Greeks in the Morea rebelled, but the Russians failed to provide their promised support and it was difficult to co-ordinate Greek action. The Ottomans were able to suppress the revolt. In 1771, the Russians overran the Crimea while the Tatars were busy fighting Rumyantsev; but thereafter Russian forces were distracted by the First Partition of Poland (1772) and the Pugachev serf rising (1773–75). In 1773, the Imperial Council decided that Rumyantsev should attack the main Ottoman army south of the Danube, although the General was unhappy about doing so with a small army and with communications threatened by Turkish garrisons, especially in Silistria, which resisted assault. Accordingly, having crossed the Danube in June, Rumyantsev retreated in the following month.

MAP 1

The Russo-Turkish war of 1768–74 witnessed repeated Russian advances that combined the successful movement of large numbers of troops over substantial distances with victory in assault and battle.

1. RUSSO-OTTOMAN WAR, 1768–1774

→ Russian advances, with date

▨ territory gained by Russia, 1774

● towns captured by Russia, with date

✕ Russian victories, with date

On 5 July 1770, an Ottoman fleet of 20 ships of the line and frigates and at least 13 galleys was out-manoeuvred by a smaller Russian squadron in the channel between Chios and the Anatolian coast. The fleet was attacked in Ches-mé harbour and almost totally destroyed by fire-boats covered by Russian naval gunfire. About 11,000 Turks were killed.

In 1774, Rumyantsev proposed to seize the major Otto-man forts at Silistria, Rushchuk, and Varna, and then to advance on the Turkish headquarters at Shumla. After abortive peace negotiations, he was instructed to pursue this plan and his forces again crossed the Danube. In June, their advance guard under Generals Kamensky and Suvorov routed the main Ottoman army near Kozludzhi. The Ottomans' fortresses were left isolated and vulnerable, and the Turks hastily made peace by the Treaty of Kutchuk-Kainardji (1774): Russia gained several Crimean forts and territory to the north of the Black Sea and in the Caucasus region, and in addition was allowed to fortify Azov, to nav-igate on the Black Sea, and to send merchant vessels through the Dardanelles.

RUSSIAN SUPREMACY

Eastern European warfare at the end of the eighteenth cen-tury was dominated by Russia. Catherine the Great's forces were more successful than those of her ally, Joseph II of Austria. In 1788–90, Russian forces were able, albeit with some difficulty, to sustain war on two fronts – against the Ottomans and against the Swedes. In addition, Catherine was not intimidated when threatened in 1791 by Anglo-Prussian military coercion to accept only modest territor-ial gains from the Ottoman Empire.

The most spectacular Russian successes were against the Ottomans. Victories in battle relying on firepower and square or column formations, such as Fokshani (1789), and Machin (1791), were accompanied by the storming of major Ottoman fortresses, especially Ochakov in 1788 and Izmail in 1790 (map 2). In the last, the ditches were filled and the walls scaled by ladders, as if Suvorov were oper-ating in the pre-gunpowder age: more than one-third of the Russian force, and two-thirds of their officers, were killed or wounded.

The Russians had learned how to campaign effectively in the vast and often barren expanses to the north and west of the Black Sea. Suvorov, like Rumyantsev before him, pur-sued an offensive strategy complemented by using com-pact, mobile forces with advanced supply bases, by storm-ing rather than beseiging fortresses, and by attacking in for-mations of mutually-supporting squares or rectangles which benefited from crossfire.

The Ottomans took the initiative in 1787, aiming to seize Kinburn and Kherson, to reconquer the Crimea, and to instigate rebellion in the Kuban, but their amphibious attacks on Kinburn were repulsed in hand-to-hand fighting. In 1788, the Russians moved onto the attack, focusing on the powerful fortress of Ochakov which overlooked the entrance to the Bug and the Dnieper. Catherine's favourite, Potemkin, led the besieging army, while bitter naval engagements took place offshore as the Russians struggled to create an effective blockade. After lengthy bombardment, Ochakov was stormed in December.

In 1789, the main Russian army under Potemkin ad-vanced to the Dniester with naval support, capturing Gad-zhibey, Akkerman and Bender. The line of the Dniester had been won, and the Ukrainian army was instructed to co-operate with the Austrians under the Prince of Coburg. The Ottomans sought to prevent this co-operation, but Suvorov joined Coburg in routing them at Fokshani and Rymnik. The cohesion of the Ottoman war effort was weakened by the political changes introduced by the new Sultan, Selim III. In 1790, the Russian Black Sea fleet defeated its Ottoman rival, while Russian troops cleared the forts in the Danube delta, capturing Kilia, Izalchi, and Izmail. In 1791, the Russians advanced south of the Danube, defeating the Ottomans at Babadag and Machin, and captured Anapa, the Ottoman base in the Kuban. Selim III's vulnerability had been demonstrated, and he hurried to make peace. By the Treaty of Jassy (1792), the Ottomans recognized the Russian annexation of the Crimea in 1783, and yielded Ochakov and the lands between the Dniester and the Bug.

THE AUSTRIAN ADVANCE

The Austrians had less success than their Russian allies. An attempt to surprise Belgrade early in 1788 failed, the Austrians losing their way in the fog. Deploying 140,000 men, Emperor Joseph II hoped to conquer Serbia, Moldavia, Wallachia, and most of Bosnia, but the Ottomans concentrated their efforts against him and not, as he had hoped, against the Russians, who were besieging distant Ochakov. Joseph II proved an indecisive commander-in-chief, dis-

ease debilitated the inactive Austrians, and the Ottomans were able to force them onto the defensive. Invading the Banat of Temesvár in August, Ottoman forces under the Grand Vizier Yussif Pasha, defeated the Austrians in an attack on their camp at Slatina from which Joseph only narrowly escaped. The Ottomans were finally halted by their own supply problems rather than by Austrian resistance.

By contrast, the Austrians in Bukovina had been more successful. Helped by the Hospodar of Moldavia, they captured Khotin in September 1788, while Loudon captured Dubitza and Novi on the Croatian border. The Austrians made further gains in 1789. In place of the linear tactics

MAP 2

Conflict in eastern Europe in 1787–92 involved a number of distinct but related struggles that led to a significant increase in Russian power. If Britain and Prussia had intervened against Russia, as they planned to do in 1791 in order to force Russia to restore gains made from the Turks, war would have become more general. However, neither side pushed their confrontation with Catherine the Great to the point of fighting.

WAR IN THE BALTIC

Fighting in northern Europe was on a much smaller scale than the Balkan and Black Sea actions, but a series of hard struggles in the Baltic thwarted Gustavus III of Sweden and led him to sue for peace. On land, Gustavus invaded Russian Finland in 1788, bombarded Fredrikshamn, and unsuccessfully besieged Nyslott, before retreating in the face of his own officers' political hostility. But at sea, thanks to new ships of the line and other types of vessel, especially versatile oared gunboats, Sweden was a formidable challenge to Russian power. Furthermore, the strategic situation was exactly that sought by earlier advocates of war with Russia: Catherine was heavily committed against the Ottoman Empire. Unfortunately for the Swedes, unlike 1769–70, the Russian Baltic fleet had not sailed to the Mediterranean, largely because the British had refused to provide their previous supply facilities.

Gustavus attacked in 1788. A naval battle off Hogland in the Gulf of Finland (17 July), in which the Swedes were hindered by ammunition shortages, resulted in a draw. This denied the Swedes the crucial control of the Gulf required both for military operations from Finland and for an amphibious attack on St Petersburg. Gustavus' forces lacked tactical training in offensive warfare, and in 1790 his attempt to retake south-eastern Finland, lost by the Swedes in 1743, was similarly unsuccessful. In May and June, a series of amphibious attacks under the King's personal command against Russian forces north of the Gulf of Finland failed to defeat the Russian army or force it to retreat to defend St Petersburg. An attack by the Swedish battle fleet on the Russian Reval squadron on 13 May failed, while a major engagement close to Kronstadt on 3–4 June was inconclusive. On 9 July, a major engagement between the two large archipelago (or oared) fleets took place at Svensksund, and the Russians suffered a defeat with very severe losses. Both sides had now exhausted their abilities for further offensive warfare during 1790. Britain and Prussia had not attacked Russia as Gustavus had hoped, so he felt obliged to negotiate the peace at Verela (1790) without making any territorial gains.

they had adopted against the Ottomans in 1737–39, they now used infantry squares arranged to offer mutual support. This brought victory at the Battle of Mehadia, which was followed by the crossing of the Sava and the Siege of Belgrade. After the field army that might have relieved the city was defeated at Rymnik, and Loudon mounted a massive bombardment, Belgrade surrendered in October. Bucharest fell soon afterwards and the Austrians occupied Wallachia and Serbia. They returned their gains when the Treaty of Sistova was concluded in 1791.

The Battle of Fokshani, 31 July 1787. The Ottoman Turks, under the Grand Vizier Osman Pasha, were routed as they sought to prevent the junction of Austrian troops, under Josiah of Saxe-Coburg, and Russians under Alexander Suvorov. The Turks were driven from Moldavia.

VI

WARFARE IN THE WIDER WORLD, 1700-1792

I n his *Decline and Fall of the Roman Empire,* Gibbon argued that military developments had changed the balance between civilization and 'barbarism': 'the military art has been changed by the invention of gunpowder; which enables man to command the two most powerful agents of nature, air, and fire. Mathematics, chemistry, mechanics, architecture, have been applied to the service of war; and the adverse parties oppose to each other the most elaborate modes of attack and of defence…Cannon and fortifications now form an impregnable barrier against the Tartar horse; and Europe is secure from any future irruption of Barbarians; since, before they can conquer, they must cease to be barbarians. Their gradual advances in the science of war would always be accompanied, as we may learn from the example of Russia, with a proportionable improvement in the arts of peace and civil policy; and they themselves must deserve a place among the polished nations whom they subdue.'

Gibbon's argument that military technology had permitted the European powers to break free from a cyclical process of growth and then collapse at the hands of 'barbarians', appeared justifiable in the eighteenth century. It was European superiority in gunpowder weapons that was partly responsible for their advances. European military innovations, such as the bayonet, the flintlock musket, and accurate and mobile grape- and canister-firing field artillery, opened up a major gap in capability among armies armed with firearms. This was more than a matter of technology. The European advantage in military technique and infrastructure, which was especially apparent in naval terms, rested on the foundations of centuries of European economic, social, and institutional change.

The European impact in the Orient was limited, and China itself was one of the most expansionist powers of the century. Yet elsewhere, the European military impact was increasingly apparent. Thanks to its successes against the Ottomans in 1736–9, 1768–74, and 1787–92, Russia came to control the lands to the north of the Black Sea, the traditional route of nomadic irruption into Europe. Trans-oceanic initiatives rested with the Europeans: the advances of the British in India are well-known, but there were many other less prominent moves, such as the development of a French base at Cayenne in South America, or the capture in 1785 by a Dutch fleet of Riouw, an island that controlled the eastern approach to the Strait of Malacca, and of Kuala Selangor.

In addition, European military experts and arms were used by aggressive non-European rulers, for example the Marathas in India, and by Kamehameha I, who fought his way to supremacy in the Hawaiian archipelago in the 1790s: guns there replaced spears, clubs, daggers, and slingshots, and led to convincing victories such as that of Nuuanu (1795), which made Kamehameha ruler of all the islands except Kauai and Niihau.

CHINA AND SOUTHEAST ASIA

ONE OF THE MOST dynamic military powers of the eighteenth century was China. The Chinese population rose dramatically, from about 100 million in 1650 to 300 million in 1800. Combined with greater domestic stability from the 1680s, this generated widespread imperial expansion.

ADVANCE ON SEVERAL FRONTS

In the 1680s and 1690s, the Chinese drove the Russians from the Amur region (pages 34–36) and took control of Outer Mongolia. They intervened in Tibet in 1718, later making it a protectorate, and in 1730 assumed suzerainty over Bhutan, a Tibetan vassal. An invasion of Tsinghai led to the Chinese assuming control from 1724. In the 1750s, Chinese power was extended to Lake Balkhash and to Muslim east Turkestan; Kashgar fell in 1759 (map 1). Non-Chinese peoples, especially the Muslims, staged a number of unsuccessful risings in western Szechwan (1746–49),

in the Lake Balkhash area (1765), in Kansu (1781–84), and Taiwan (1787–88).

The Chinese had less success extending their power into Southeast Asia. Invasions of Burma (1766–69) and Tongking (1788), prompted by concern at Burmese expansion into Laos and Siam, made little progress. Attacks from Szechwan into the valley of the Irrawaddy (1766–69) reached only Kaungton, while an expedition further south from Yunnan (1765–66) stopped at Kengtung. In 1767–68, the Chinese advanced via Hsenwi towards Mandalay, but were unable to hold the territory gained, although their repeated attempts did weaken the Burmese in the east. In 1792, a Chinese expedition penetrated to the Katmandu area, and the British refused to help Nepal against the invaders. In the eighteenth century there was little of the vulnerability to be exhibited by the Chinese empire in the nineteenth century.

SOUTHEAST ASIA

The Dutch East India Company played an important role in the East Indies, although its army was weak and its power was largely restricted to the coastal regions. By a treaty of 1749, the Dutch acquired sovereignty over the inland Javan

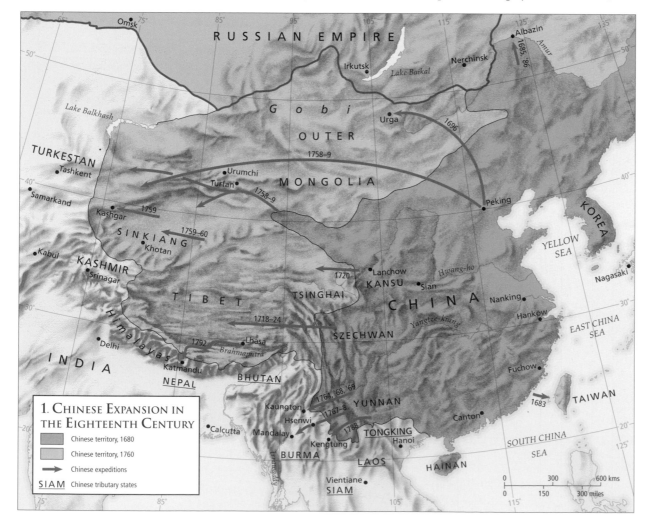

MAP 1
Manchu China achieved a degree of control over its neighbours greater than that enjoyed by the Ming.

1. CHINESE EXPANSION IN THE EIGHTEENTH CENTURY

- Chinese territory, 1680
- Chinese territory, 1760
- → Chinese expeditions
- SIAM Chinese tributary states

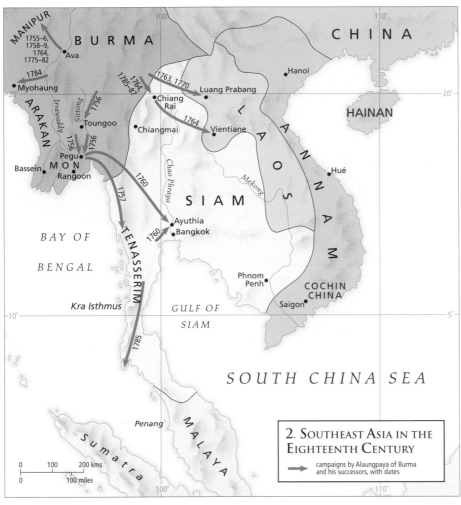

2. SOUTHEAST ASIA IN THE
EIGHTEENTH CENTURY

→ campaigns by Alaungpaya of Burma
and his successors, with dates

kingdom of Mataram, but this authority amounted to little in practice.

On the Asian mainland, European power was of little consequence. Burma was particularly volatile (map 2). The Mon (Talaing) rebellion of 1740–47 threw off the rule of the Toungoo (Burmese) dynasty and led to the establishment of a Mon kingdom based on Pegu. The Mon conquered the Burmese capital of Ava in 1752, but Burmese power was rebuilt by a local official, Alaungpaya (1714–60), who recaptured Ava in 1753, and defeated the Mon and their French allies in 1754–57.

Alaungpaya founded a new dynasty, the Konbaung, and destroyed the power of the state of Manipur in 1759. He overran Tenasserim in 1757, but was fatally wounded in 1760 in an unsuccessful attack on the Siamese capital of Ayuthia. Siam was invaded again in 1766–67 and the capital destroyed. The Burmese also thrust east to Luang Prabang in 1763 and 1770, and to Vientiane in 1764. In 1784–85, the Burmese conquered Arakan, regained part of Laos, overran the Kra Isthmus, and advanced on Chiangmai.

Another dynamic power emerged in Vietnam. Nguyen Anh (1762–1820), the son of one of the claimants to Cochin China (the Mekong delta region), was initially dependent on Chinese pirates and Cambodian mercenaries. With the help of French merchants, he hired French advisers to train his troops in European methods in order to conquer Cochin China. They captured the Tay Son capital at Hué, and by 1802 the whole of Vietnam was united under one rule for the first time in its history; Nguyen Anh proclaimed himself Emperor Gia-Long.

MAP 2

Burma was a dynamic power in the later eighteenth century, an apparent threat to European interests. The Burmese conquest of Arakan in 1784–85 created a tense situation in relations with the domain of the British East India Company in Bengal.

Manchus under Nurhachi (1559–1626) storming a Chinese city (right, far right), from *Manchou shih-lu* by Men Ying-Chao. When Nurhachi attacked China in 1618, his horse archers were successful against the Chinese with their firearms and fortifications. By the late seventeenth century, the Manchus were benefiting from the fusion of the two military inheritances.

INDIA AND AFGHANISTAN, 1707-1790

AFTER THE DEATH of *Aurangzeb* in 1707, Mughal power declined rapidly, not with European conquest, but rather through the emergence of a number of independent principalities, including the British possessions in India. The most important of these was the Maratha Confederacy, and for much of the period the most powerful threat to India came from *Afghanistan*.

MARATHA EXPANSION

The Hindu Marathas, with their army of highly mobile cavalry, expanded their territory as Mughal power declined, and staged extended raids to collect taxes. From their base area in western India, where the capital after 1750 was at Poona, the Marathas extended their control over much of central India (map 1), and for a while it seemed as though they might supplant the Mughals. In south-central India they were resisted by the Nizam of Hyderabad, heir to the Mughal *subahdarship* of the Deccan and from 1724 effectively independent. Further north the Rajput princes and the rulers of Bengal and Oudh were effectively autonomous from the Mughals from the 1700s and the 1720s respectively.

In mid-century, Maratha power expanded further, mainly at the expense of the Nizam. By the Treaty of Bhalki (1752), the Nizam ceded West Berar, Khandesh, and Baglana. After a defeat at Udgir (1760), he ceded further territories around Burhanpur, Ahmadnagar, and Bijapur. Elsewhere, the Marathas had seized Bassein from the Portuguese in 1739 and Chaul in 1740, had extended their control east to Orissa by 1752, and had occupied Ahmadabad in Gujarat by 1756 and Lahore by 1759.

AFGHAN PRESSURE

This expansion was checked by the Afghans. In 1739, Nadir Shah, who had already gained control of Persia (pages 142-143), annexed Kashmir and sacked Delhi. The Mughals had then ceded Sind and all the territories west of the Indus, and Nadir Shah had concentrated on Bukhara and the Ottomans. After his assassination in 1747, the Abdali chief Ahmad Khan was chosen by the Ghilzais and Abdalis as King of a united Afghan nation and founded the Durrani dynasty. The Afghans pressed hard on India, annexing the Punjab and Kashmir in 1752, and Sirhind in 1757. In 1761, at the third Battle of Panipat, the Afghans inflicted a severe defeat on the Marathas. Possibly 100,000 Marathas perished. Although this victory was not exploited, it gravely weakened Maratha power in northern India, and increased tendencies towards regionalism. There was no revival of Mughal power, but neither was it replaced by the Afghans, who found it difficult to control the Punjab. The Maratha

chieftains, particularly Sindhia, increasingly followed independent policies, which weakened the cohesion of the Confederacy, though the Marathas recovered sufficiently from Panipat to defeat the Nizam at Rakshasbhavan in 1763. To the south of Hyderabad, another regional power emerged when Haidar Ali, who had fought against the Marathas and Hyderabad, usurped the Hindu throne of Mysore in 1761. In 1763, he conquered Kanara, gaining Mysore a coastline.

British consolidation of a regional power base in Bengal and Bihar came after victories at Plassey in 1757, and Patna and Buxar in 1764 (pages 160–63). Victory over Kandy (1761–65) led to the Dutch gaining control of all Ceylon's coastal regions. In the Punjab, a Sikh confederation arose to challenge both Marathas and Afghans. The Gurkhas, who had failed to conquer Nepal in 1736–48, gained Katmandu in 1767–69 and then overran much of the Himalayan chain, including Sikkim in 1789 and Kumaun in 1790.

MAP 1

Although the British became a more important Indian military power from the mid-eighteenth century, the most dramatic military interventions in India were those of Nadir Shah of Persia and the Afghans. The Marathas greatly expanded their territory, particularly in rivalry with the Nizam of Hyderabad.

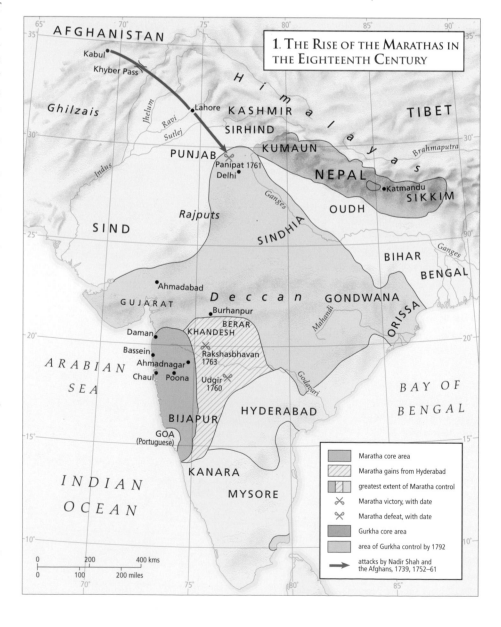

1. THE RISE OF THE MARATHAS IN THE EIGHTEENTH CENTURY

AFGHANISTAN

Kabul
Khyber Pass
Ghilzais
Lahore
KASHMIR
Himalaya
TIBET
SIRHIND
Jhelum
Ravi
Sutlej
Indus
PUNJAB
KUMAUN
Panipat 1761
Delhi
NEPAL
Ganges
Brahmaputra
Katmandu
SIKKIM
Rajputs
SINDHIA
OUDH
SIND
BIHAR
Ganges
BENGAL
Ahmadabad
Deccan
GONDWANA
GUJARAT
Burhanpur
BERAR
Mahanadi
ORISSA
Daman
KHANDESH
Bassein
Rakshasbhavan 1763
Ahmadnagar
Godavari
ARABIAN SEA
Chaul Poona
Udgir 1760
BAY OF BENGAL
BIJAPUR
HYDERABAD
GOA (Portuguese)
KANARA
INDIAN OCEAN
MYSORE

	Maratha core area
	Maratha gains from Hyderabad
	greatest extent of Maratha control
✕	Maratha victory, with date
✕	Maratha defeat, with date
	Gurkha core area
	area of Gurkha control by 1792
→	attacks by Nadir Shah and the Afghans, 1739, 1752–61

0   200   400 kms
0   100   200 miles

PANIPAT 14 JANUARY 1761

At Panipat, on the plains north of Delhi, the Afghan forces, under Ahmad Shah Abdali, consisted largely of heavy cavalry equipped with body armour and muskets. Their Maratha opponents included the traditional mobile light cavalry, armed with swords, shields, battle axes, daggers, and lances, and the trained infantry of one Maratha commander, Ibrahim Gardi. The Marathas had little experience in integrating the different military capabilities of their various units, in particular the need to combine the offensive characteristics of their light cavalry with the more stationary tactics required by the artillery and infantry, which needed the cavalry to defend their flanks from opposing cavalry.

The Marathas, blockaded in a fortified position by the Afghans, had lost their mobility. They came out of their positions, their faces anointed with saffron, a sign that they had come out to conquer or to die on the field. The front was about 7.4 miles (12km) long. The battle began at dawn after a fierce discharge of artillery and rockets in which the Maratha gunners, probably deceived by the light, fired high; a weapon on which the Marathas had partly relied had failed. The Marathas pushed back the Afghans, and the latter were initially only able to hold their own on their left flank. However, while the Maratha infantry advanced effectively in disciplined order, there was no co-ordination between the infantry and the cavalry: the cavalry was undisciplined, and the heavy artillery was slow, immobile, and inaccurate. The absence of a good command structure exacerbated problems of control caused by the composite nature of the Maratha army.

In the late afternoon, Abdali committed his 5,000-strong cavalry reserves, and Afghan counter-attacks were simultaneously launched all along the line. The Marathas were exhausted. Their men and horses had had little food for weeks, and none since dawn. Nevertheless, they fought hard until resistance collapsed at about 4 p.m. The Maratha centre collapsed in the face of Afghan cavalry attacks, leading to a general rout of the entire army. The Afghans pursued the fleeing Marathas all night, killing many. The following morning the camp was stormed and many other Marathas killed. The prisoners were all beheaded.

Panipat was not, however, followed by a permanent Afghan presence in northern India. On 22 March 1761, after ransacking Delhi, Ahmad Shah Abdali left India under pressure from his troops who hated the heat of the sub-continent.

A figure wearing Indian arms and armour of the late eighteenth century.

An Indian matchlock from the late eighteenth century.

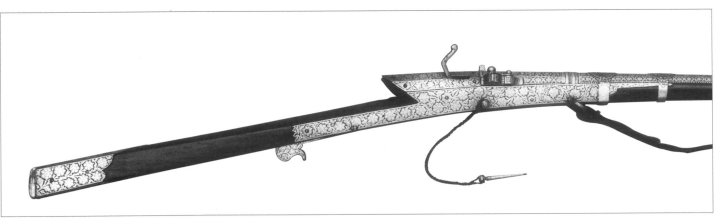

THE STRUGGLE FOR PERSIA, 1709-1785

AFTER THE FALL of the Safavids, Persia was invaded from the east by a series of rival Afghan dynasties and from the west by the Ottomans. From 1730, under Nadir Shah, a new Persian empire was built, but it fell apart after his death. From the 1780s, Russian pressure became more important in the Caucasus region, although the region proved difficult to control.

THE AFGHAN INVASION

The Safavid dynasty in Persia collapsed in the 1720s as a result of an Afghan rising. The Abdalis of Herat successfully rebelled in 1709–11, to be followed in 1717 by the Ghilzais under Mahmud, who had already seized power in Herat. The Afghans captured Kandahar and in 1719 advanced as far as Kirman, but Mahmud was forced to turn back by problems in Afghanistan itself. He advanced into Persian territory again in 1721. Failing to take Kirman and Yazd, he nevertheless marched on the Persian capital of Isfahan. At Gulnabad (March 1722), Mahmud encountered the Persian army, which was not only far larger than his own but also included artillery, which the Afghans lacked. Initial Persian success was not exploited due to the lack of unified command, and the better coordinated Afghans eventually prevailed. Gulnabad was followed by a siege of the poorly prepared Persian capital, Isfahan. After seven months, food shortages led the Shah to surrender and abdicate, declaring Mahmud his successor.

The Ghilzai Afghans were unable to maintain the Safavid state. The Ottomans overran much of the west, reaching as far as Hamadan and Kirmanshah, while Mahmud was murdered in 1725 and his succession contested by his son and a nephew. Both were overthrown in 1729–30 by Nadir Shah (1688–1747), a general from the Afshar tribe of Khurasan, who ruled Persia behind Safavid puppets until 1736, when he declared himself Shah.

NADIR SHAH

Having gained control of Persia in 1730, Nadir Shah immediately embarked on a programme of expansion in all directions. His first target was the Ottoman Empire, which had benefited from Persian instability by making conquests in the west. In 1730, he drove the Ottomans from western and northern Persia, defeating their army at Nahavand, and in 1732–33 unsuccessfully besieged Baghdad before turning east. Kandahar was taken from the Afghans in 1738, and Persian forces then seized the Mughal outposts of Ghazni, Kabul, Jalalabad, and Peshawar, which guarded the route to India. In 1739, Nadir advanced to seize India's wealth. Having taken Lahore and defeated the Mughals at Karnal, his forces sacked Delhi and returned home with fabulous spoils including the Mughals' Peacock Throne.

In 1740, he attacked the Uzbeks, capturing the cities of Bukhara and Khiva, and leaving the Khan of the former as a subject ruler. The lands up to the Amu Darya, including Balkh, were annexed to Persia. In 1737, the Arab mercantile state of Oman was attacked. Nadir Shah's forces set sail from Bushire and overran much of Oman in 1737–38, but failed to capture its capital, Muscat. Further campaigns were launched in 1740–44, but a lack of reinforcements led to the abandonment of the Persian presence in 1744: wars with the Uzbeks and the Turks were more important. In 1743, Nadir resumed hostilities with the Ottomans, but his attacks on Kirkuk, Mosul, and Baghdad were beaten back. He was more successful in the Caucasus, but in 1746 the lack of decisive victory led to a compromise peace.

Nadir's oppressive policies and his attempt to alter Persian Shi'ite Islam made him unpopular, leading to his assassination in 1747. His empire split between Bukhara, which regained its independence; Balkh (briefly); Khurasan, where his family retained power; Afghanistan, where Ahmad Khan established the Durrani dynasty; and Persia where the Luristan chief Karim Khan Zand established the Zand dynasty

Nadir Shah (1668–1747) was a Khurasan brigand who rose to dominate Persia. He was a spectacular conqueror who created an impressive army of Persians and Afghans and gave Persian power an eastward orientation, moving the capital to Meshhed. But Nadir failed to integrate Shi'ism into Sunn'ism. His heavy taxation led to revolts and he was increasingly seen as cruel and dangerous, which led to his murder in 1747.

Kandahar was bitterly contested between Mughals and Persians in the seventeenth century. In the eighteenth century it fell under Afghan control, but was seized by Nadir Shah in 1738.

based on Shiraz. Zand ruled southern and central Persia from 1750 until his death in 1771. He was not interested in foreign conquest, with the exception of an invasion of southern Iraq in 1775–76 which culminated in a successful siege of Basra in April 1776. The Persians were driven out in the following decade. The death of Karim Khan Zand was followed by the rise of the Qajar tribe under Aga Muhammad Khan, who succeeded by 1794 in establishing a state based on Teheran. Aga Muhammad Khan ousted the Zand Khans but it took many years of fighting to reimpose order in Persia.

Peter the Great's conquests to the south of the Caspian were abandoned in 1732: the Russians found them of little value and lost large numbers of troops to disease. However, Russian pressure in the Caucasus and interest in Persia resumed in the 1780s. In 1781, Catherine the Great established a base in the Gulf of Asterabad (Gorgon) on the south-eastern shore of the Caspian Sea because of its location on the trade route to Bukhara and India. The Caucasus was a region where Turkey, Russia, and Persia had long competed for control or influence, and where there were religious and ethnic rivalries, an absence of clearly defined boundaries, and a lack of control over rival local protégés. Russia had moved into an area that Persia and Turkey had been disputing since the sixteenth century. In 1783, Erekle II, ruler of Kart'li-Kakhet'i, the principal Georgian state, placed himself under Russian protection and Russian troops entered Tbilisi. In 1784, a military road through the Dariel Pass, linking Russia and eastern Georgia, was completed. Russian pressure was to help define much of Persia's subsequent history. Yet the Russians also found the Caucasus a difficult region to influence or conquer. In 1785, a Russian force was encircled and annihilated on the bank of the river Sunja by north Caucasian Muslims taking part in a holy war against Russia.

MAP 1

Persia under Nadir Shah was a dynamic power, able to act effectively against all its neighbours. After Nadir Shah's death, the international situation in the region became less volatile. The rise of Russian power was important for Persia's future development.

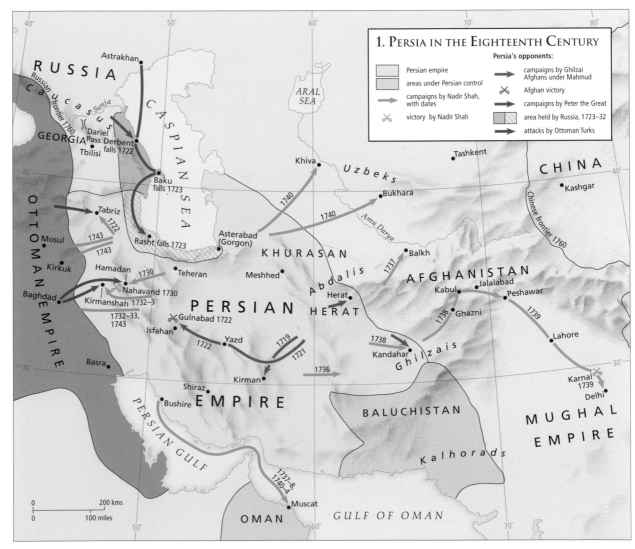

WARFARE IN AFRICA

THE EIGHTEENTH century was the last for which the history of most of Africa could be written without reference to Europeans. The rise and fall of African polities owed little to non-African states: firearms and dynamic leadership were more important. The European presence was restricted to a few coastal regions.

DYNAMIC AFRICAN POWERS

The Sudan in the eighteenth century continued to be a zone of conflict exacerbated by the clash between Islam and other religions. In the west, the theocratic Islamic states Futa Toro, Futa Jallon, and Khasso were established, the first being the consequence of the conquest of the Fulbe people by the Toucouleurs. The Pashalik of Timbuktu declined under pressure from the Tuareg and was destroyed by them in 1787. In its place the Bambara people, whose principal town was Segu, extended their power down the Niger river.

Further east, Kordofan was conquered, first by Funj in c.1750, and then by Darfur (1790). In East Africa, the Masai moved south from Lake Turkana, while the Tutsi moved from the upper White Nile to Rwanda and Burundi where they conquered the Hutu. In central Madagascar, the Merina expanded, making effective use of firearms, and by 1790 they could raise an army of 20,000 men. The Kingdom of Buganda developed to the north-west of Lake Victoria. Ethiopia was riven by internal struggles, and from 1769 to 1855, during the *Zamana Masafent* (the 'age of the Princes'), the emperors were essentially powerless, and Ethiopia was dominated by the nobility. On the Gold Coast, the Asante came to dominate the Akan peoples.

The use of firearms increased in Africa during the eighteenth century. In West Africa muskets, powder, and shot were imported, and were particularly important in purchasing slaves. There is little evidence that Europeans provided real training in the use of firearms, although rulers showed a keen interest in seeing European troops and their local auxiliaries exercise in formation. The auxiliaries were probably the key figures in the transfer of expertise. Since they worked seasonally for the Europeans and were trained to use firearms in the riverboat convoys, they had ample opportunities to sell their expertise to local rulers. There is evidence that the troops of some African kingdoms trained in formation. There are a few cases of Africans capturing European cannons and putting them to use, but field pieces were not sold to them. West African blacksmiths could make copies of flintlock muskets, but casting cannon probably exceeded their capacity.

The ability of Bekaffa of Ethiopia, who ruled between 1721 and 1730, to regain control over rebellious provinces owed much to his recruitment of new units whom he armed with muskets. In the 1760s, Mikail Sehul, the Ethiopian imperial *Ras*, built up an army, 8,000 of whom he equipped with muskets. In 1769, he defeated his master, the Emperor Iyoas.

CONFLICT IN NORTH AFRICA

Ottoman authority declined in North Africa during the eighteenth century: Algeria, Tunisia, and Tripolitania threw off Ottoman rule in 1710, 1705, and 1714 respectively. The Mameluke Beys of Egypt were effectively autonomous, and Ali Bey ul-Kebir, who controlled Eygpt from 1760 to 1773, extended his power by overrunning Upper Egypt, the Hejaz, and Syria. The Ottomans did not reimpose control until 1786.

The Barbary states along the north coast of Africa engaged in numerous small-scale wars, both against each other and against the European possessions in North Africa. In 1756, the Algerians profited from the civil war in Tunisia, by establishing their overlordship which was not overthrown

A shrine figure depicting a warrior in the full battle dress of the nineteenth-century Yoruba wars, carried on the shoulders of a retainer. These figures were still in use in the 1960s when they were found in a cult house in Isare, a town in the Yoruba area.

Map 1

Mapping Africa highlights two problems: actually determining if boundaries as we understand them existed at all; and locating, through historical sources, where boundaries actually lay. Larger political units typically agglomerated 'mini-states', either by charging them tribute or by interfering in their institutional, judicial, or leadership functions.

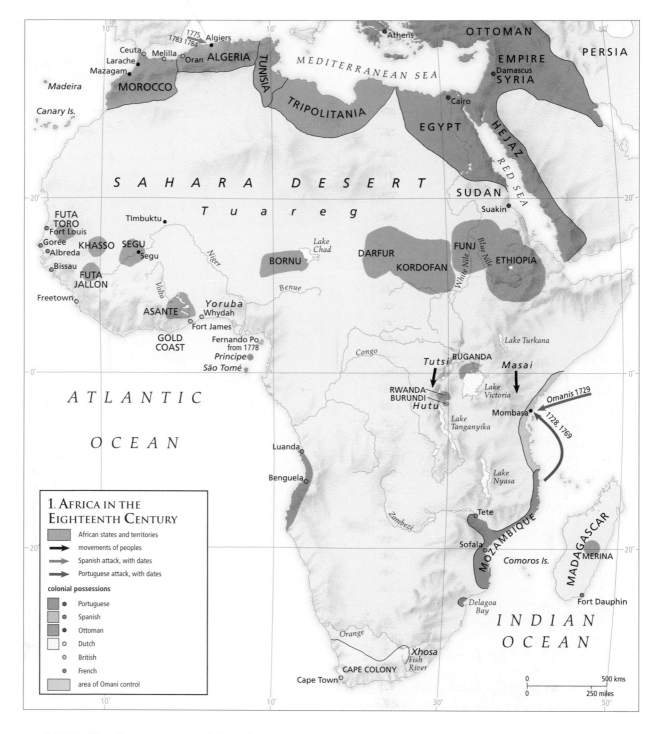

1. AFRICA IN THE EIGHTEENTH CENTURY

- African states and territories
- → movements of peoples
- → Spanish attack, with dates
- → Portuguese attack, with dates

colonial possessions

- Portuguese
- Spanish
- Ottoman
- Dutch
- British
- French
- area of Omani control

until 1790. The Algerians captured Oran from Spain in 1708, only to lose it again in 1732. The Spaniards evacuated it in 1792. Major Spanish attacks on Algiers were repelled in 1775, 1783, and 1784: in the first of these, the Spanish suffered severe casualties as their exposed troops were subjected to heavy fire while their artillery was delayed by the coastal sand.

EUROPEANS AND EAST AND SOUTH AFRICA

On the coast of East Africa, the Portuguese regained Mombasa in 1728 after a mutiny by African soldiers against Omani control, but it was lost again in 1729: although the Omani besiegers had no artillery and few firearms, the garrison capitulated as a result of low morale and food short-

age. In 1769, the Portuguese Governor, who had overcome native tribes in the south of Mozambique, failed to reconquer Mombasa.

In southern Africa, the Dutch, expanding east from Cape Colony, encountered the Xhosa. Raiding led to the First Kaffir War between 1779 and 1781. In Cape Colony, the Dutch were faced with serious resistance from the Xhosa, but defeated them on the Fish River. In West Africa, the European colonists were restricted to a few disease-ridden coastal possessions. The British Governor of Fort Louis reported in 1761, 'the troops here are exceedingly sickly, and we have lost many officers and men, the whole garrison has suffered prodigiously...it is not in my power to mount an officers' guard'.

THE AMERICAS IN THE EIGHTEENTH CENTURY

THE EUROPEANS' colonization of North and South America was by no means a straightforward matter of military conquest. It also involved a gradual and complex mixture of trade and alliance, in which the rivalries between the native tribes and between the incoming Europeans often played as important a role as that of direct confrontation.

SOUTH AMERICA

The western hemisphere saw the most rapid expansion of European territorial control in the eighteenth century. The Spanish made advances south in both Chile (map 1), where San Carlos de Ancud was founded in 1763, and Patagonia, where Carmen de Patagones was founded in 1779. But more important was the expansion into the interior of South America by the Portuguese in Brazil and by the Spanish east of the Andes and north from Buenos Aires. The discovery of gold and diamonds in Minas Gerais, in the interior of Brazil, led to extensive colonization. The military potential of the colonies was also developed. The colonial powers created militia units; in the 1760s and 1770s, for example, auxiliary cavalry and infantry regiments were raised throughout Brazil, and black and mulatto Brazilians were recruited into companies of irregular infantry. These units were useful in campaigns against native peoples, but they also served as potential bases for hostility towards the mother countries.

European control of firearms production was decisive in most of the conflict with Native Americans, but not in all. In central Amazonia in the 1760s and 1770s, the Portuguese were unable to defeat the guerrilla attacks of the mobile Mura, who staged numerous ambushes on Portuguese canoes and raids on isolated settlements. The Mura did not adopt firearms and remained effective with bows and arrows, but nevertheless they could not defeat the Portuguese and were obliged to agree a peace in 1784. In 1780, at Arequipa in Peru, Spanish firepower defeated local rebels armed with lances, sticks, and the traditional Andean weapon, the sling. However, in the 1770s on the Guajira Peninsula in Colombia, the Spanish forces failed to subdue the Indians despite their superior weaponry.

NORTH AMERICA

The native North American tribes resisted the 'European' Americans effectively until almost the end of the eighteenth century (map 2). There was resistance near the eastern sea-

board, where the Yamasee, with Creek support, nearly destroyed the British colonies in the Carolinas in 1715, along the northern border of French expansion from Louisiana, and against Spanish expansion north from Mexico. The Yamasee were only defeated in 1715 because the Cherokee supported the colonists; with their help, the Yamasee were defeated and most of them were killed or enslaved. Four years earlier, the Yamasee had helped the

MAP 1

Spain and Portugal considerably increased their territorial control in South America during the eighteenth century.

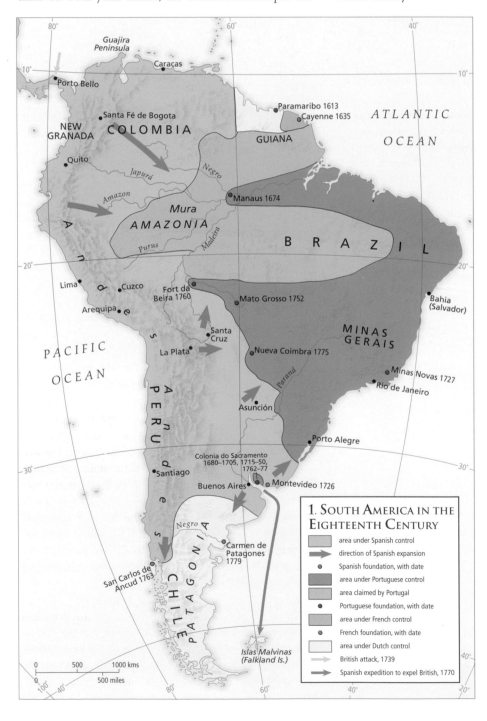

1. SOUTH AMERICA IN THE EIGHTEENTH CENTURY

- area under Spanish control
- → direction of Spanish expansion
- • Spanish foundation, with date
- area under Portuguese control
- area claimed by Portugal
- • Portuguese foundation, with date
- area under French control
- • French foundation, with date
- area under Dutch control
- → British attack, 1739
- → Spanish expedition to expel British, 1770

Tupac Amaru, the Indian Lord, taken prisoner by Spanish forces. The rigorous collection of taxes led to a general insurrection in Peru in 1780–81, headed by Tupac Amaru, who was a descendant of the last Inca rulers. He sought the support of the local whites, but was defeated and executed.

North Carolinians defeat an attack by the Tuscaroras, whose initial friendliness had been lost as a result of advancing white settlement. Tuscaroras numbers fell from 5,000 to 2,500; many took refuge with the Iroquois and those that remained were grouped by the colonists in a reservation which, by 1760, contained only about 300 people.

The French developed Louisiana, founding settlements near Biloxi Bay in 1699, New Orleans in 1718, and Baton Rouge in 1722. They suffered defeat at the hands of the Chickasaw in the late 1730s, and were affected by Chickasaw raids in 1747–48 and 1752, although the use of devastation, destroying native villages and crops, forced them to terms in 1752. An 800-strong French force in Louisiana savagely crushed the Natchez in 1729–31, in a campaign of systematic extermination. Most of the prisoners were shipped to Santo Domingo in the Caribbean, where they became slaves. The Natchez were weakened by their failure to win support from other tribes.

The Spanish attempted to create an impregnable cordon of *presidios* (fortified bases), but Native American war parties bypassed them without difficulty. The Apache, Comanche, and other Plains tribes were well mounted and armed, their firearms coming from trade with British merchants and with Spanish Louisiana, where the established policy was to win them over by doing business with them. The native tribes were able to respond with considerable flexibility to Spanish tactics. Spanish expeditions, such as those against the Apache in 1732 and 1775, were hindered by the lack of fixed positions for them to attack. The Yuma rebellion of 1781, in which Spanish positions were destroyed, thwarted plans for expansion through the Colorado valley and into central Arizona. By contrast, the Native Americans on the Pacific coast lacked both guns and horses, and Spanish power in California expanded rapidly in the 1770s, although in 1775 the Ipais burnt the mission at San Diego. Spanish involvement during the American Revolution

ensured that no more troops could be sent for operations against the Native Americans. Nevertheless, there was scant sign that Spain was in decline at this point, and the Spanish imperial position was to recover after the war.

FIREARMS, HORSES, AND TRADE

Warfare in North America was greatly conditioned by the diffusion of European developments, particularly of firearms and horses. Native Americans living near the Spanish settlements in the early seventeenth century had first acquired the horse, and it spread northward, by trade and theft, to the Rocky Mountains and the Great Plains. The Apache and Comanche had the horse before the end of the century, the Cheyenne and Pawnee by 1755. In the eighteenth century, more horses were acquired from Europeans trading from the St Lawrence valley. A major horse-culture developed on the Great Plains.

Tribes which acquired firearms in quantity, such as the Cree and Chipewayo, were able to establish trading and fur-trapping empires at the expense of rivals. Once the Chipewayo had matched the armaments of their rivals the Cree, they could block Cree expansion northward to the west of Hudson Bay. Further south, the Cree fought the Dakota Sioux west of Lake Superior. Jonathan Carver, a captain of the Massachusetts militia, who wintered with the Dakota Sioux in 1766–77, found few horses, guns, and flints had reached the lands west of the Mississippi. He noted that prisoners-of-war were tortured to death.

ANGLO-FRENCH RIVALRY

Warfare between native tribes was often related to commercial or political rivalry between the British and the French colonizers, who actively competed for trade in the interior. Suspicious that the Fox tribe from the Mississippi-Illinois region were plotting with the British, the French launched five attacks on them in 1712–34, finally breaking Fox resistance. In 1724, Governor Shute of Massachusetts sent an expedition to the north to destroy the mission of the French Jesuit Sebastian Rale, and thus French influence among the Norridgewock Indians. French attempts in the 1740s to prevent their native allies from trading with the British led to British-incited resistance: the Miami sacked Fort Miami (1747) and Fort Vincennes (1751), while the Huron burnt Detroit. The French responded vigorously, forcing the Miami back into alliance (1752) and establishing new posts in the upper Ohio (1753–54), which helped to provoke the Seven Years' War with Britain, a conflict known in North America as the French and Indian War. The war was won by the British, but British American settlers then moved into native lands. This led to Pontiac's Rising (1763–64) which involved a number of tribes, especially the Ottawa under Pontiac. Successful attacks were made on a number of British forts, while the British were forced to abandon several others; British field forces were also successfully ambushed. The British were less effective at fighting in the frontier woodlands than their opponents and British dependence on supply routes made them more vulnerable to ambush. However,

A fanciful picture of Pontiac uniting the tribes against the British. Pontiac was the leader of the Ottawa tribe. In Pontiac's rising (1763–64), he united a number of tribes in attacks against British forts.

owing to the British conquest of Canada, the natives had no source of firearms other than captures, and some British positions, such as Detroit, Niagara, and Fort Pitt, successfully resisted attack. The British also distributed clothes infected with smallpox, causing an epidemic among the tribes who were vulnerable to the disease. In the late summer and autumn of 1764, the Native Americans, who found it difficult to sustain long conflicts, were obliged to submit.

THE AMERICAN REVOLUTION

The military potential of the tribes was confirmed during the American Revolution (pages 154–59), when those allied to Britain made serious attacks on the colonists. The Native Americans were well-suited to fighting in the terrain of the backcountry, an area in which the British military presence was sparse. Their military potential was considerable given their hunter-warrior training and their substantial numbers, especially compared to the backcountry whites. The independence that made them the great warriors they were, however, also made them uncontrollable in conjunction with regular forces. In addition, the Native Americans were divided and their politics were often factionalized. They were uninterested in a defensive strategy which involved garrison duty, and were disinclined to abandon the winter hunt for campaigning. They were also vulnerable to smallpox, which affected the Creek in 1779. Most of the Native Americans fought on the British side and their attacks put considerable pressure on the Americans. Advances by Native Americans into New York State and Pennsylvania in 1778, took them to within striking distance of the main centres of American power. Counter-attacks by George Rogers Clark into the Illinois country in 1778 and 1779 and by John Sullivan into western New York in 1779 brought success, such as Clark's capture of Vincennes in February 1779, but they were indecisive, and the Native Americans maintained

the pressure in New York, on the Upper Ohio, and in Kentucky until the end of the war.

Once that war was over, American pressure on the native peoples increased, although on 4 November 1791 the Native Americans won a crushing victory over Major-General Arthur St Clair near present-day Fort Wayne, where St Clair lost three times the number of men who were to die with Custer in 1876. However, the Americans' superior firepower, numbers, and organization led to Anthony Wayne's victory over the native tribes at the Battle of Fallen Timbers

Notch-ee-ming-a, the principal chief of the Iowa tribe, painted by George Catlin in 1831. The face paint probably indicates that he killed an enemy in hand-to-hand combat.

MAP 2

Colonial expansion in
North America increas-
ingly affected the Native
Americans living west
of the Mississippi (right).
The northern frontier of
New Spain was advanced
during the eighteenth
century, especially in the
1770s (inset, below). Spain's
involvement in the Amer-
ican Revolution ensured
that no more troops could
be sent to New Spain, and
the Yuma uprising of 1781
closed the land route
through to California.

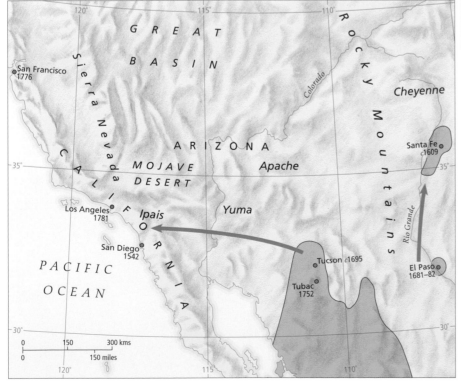

on 20 August 1794, after which the Treaty of Greenville
opened most of Ohio to white settlers. In this battle, the
native warriors were put to flight by a well-aimed volley
followed by a bayonet charge; difficulties withstanding,
the American cavalry was also cited as a reason for the
Native defeat.

In the east, the Native Americans were overwhelmed
largely by greater European-American numbers, but this
was not yet the case in the west. Armed and on horseback,
the native tribes of the Plains remained a formidable military challenge, as the Spaniards were well aware. On the
north-west coast of North America, firearms were introduced by European and American traders in the 1780s and
the natives quickly adopted them in place of bows and
arrows, using them for warfare among themselves as well
as against whites. Yet, despite their adaptability in war, the
situation of Native Americans steadily deteriorated as the
demographic balance in North America moved towards
those of European descent.

THE ANGLO-BOURBON STRUGGLE, 1739-1763

THE EUROPEANS' struggle for maritime supremacy and colonial dominance was decisively won by the British in mid-century. The French empire was overthrown in the Seven Years' War, and the Spanish empire was badly battered. Britain emerged as the leading European power in North America and South Asia.

THE FRANCO-SPANISH CHALLENGE

Whatever the strength and resilience of non-European peoples, the European states were dominant at sea, and none more so than Britain. Britain had emerged from the Nine Years' and Spanish Succession Wars with the strongest navy in Europe, a situation further enhanced by alliance with France in 1716. However, poor relations with France from 1731 and with Spain from 1733, and closer relations between these two Bourbon powers prompted serious con-

cern in Britain, as did the build-up of the French navy. The uncontested naval hegemony that Britain had enjoyed in the 1710s and 1720s was challenged in mid-century wars with both France and Spain. The British won chiefly because their navy had a stronger organizational and mercantile base. The great expansion of British trade produced a larger pool of sailors from whom the navy could be manned, albeit often by the use of the press gang. Helped by a rising customs revenue, the government provided the necessary funds, and there was no crisis in naval funding comparable to that suffered by France during the Seven Years' War.

War broke out with Spain in 1739 over Spanish attempts to preserve their commercial system in the West Indies and to prevent illegal trade. Allegedly Spanish coastguards had cut off the ear of an English merchantmen captain, Robert Jenkins. In 1739, the British easily took Porto Bello on the Caribbean coast of Panama, but their failure to seize the Spanish base of Cartagena in modern Colombia in 1741 ended their hopes of easy conquests in the West Indies. The British fleet on the Cartagena expedition – twenty-nine

MAP 1

British military pressure on Canada was ultimately successful because of a number of factors: numerical superiority, naval control, logistical strength, Wolfe's bold generalship, and victory in the different regions of British advance.

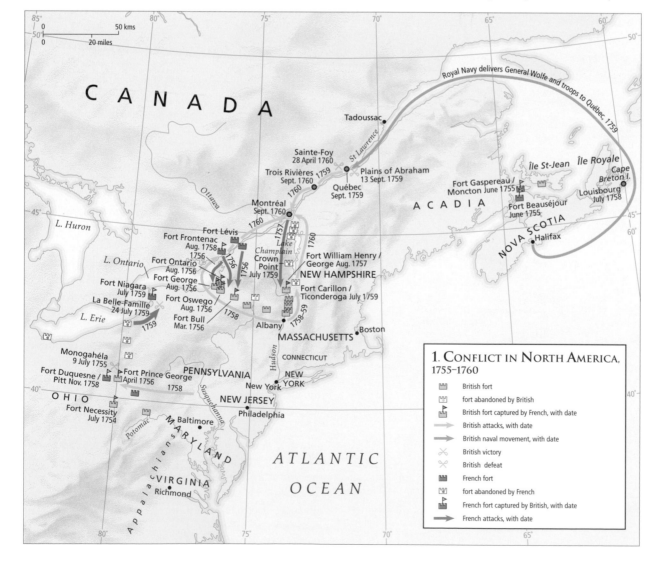

QUÉBEC 26 JUNE – 18 SEPTEMBER 1759

In 1759, the Royal Navy brought a force of 8,600 men under Wolfe to Québec. Wolfe arrived on 26 June, but his operations along the Beauport shore were initially unsuccessful: on 31 July an attack on French positions was repelled by Montcalm's larger army.

As winter approached, Wolfe risked a bold move. British warships had passed beyond Québec from 18 July onwards and made upriver raids on 8 August. On 1–3 September, British troops left the Montmorency camp and moved along the southern bank of the river opposite Québec. On 10 September Wolfe, having reconnoitred the channel, decided to land at Anse au Foulon, close to the city.

After delays due to the weather, the British landed in the early hours of 13 September. Some 200 light infantry scaled the cliffs and successfully attacked a French camp of 100 men. The rest of the British force, less than 4,500, then landed and assembled on the Plains of Abraham to the south-west (1).

Montcalm, with 13,000 men in the area, was in a strong position but, instead of waiting on the defensive and uniting his forces, he chose to attack with the men immediately available. The French advanced in columns, but their centre veered to the right, allowing the British centre to fire methodical volleys. The French formations became disorganized and the British waited until they were about 100 feet (30m) away (2), and opened fire. This close-range onslaught caused the French columns to disintegrate and retreat (3). Wolfe had already been fatally wounded before the charge; and Montcalm's troops retreated after he too was killed.

French and British casualties were comparable, about 650 each, but French morale was shattered. Although Québec had not been captured and more French troops arrived immediately after the battle, at a council of war the French officers decided not to risk battle again, but to retreat upriver. This decision to retreat was reversed a few days later but, as a French force approached the city, it surrendered on 18 September.

The Taking of Québec, engraving by J. & C. Bowles.

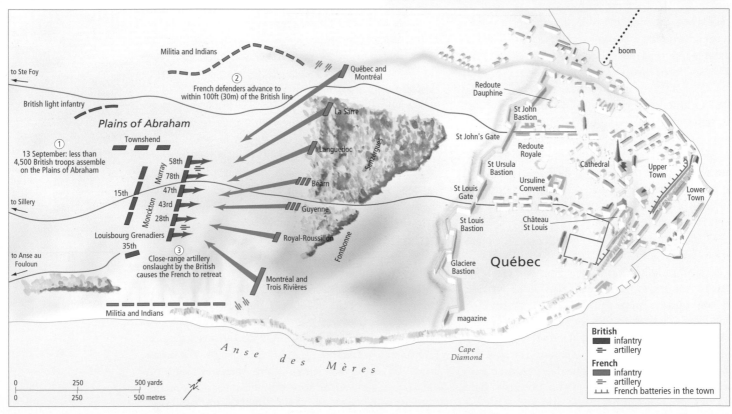

THE FALL OF HAVANA

A British force of 12,000 under the Earl of Albemarle landed to the north of Havana on 7 June 1762. Operations were concentrated against Fort Moro which commanded the channel from the sea to the harbour and was protected by a very deep landward ditch. The summer passed in siegeworks which were hindered by the bare rock in front of the fortress and artillery duels, supported by naval bombardment. Thousands of British soldiers died from disease. On 30 July, the British exploded two mines on either side of the ditch, creating an earth ramp across it and a breach that was stormed successfully, enabling the British artillery to dominate the city, which surrendered on 12 August.

British troops enter the breach of Fort Moro in 1762, by Philip Orsbridge.

ships of fifty to eighty guns – was larger than any European force yet seen outside European waters.

THE WAR OF THE AUSTRIAN SUCCESSION

When France formally entered the war against Britain in 1744 (*page 120*), British maritime and colonial concerns found a new focus. A New England force captured the major French-Canadian base of Louisbourg on Cape Breton Island. Its fortifications were designed to resist artillery bombardment, especially from the sea, but it was attacked by land where its defences were weakest: bombardment for about six weeks breached the walls, leading to the garrison's surrender. In the following year, the French failed to regain the island: d'Enville's fleet returned to France, victims of disease and shipwreck. The British, however, retained most of their fleet in home waters, from where they mounted an unsuccessful attack on Lorient in north-west France, rather than following up the fall of Louisbourg by invading Canada. Despite the victory at Louisbourg, the main French fleet was still undefeated, and the British government was aware of the danger of the French seeking to invade Britain in support of a fresh Jacobite attempt. In these circumstances it did not seem appropriate to devote substantial resources to extra-European attacks.

In 1747, British naval victories ensured that the French capacity to launch initiatives was dramatically reduced: Anson defeated La Jonquière off Cape Finisterre (14 May) and Hawke won the most brilliant action of the war, the Second Battle of Cape Finisterre (14 October), in which six of L'Étenduère's eight ships were captured. However, the British had to hand Louisbourg back in the subsequent Peace of Aix-la-Chapelle (1748) in order to regain Madras, which had fallen to the French in 1746. Under Dupleix, the French were in the ascendant among the European powers in India in the 1740s, and in 1747 a British attempt to reverse this by capturing the French headquarters at Pondicherry was unsuccessful.

BRITISH OFFENSIVES IN CANADA

Relations between the two powers were uneasy despite the coming of peace, and competing interests in North America led to a renewed outbreak of hostilities in 1754. The French successfully blocked an attempt to challenge their position in the Ohio valley: a superior French force obliged the surrender of American provincial troops at Fort Prince George and Fort Necessity, the latter under George Washington. The British government then sent regular forces under Major-General Edward Braddock. These, however, were defeated near Fort Duquesne (9 July 1755) by the French and their Indian allies, who made excellent use of tree cover to fire at the exposed British force which had no experience in 'wilderness warfare': the British lost 1,000 dead or wounded, the French 40. Only an attack on Fort Beauséjour in Acadia was successful (16 June) .

War formally broke out in 1756. Greater French interest in Canada had led to a growth in the size of the Louisbourg garrison to 2,500 regulars with a supporting naval squadron, but they faced a British North American army of 23,000 regulars. Nevertheless, the French took the initiative in 1756, driving the British from Lake Ontario and capturing Forts Bull, George, Ontario, and Oswego. In the following year, the French advanced towards the Hudson, capturing Fort William Henry after heavy bombardment. A British plan for an attack on Louisbourg had been deterred by French naval forces.

The British war minister, William Pitt the Elder, had the commanders he blamed for the failures removed, and in 1758 he took a leading role in planning a three-pronged offensive on Canada. Separate forces were to attack Carillon (Ticonderoga), Louisbourg, and Fort Duquesne. The largest army was sent under General James Abercromby against Carillon, but it was the smaller Louisbourg force under Generals Jeffrey Amherst, James Wolfe, and Admiral Boscawen which was successful. They landed on Cape Breton on 8 June and, as in 1745, concentrated on the landward defences. Louisbourg surrendered on 26 July. The British force of 13,000 had suffered 560 killed or wounded, but 3,000 French were taken prisoner. In addition, the French naval squadron was lost.

The main offensive at Carillon on 8 July 1758 was a costly failure: out of 9,000 American provincials and 6,400 regulars, the British lost 1,900 killed or wounded to the mere 400 French, a serious setback for a European army in transoceanic operations.

The third offensive was successful. An army of 7,000, mostly American provincials, advanced on Fort Duquesne, and the 300 defenders withdrew on 30 November. The rebuilt fort was named Fort Pitt. The French position was weakened when, in October, Pennsylvania authorities promised the Ohio tribe that they would not claim land west of the Appalachians. The tribe abandoned the French, obliging them to give up the Ohio region. In August, another British force had destroyed crucial French supplies at Fort Frontenac. Nevertheless, British strategy was weak in 1758. The three offensives failed to provide mutual support and the French commander, the Marquis de Montcalm, had been able to concentrate his efforts against Abercromby, ensuring that he was defeated when he attacked Carillon.

THE FALL OF FRENCH CANADA

In 1758, the British had made the Hudson-Lake Champlain axis their first priority; in 1759, it was to be the St Lawrence, where British naval power could be used most effectively. There were other advances in 1759. From Albany the British advanced to Lake Ontario, and the French, short of Indian support, abandoned some of the forts there and near Lake Erie. The French contested the Niagara position, but were defeated at an engagement at La Belle-Famille (24 July) and Fort Niagara surrendered to a large British force two days later. Carillon was abandoned on 27 July and renamed Ticonderoga. Crown Point followed four days later, and Wolfe's campaign against Québec came to a successful climax in September (*page 151*).

Six months after the fall of Québec, the substantial French army still in Canada under Lévis advanced to recapture it.

James Murray repeated Montcalm's mistake, engaging on the Plains of Abraham when it would have been wiser to remain in the city. In the Battle of Sainte-Foy (28 April 1760), the French carried the day with a bayonet charge and the British retreated with heavier casualties into Québec. The city was then besieged until a British fleet arrived with reinforcements on 16 May and forced the French back to Montréal. In the summer of 1760, the three-pronged British advance finally worked. British troops advanced from Québec, Crown Point, and, in largest numbers, from Lake Ontario. The outnumbered French abandoned most of their positions, although there was fighting round Fort Lévis. On 8 September, the 3,520 French in Montréal surrendered to Amherst's force of 17,000. Canada had fallen.

TRIUMPHS ACROSS THE GLOBE

British amphibious forces were successful elsewhere during the Seven Years' War. In 1758, Forts Louis and Gorée, the French bases in West Africa, were easily taken. In the West Indies, Guadeloupe was captured in 1759 and Martinique in 1762, with naval firepower playing a major role. The French were defeated in India (*page 160*). They successfully besieged Fort St David in 1758, but their attack on Madras in 1759 was unsuccessful; the British were superior in artillery and were relieved by sea. In 1760, Lally was defeated by Sir Eyre Coote at the Battle of Wandewash on 22 January, in which the British artillery played a crucial role. Wandewash was followed by the rapid fall of hostile positions such as Cuddalore. The remaining French posssessions in India were captured by early 1761; Pondicherry surrendered on 15 January after an eight-month siege. The entry of Spain into the war led in 1762 to British attacks on Manila and Havana, the former mounted from Madras, where its commander, Colonel William Draper, complained that the small numbers he had been allocated 'will sufficiently evince the impossibility of my acting against the place with the formalities of a siege. My hopes are placed in the effects of a bombardment, or *coup de main*'. Landing on 25 September, Draper captured Manila on 6 October after a vigorous advance. Havana had fallen by 12 August.

THE ROYAL NAVY

Britain's triumphs in the Seven Years' War rested on naval power. By 1762 the navy had about 300 ships and 84,000 men, a size that reflected the growth of the British mercantile marine, population, economy, and public finances, as well as its heavy shipbuilding programme during the war. There was good naval leadership. An experienced admiral, George, Lord Anson, was First Lord of the Admiralty (1751–62), while admirals such as Boscawen, Hawke, Pocock, and Rodney were bold and effective commanders.

Britain needed to destroy her opponents' fleets, as both France and Spain were expanding their sea power. Together they launched

warships with a total displacement of around 250,000 tons in 1746–55, while Britain launched only 90,000, losing its previous superiority over the two Bourbon powers. Fortunately for Britain, Spain did not join the war until 1762 and by then France, involved in the Seven Years' War on the Continent, had been defeated at sea, losing about 50,000 tons of warships to British captures.

Thanks to captures and shipbuilding, the British navy in 1760 had a displacement tonnage of about 375,000 (381,000 tonnes), at that point the largest in the world. The British had become the leading global naval power.

THE AMERICAN REVOLUTION

THE AMERICAN Revolution was the only successful rising within the eighteenth-century British world. The British state controlled a formidable war machine, arguably the strongest in the world at that point, with the largest navy and the best system of public finance, but it was nevertheless unable to suppress the revolution in the Thirteen Colonies.

THE BRITISH ATTEMPT TO ISOLATE NEW ENGLAND

Relations between Britain and a large section of the population in the Thirteen Colonies on the eastern seaboard of the modern USA broke down in the 1760s and early 1770s as disputes over taxation led to a stubborn rejection of British authority. The Seven Years' War had left the British government with an unprecedentedly high level of national debt and it looked to America to meet a portion of the burden. The Americans, however, no longer felt threatened by French bases in Canada, and were therefore unwilling to see British troops as saviours. The Stamp Act of 1765 led to a crisis as Americans rejected Parliament's financial demands, and thereafter relations were riven by a fundamental division over constitutional issues.

Fighting between the British and their North American colonists broke out in Massachusetts, the centre of opposition to British rule, when the British sought to seize a colonial arms dump at Concord and encountered militiamen at Lexington (19 April 1775). The shedding of blood outraged New England, and a substantial force, largely dependent on their personal arms, soon encircled the British in Boston. On 17 June 1775, the British attacked at Bunker Hill (page 155), advancing in traditional order, and the entrenched Americans inflicted heavy casualties. Only at the third attempt, when the Americans were running short of ammunition, did the British drive them back, sustaining heavy casualties in the process.

In order to prevent a British advance to the Hudson which would cut off New England from the other colonies, the Americans decided in autumn 1775 to invade Canada. Their main army, 2,000 strong, under the command of Richard Montgomery, advanced via Lake Champlain (map 1). Fort St-Jean fell after a six-week siege (2 November), and the smaller British forces in Fort Chambly (17 October) and Montréal (13 November) surrendered. The Governor of Québec, Guy Carleton, fled from Montréal to Québec.

Meanwhile, another American force under Benedict Arnold crossed Maine to arrive, after much hardship, opposite Québec on 14 November. Montgomery advanced on Québec down the St Lawrence and the combined American force besieged the city. An attack on the Lower Town on

the night of 30–31 December was beaten back with heavy American casualties, including Montgomery, and no progress had been made by the time a British relief force arrived on 6 May. The Americans then retreated and mounted an unsuccessful counter-attack at Trois Rivières on 8 June.

In March 1776, the British withdrew from Boston to refit at Halifax. Under General William Howe, they landed on Staten Island, at the entrance to New York harbour, on 3 July. This began a second stage in the war that was more widespread, bitter, and sustained than had at first seemed likely. This was the equivalent of the British riposte after the Jacobite advances in 1715 and 1745; unlike the Jacobites, the Americans had the space and resources to cope, although the British home base was not exposed to American attack.

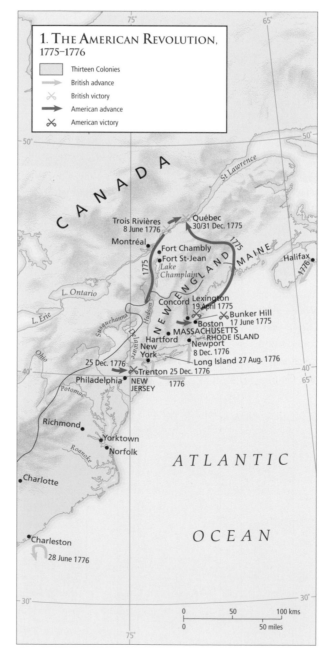

MAP 1

In 1775, British authority collapsed in the Thirteen Colonies, but in 1776 the British mounted a powerful riposte in the Middle Colonies. The American attempt to conquer Canada had already failed.

MAP 2

British operations failed in 1777 as Burgoyne's unsupported advance collapsed. Howe's successful capture of the American capital Philadelphia was a major achievement, but it was abandoned the following year when the French entered the conflict.

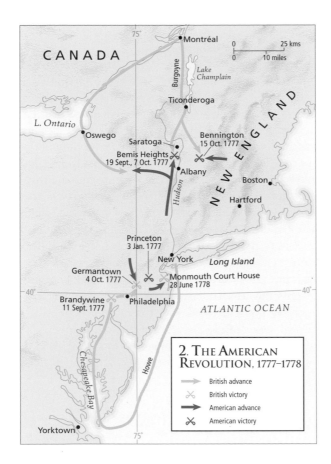

2. THE AMERICAN REVOLUTION, 1777–1778

→ British advance
✕ British victory
➔ American advance
✕ American victory

(8 December), and overran New Jersey, reaching the Delaware at Trenton (8 December). However, a surprise American counter-attack at Trenton led the British to abandon much of New Jersey.

In 1777, Howe approached Philadelphia via a lengthy voyage to the Chesapeake (map 2). George Washington, the American commander, sought to block him at Brandywine Creek (11 September), but was outflanked and defeated. Philadelphia fell (26 September), and an American surprise attack was beaten off at Germantown (4 October). Howe, though, had been unable to provide support for Burgoyne's advance south from Canada. Ticonderoga fell in June, but Burgoyne found it difficult to advance through the forests to the Hudson, and was soon faced by a much larger American army.

Burgoyne foolishly pressed on, attacking the Americans at Bemis Heights (19 September), where he suffered heavy casualties from American riflemen. Another British attack was repelled on 7 October. An attempt was made to relieve Burgoyne from New York, but it was unsuccessful, and on 17 October he surrendered at Saratoga. The British strategy of cutting the Thirteen Colonies in half along the Hudson corridor had failed.

FRENCH INVOLVEMENT

In 1778, the entry of France into the war on the American side changed the nature of the conflict. In America it led the British to abandon Philadelphia. Their interest was increasingly focused on the South (map 3). Savannah fell to a British amphibious force in December 1778, as did Charleston in May 1780, one of the most serious American

The British outflanked and defeated the Americans at the Battle of Long Island on 27 August (page 156), before driving them from New York. Successive blows weakened the Americans, while the British seized Newport, Rhode Island

---

BUNKER HILL 17 JUNE 1775

On the night of 16-17 June, the Revolutionaries marched to Breed's Hill on the Charlestown peninsula and began to fortify the position, which commanded the heights above the city of Boston; the Battle is named after the more prominent hill behind Breed's Hill. The British commander, General Gage, decided on a landing at high tide that afternoon, followed by an attack on the American entrenchments. Gage moved ponderously, spending about two hours deploying his men and advancing in a traditional open-field formation. There was considerable confusion among the British artillery, who failed to harm the American positions significantly. The Americans waited until the advancing British were almost upon them before shattering their first two assaults with heavy fire. An attempt to turn the American flank was repelled. The Americans were running short of ammunititon and a third British attack took the American redoubt; but the exhausted British, harassed by sharpshooters, were unable to stop the Americans from retreating.

Battle of Bunker Hill (contemporary painting).

defeats of the war. The British, however, found it difficult to consolidate their position in South Carolina. Thanks
to the poor quality of the Virginia and North Carolina militia, Cornwallis defeated the American southern army under
Horatio Gates at Camden (16 August), but it proved impossible to control the backcountry, and Colonel Banastre
Tarleton was defeated at Cowpens (17 January 1781).

By 1780, the Americans faced growing exhaustion, and
war-weariness. The limited creditworthiness of Congress
and the reluctance of the states to subordinate their prior-
ities and resources to Congress meant that the army had to
live from hand to mouth. In January 1781, short of pay,
food, and clothes, and seeking discharge, both the Pennsylvania line and a total of three New Jersey regiments
mutinied. The Pennsylvania mutiny was ended only by
concessions, including the discharge of five-sixths of the
men. The episode was a salutary warning to the Revolutionary cause and can only give rise to speculation as to
what would have happened if the army had been obliged
to endure another harsh winter without the prospect of a
victorious close to the conflict.

Early in 1781, Cornwallis invaded North Carolina: on 15
March he defeated the larger army of Gates' replacement,
Nathaniel Greene, at Guildford Court House, although the
Americans fought well and the battle was no rout. Cornwallis' report on the battle offers a valuable indication of
how he saw the conflict: 'Their invincible patience in the
hardships and fatigues of a march of above 600 miles, in
which they have forded several large rivers and number-
less creeks, many of which would be reckoned large rivers
in any other country in the world, without tents or covering against the climate, and often without provisions…The
Second Battalion of Guards first gained the clear ground
near Guildford Court House, and found a corps of Continental [American] infantry much superior in number,
formed in the open field on the left of the road. Glowing
with impatience to signalize themselves, they instantly
attacked and defeated them, taking two six-pounders; but
pursuing into the wood with too much ardour, were
thrown into confusion by a heavy fire, and immediately
charged and driven back into the field by Colonel Washington's Dragoons, with the loss of the six-pounders they

LONG ISLAND 27 AUGUST 1776

The Americans on Long Island were divided
between entrenchments at Brooklyn and a force
strung out along the Heights of Guan, a ridge in
advance of this position. The American troops
guarded the coastal flank of the Heights on
Gowanus Bay and the Flatbush and Bedford passes,
but a failure to guard Jamaica Pass on the left of the
American line was exploited by the British, who
outflanked the outnumbered Americans, while the
left of the British army engaged the American front.
The Maryland and Delaware troops on the American
right, under 'Lord' Stirling mounted a rearguard
action, but were captured or dispersed as the
Americans fell back to their positions on Brooklyn
Heights. The British commander, Lord Howe, failed
to order their storming and, instead, decided on
'regular approaches'. With hindsight, it is argued
that Howe should have pushed his men, who were
ready and willing to keep advancing, at the
American lines. But he was unwilling to waste
valuable British soldiers when, as soon as the winds
abated, his brother Admiral Howe could bring his
fleet up the East River and cut the Americans off
from either Manhattan or the mainland. In fact,
when the wind abated, a fog rolled in and, even as
the British fleet was lifting anchor preparatory to
sailing, Washington used the cover of the fog to
row his men across the river to Manhattan.

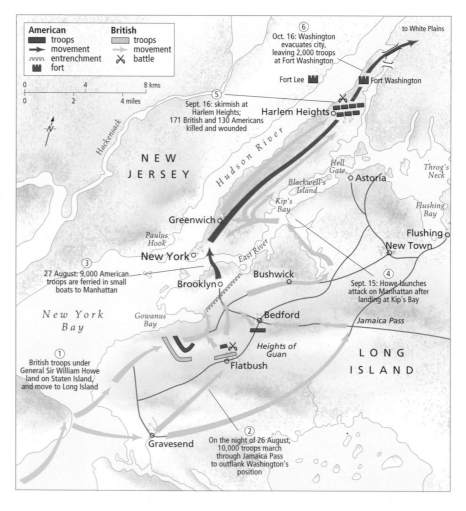

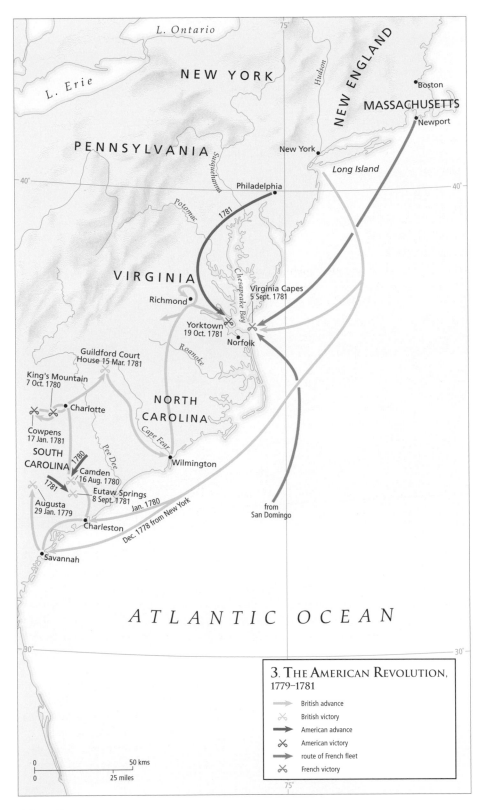

line. At this crucial juncture, however, the movement from the West Indies of the French fleet under de Grasse denied the British command of the sea, and Washington and a French expeditionary force under Rochambeau were able to achieve a concentration of strength which placed Cornwallis in an untenable position. Blockaded, under heavy bombardment, and without relief, Cornwallis surrendered on 19 October 1781. Although the British still held Charleston, New York, and Savannah, this was effectively the end of the war in North America. News of the defeat led to the replacement of Lord North's ministry by a British government more ready to accept American independence. Thereafter, the British concentrated on their conflict with the Bourbons.

A major strength of the American cause was that it was based on the free association of different communities. Collectively, the American economy was very strong with a standard of living higher than in the British Isles. In addition, each colony or state had military and economic resources of its own, so that a British victory in one part of America had only a limited effect elsewhere. The fall of Charleston did not make that of Boston more likely.

Clearly the Middle Colonies were more crucial, because of their geographical position. Here again, however, the Americans suffered severe blows, but not fatal ones. In 1776, they were defeated at Long Island and lost New York (*map* 1); and in 1777 they were defeated at Brandywine and lost Philadelphia (*map* 2). Yet in neither case did this lead to the collapse of the revolution. The Americans were largely helped by the fact that their defeated forces were able to retreat. There was no total loss, as the British suffered when they surrendered at Saratoga and Yorktown. Even if the British had achieved a more decisive victory either at Long Island or Brandywine, they would still have had to face an undefeated New England and South. Compared to the Jacobites in their failed confrontation with the British government in the first half of the eighteenth century, the Americans benefited from having a diffuse leadership and more military and political autonomy.

THE WAR AT SEA

Although American privateers caused many problems for British trade, the Americans did not pose a naval threat to the British, who were able to move their forces readily along the Atlantic seaboard, evacuating Boston (17 March 1776) and landing at Staten Island (2 July 1776), and in the Chesapeake (August 1777) without difficulty.

The American victory at Saratoga and Washington's ability to mount a riposte to the fall of Philadelphia at Germantown led France to enter the war in 1778. Thereafter the threat of French naval action was a major factor in operations in North America. The entry of the Spanish (1779) and the Dutch (1780) further complicated the position. Thanks to much shipbuilding in the late 1760s and 1770s, especially by Spain, France and Spain combined had a quantitative superiority in naval tonnage over Britain of about twenty per cent by 1775, and twenty-five per cent by 1780.

MAP 3

British operations in the South initially met with success, but it proved impossible to control the Carolina backcountry. Cornwallis' advance into Virginia led to a British disaster at Yorktown.

had taken. The enemy's cavalry was soon repulsed by a well directed fire from two three-pounders...and by the appearance of [fresh troops]...The excessive thickness of the woods rendered our bayonets of little use, and enabled the broken enemy to make frequent stands with an irregular fire, which occasioned some loss.'

Cornwallis then moved north to the Chesapeake, establishing himself at Yorktown. This was a poor defensive position, but it had an anchorage suitable for ships of the

As a result, the British were unable to repeat their success of the Seven Years' War.

The Royal Navy gained control of neither European nor American waters, and in 1778 was unable to defeat the French before Spain entered the war: Admiral Augustus Keppel failed to destroy the Brest fleet off Ushant (17 July 1778). The British concentration of naval strength on defending home waters ensured that the French naval base at Toulon was not blockaded, so its fleet was free to sail to American waters and threaten the British there. In 1779, France and Spain sent a force into the Channel, and their attempt to invade Britain was thwarted by disease and poor

The Battle of Lexington, 19 April 1775, by W. B. Wollen. The war began with an attempt to seize a cache of arms reported to be at Concord, a town 16 miles (10km) from Boston, past the village of Lexington. The British reached Lexington at first light, and found about seventy militia drawn up in two lines. Heavily outnumbered, the militia began to disperse, but a shot was fired and the British fired two volleys in response, thereby scattering the militia.

THE RIFLE

In his *Rêveries*, Marshal-Saxe had recommended 'the rifled-fusée, as it is charged quicker and carries not only further, but with more exactness'. Rifles were more accurate than the common flintlock musket and more suitable for individually aimed fire.

In popular accounts, the American Revolution is often seen in terms of American frontiersmen firing with rifles from behind cover at exposed ranks of British redcoats. Riflemen were effective, particularly at Saratoga (1777), but rifles also posed serious problems for their users: they could not carry bayonets, and were therefore vulnerable to bayonet

advances. Rifles could be fouled by repeated firing and they had a slow rate of fire, one round per minute; a serious problem in close-order fighting. Rifles were more expensive than flintlocks, and their use required expertise, of which there was little, even amongst the colonial Americans. Riflemen were effective when they had good cover, either natural or artificial, but such situations arose less frequently than is commonly supposed, especially as Washington preferred the tactics of close-order fighting rather than a reliance on guerrilla action. In fact, most Americans were armed with muskets.

organization rather than by British naval action. The loss of West Florida (1781) and Minorca (1782), and the successful build up of a powerful Franco-American force around Yorktown (1781) revealed that the Bourbons could mount successful amphibious expeditions. The failure of Admiral Thomas Graves to defeat the French off the Virginia Capes (5 September 1781) was an indecisive battle in terms of casualties, but as it prevented British relief of Cornwallis' encircled army at Yorktown, it was an important success for the French. It was not until the Battle of the Saints that there was a decisive British naval victory to rank with Quiberon Bay or Lagos: the French were planning to invade Jamaica, but on 12 June 1782, off the Iles des Saintes south of Guadeloupe, the outnumbered French commander, François de Grasse, was soundly defeated by George Rodney. He broke through the French line, capturing five ships of the line, including the flagship, the *Ville de Paris*, with de Grasse himself. The planned invasion of Jamaica had to be abandoned after the battle, and the British position improved on the eve of peace.

WORLD WAR

French naval efforts on entering the American war were chiefly aimed at securing the wealthy sugar islands of the West Indies. They took Dominica, St Vincent, Grenada, Tobago, St Kitts, Nevis, and Montserrat from the British, but lost St Lucia. The Spanish conquered West Florida: Baton Rouge fell in September 1779, Mobile in March 1780, and Pensacola in May 1781. In Europe, however, the Spanish failed, despite major efforts, to take Gibraltar. Their blockade began in 1779, and a formal siege began in the summer of 1781. On 13 September 1781, a major attack was made with floating batteries, but most were sunk by British fire and thereafter the siege became a less intense blockade and bombardment.

In the latter stages of the war, the Indian Ocean also became an important sphere of hostilities. The British attempt to capture Cape Town from the Dutch in 1781 was prevented by French reinforcements under Admiral Suffren. From February 1782 until June 1783, the bold Suffren battled against Edward Hughes in the Bay of Bengal. The French co-operated with the rulers of Mysore, but the British were not driven from India. In the Treaty of Versailles (3 September 1783), Britain lost Tobago and Senegal to France, and Minorca and Florida to Spain, but emerged with much of its empire still intact. The basis for Britain's imperial revival and rapid growth was soon to be laid by William Pitt the Younger.

WASHINGTON

George Washington (1732–1799) began his military career as an adjutant in the Virginia militia in 1752. He led a militia expedition towards Fort Duquesne in 1754 (*page 152*), but was forced to surrender by the French. In 1755, he was with Braddock at the ambush of the Monogahela, but survived it and was made commander of all Virginia forces.

His experience helped him gain command of the Continental Army blockading Boston on 15 June 1775. He helped to force the British out of Boston, but was unsuccessful in defence of New York (1776), though his surprise attack across the Delaware against the Hessians at Trenton (25–26 December 1776) did stem the tide of British success.

Seeking to protect Philadelphia in 1777, Washington was defeated at Brandywine and so unable to prevent the fall of the city, but he was able to mount an attack on the British at Germantown. When Clinton retreated from Philadelphia in 1778, Washington fought a creditable if not entirely successful battle at Monmouth Court House. In 1780 the focus of attention moved to the South, but in 1781

Washington responded to Cornwallis' invasion of Virginia by blockading him in Yorktown and forcing his surrender.

Although not a particularly good field general, especially at Long Island and Brandywine, Washington was an excellent leader and a good strategist. He was instinctively aggressive, though the disasters of 1776 made him less inclined to take risks unless the prospect of success was clear. He was tactically conservative, choosing to fight in a manner to which the British were essentially accustomed, rather than to adopt the more irregular warfare advocated by Major-General Charles Lee.

John Adams criticized Washington as too cautious, but his ability to keep the undefeated Continental Army in the field denied the British victory, and was responsible for the generally immobile, defensive posture of the British forces in 1778–81. This considerable military and political achievement ultimately secured American independence.

George Washington, after Charles Peale.

BRITISH EXPANSION IN INDIA

I N 1750, the British East India Company held only small areas of India around their trading bases of Bombay, Fort St David, and Madras. By 1800, they were in control of much of southern India and of most of the eastern coast as far as Burma. This had been achieved in the face of a European rival, France, and of Indian opposition.

BRITISH-FRENCH RIVALRY

Both Britain and France came to play an important role in the internecine disputes of the rulers of south-eastern India from the 1740s. The two powers took opposite sides in the succession struggles over the Carnatic that began in 1740. The French Governor-General, Joseph Dupleix, was a skilled player in the field of south Indian politics, but he was out-manoeuvred by the British and lacked the resources to sustain his ambitions.

Dupleix's ally, Chanda Sahib, became Nawab of the Carnatic in 1749, but a rival claimant was supported by the British. Robert Clive led a diversionary force of 500 which captured Chanda Sahib's capital, Arcot, and then held it against massive odds. In 1752, both the French and Chanda Sahib surrendered. A French attempt under Lally to regain their position in the Carnatic during the Seven Years' War (map 1) was initially successful, with the capture of Fort St David in 1758, but the siege of Madras ended after Lally was defeated at Masulipatam (1759) and later routed at Wandewash (1760).

Rivalry with France also played a role in British intervention in Bengal, but Britain's opponent there was Indian, Nawab Siraj-ad-Daula of Bengal, who in 1756 had captured the East India Company fort of Calcutta and tightly confined his prisoners in the 'Black Hole'. Clive led a relief expedition which freed the prisoners, recaptured Calcutta, and then took the French base of Chandernagore. He decided to overthrow Siraj, who was seen as increasingly close to the French.

Clive defeated Siraj at Plassey in 1757 (page 163). The British position was consolidated by the Battles of Patna and Buxar in 1764. At Patna (3 May), British grapeshot halted the advance of hostile infantry and when a cavalry attack was launched by the Indians, 'a severe fire of artillery soon drove them back...we lost few men, but the enemy's loss was very great'. At Buxar (23 October), Sir Hector Munro and 7,000 men of the East India Company army, including 1,500 Europeans, defeated Mir Kasim, the Nawab of Bengal, the Mughal Emperor, and the Wazir of Oudh who together fielded a force of 50,000. The Indian army had more cannon, but British firepower was superior and their opponents lost 6,000 men. Grapeshot and bayonets blocked the Indian cavalry and the Indians were driven from the field. Nevertheless, the hard-fought battle lasted three hours and Munro's force lost 733 killed, wounded, and missing, including 69 Europeans.

Buxar was followed by the Treaty of Allahabad (1765), which recognized the British position in Bengal and Bihar. These were to provide a solid basis of revenue and manpower and were to become a centre of military power. In the late 1760s, for example, the dockyards at Calcutta

THE EUROPEANIZATION OF INDIAN WARFARE

Captain William Kirkpatrick, British Resident at the court of the Maratha leader Mahadji Sindhia, was an unsympathetic reporter of the latter's attempts to train infantry and artillery along European lines. He reported from Agra in June 1787 about the appointment of Europeans to transform the artillery and 'to form a body of troops upon the model of one of our brigades...They have together under them about 125 men whom they call Europeans; but these chiefly consist of Armenians, and the Black Christians usually though improperly called Portuguese. Each of those, I understood, is to have the command of a gun. Including calibres of all sizes, Shinde's train of artillery consists of about 200 pieces. A few of these are very good guns; but in

general they are contemptible. The number of tumbrils belonging to his [artillery] park is inconsiderable; the ammunition being for the most part transported in common hackeries...Were he opposed to an active enemy, it would almost to a certainty bring about his ruin.'

This was overly harsh. Sindhia's army proved successful in campaigns in Rajputana in the 1780s and 1790s, and his artillery captured the major Rajput fortress of Chittor in a matter of weeks. Sindhia's forces were eventually to be defeated by the British in 1803, but it is important to be cautious about viewing Indian states, as Kirkpatrick did, as 'less advanced in political and military knowledge'.

MAP 1

British power was established in Bengal and southern India in the second half of the eighteenth century. The Marathas were not defeated until the 1800s.

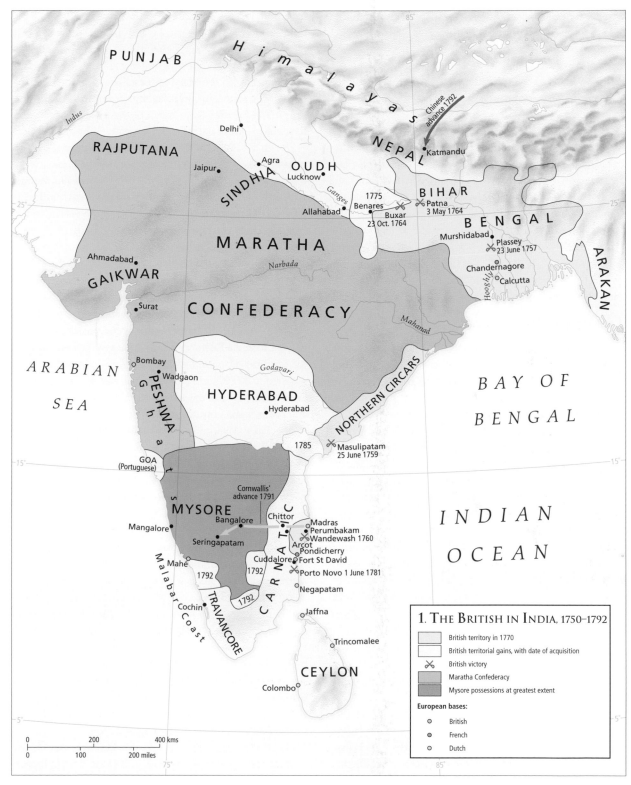

1. THE BRITISH IN INDIA, 1750–1792

	British territory in 1770
	British territorial gains, with date of acquisition
✗	British victory
	Maratha Confederacy
	Mysore possessions at greatest extent

European bases:
⊙	British
⊙	French
⊙	Dutch

were improved and the construction of ships to British design using naval shipwrights began. In 1766, the British added the Northern Circars as the price of their alliance with the Nizam of Hyderabad. Benares, gained from Oudh, followed in 1775.

THE MARATHAS

In western India, the British were drawn into struggles between the Maratha leaders in the 1770s. In late 1778, a slow-moving British army of over 3,000 men, with 19,000 bullocks pulling guns and supplies, advanced from Bombay into the difficult terrain of the Ghats, moving less than a mile a day. As it ran out of supplies, it began to retreat. The Marathas surrounded the British at Wadgaon (February 1779) and forced them to accept terms. Another army marched from Bengal to Surat safely and its rapid breaching of the walls of Ahmadabad demonstrated the effectiveness of British artillery. Britain and the Marathas fought again inconclusively in 1781–82, the Marathas emulating the infantry and artillery combinations of European armies.

The Treaty of Salbai (1782) ended the war and committed both powers to unite against Mysore.

The expansionism of Haidar Ali of Mysore, and his co-operation with the French, greatly worried the British. In 1780 he invaded the Carnatic, destroying a force under William Baillie at Perumbakam. The French landed 3,000 men to help Haidar Ali and jointly they captured Cuddalore. However, in 1781 the Mysore army was defeated by Sir Eyre Coote in hard-fought battles at Porto Novo and Perumbakam, and routed at Sholingurh. This saved Madras, but Haidar's son Tipu Sultan, who succeeded in 1782, pressed the British hard, capturing Mangalore in 1784 after a ten-month siege. After Britain and Tipu negotiated peace that spring, Tipu used his trained infantry and artillery to take Hyderabad and threaten the Marathas. The French, who made peace in 1783, had been handicapped by the limited military forces they could deploy and by the mutual antipathy of their potential allies, Mysore and the Marathas.

THE DEFEAT OF MYSORE

War between Britain and Tipu revived after he attacked a British ally, the Rajah of Travancore, late in 1789. Seeking to isolate Tipu, the British were allied to both Hyderabad and the Marathas, and they provided cavalry and supplies, although the Marathas proved unreliable because they did not wish to see Mysore crushed. In the 1790 campaign, General Medows made little impact and at the end of the year Cornwallis, now Governor-General and Commander-in-Chief in India, took personal charge. He was convinced that Tipu's destructive raids on the Carnatic could only be stopped if Mysore was invaded. Cornwallis believed in methodical planning; in January 1791 he wrote to Medows: 'I conceive that we can only be said to be as nearly independent of contingencies, as can be expected in war, when we are possessed of a complete battering train, and can move it with the army; and whilst we carry a large stock of provisions with us, that ample magazines shall be lodged in strong places in our rear and at no great distance from the scene of our intended operations...I hope that by a systematic activity and vigour, we shall be able to obtain decided advantage over our enemy before the commencement of the ensuing rains'.

The British succeeded in combining the firepower that was so effective against Mysore's fortresses with a reasonable degree of mobility. Cornwallis stressed the importance both of cavalry and of bullocks to move the artillery, themes voiced earlier by Sir Eyre Coote in the Second Mysore War. Britain's failure to obtain victory in the First Mysore War (1768) was attributed to a lack of cavalry. Like Coote, Cornwallis was also well aware of the logistical problems.

Cornwallis proposed seizing Bangalore to improve communications with the Carnatic, and thus the creation of a reliable supply system for an advance on the Mysore capital of Seringapatam. The citadel of Bangalore was stormed on 21 March, and on 13 May Cornwallis was within 9 miles (14.5km) of Seringapatam; but it was too near the rainy season to besiege it, so he fell back to Bangalore.

Late in 1791, Cornwallis captured a series of hill forts hitherto thought impregnable, and in 1792 he advanced rapidly on Seringapatam, being joined there by Sir Robert Abercromby, the commander-in-chief at Bombay, who had already occupied the Malabar coast. The rapid progress of the siege led Tipu to surrender and cede much of his territory. The British gained much of the Malabar coast, and their allies – the Marathas and the Nizam – also made gains.

French weakness at the time of the Revolution greatly helped British operations in India because the French were unable to assist Tipu Sultan. In 1788, Cornwallis wrote, with reference to a proposed attack on the French in India, 'unless we have a fleet capable of looking the enemy in the face, we must not hazard a considerable body of troops'. The British had been handicapped in India in the early 1780s by hostilities with both the French and the Dutch but, a decade later, France was weak and the Dutch were now British allies. The British presence in the Indian Ocean was growing. In 1786, the flag was hoisted on what was called, after the Governor of Bombay, Governor Boddam's Islands, now the Salomon Islands. That year Penang became the first British base in Malaysia. The Andaman Islands were acquired in 1789, and Port Cornwallis was established there. Cornwallis felt that the base would be very important in any future naval conflict with France.

The Third Mysore War was followed in 1794 by the Second Rohilla War, in which Abercromby with a small force won the Battle of Battina against a far larger army under Gholam Mahommed. In the Fourth Mysore War (1799), Seringapatam was successfully stormed; Tipu died in its defence. Most of his territories were subsequently annexed by the British.

In response to the new weapons and tactics introduced by the Europeans in mid-century, Maratha armies became bigger and more professional, so that a strategy based on living off the land became less possible. The new infantry and artillery units proved expensive. This forced development of revenue administration, banking, and credit. There was a considerable shift in power from the centre to the peripheral Maratha states, and the Marathas were greatly weakened by periods of civil war that in general reflected disputed successions. British successes did not mean that the Indians were unable to face them in battle: during the Second Maratha War, the Maratha artillery was particularly effective at the Battles of Assaye and Argaum (1803). Furthermore, much of the East India Company's British army was composed of Indians: over 100,000 in 1782. The army rose from 18,200 strong in 1763 to 115,400 in 1782 and 154,500 in 1805. The fusion of European training and Indian manpower was potent. In 1787, Cornwallis noted the great 'facility of obtaining good recruits' and wrote of one brigade of sepoys (British-trained Indians): 'Major Hay's regiment is one of the finest in every respect that I ever saw in any country'. Naval power had given the Portuguese dominance in the Indian Ocean, but the British had discovered the means of becoming the greatest land power in southern Asia.

PLASSEY 23 JUNE 1757

Plassey was a relatively minor engagement with important consequences, at which Robert Clive, at the head of 3,200 men, defeated 50,000 Indians under the Nawab of Bengal, Surajah Dowla. The newly-acceeded Nawab stormed Fort William at Calcutta on 20 June 1756 after a brief siege. Robert Clive was sent from Madras with a relief expedition of 850 Europeans and 2,100 Indian sepoys, an important deployment of British strength. Fort William was regained largely thanks to the guns of the British naval squadron under Vice-Admiral Charles Watson. The Nawab then advanced on Calcutta but was checked by Clive in a confused action fought in a heavy morning fog. Watson had added about 500 seamen to Clive's force. This led the Nawab to agree terms of peace, and on 9 February, Surajah Dowla recognized Calcutta as British. Concerned about the French presence in Bengal, Clive then attacked their fort at Chandernagore. Close-range fire from Watson's warships was instrumental in its fall on 23 March. The French did not have an appreciable military presence in Bengal and, in the face of British pressure, were thus dependent on the Indians. Clive was suspicious of intrigues between the French and Surajah Dowla, who was indeed seeking Maratha support. He determined to replace the Nawab and reached an agreement with one of his generals, Mir Jaffir. Clive then marched up the river

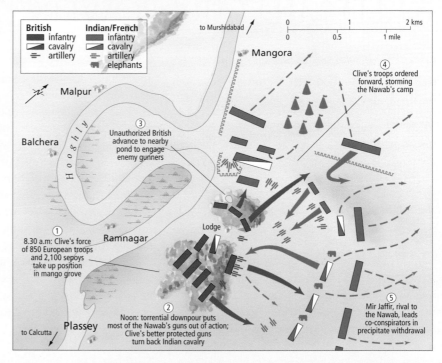

Hooghly towards the Nawab's capital at Murshidabad. He easily took the fort at Cutwa, 40 miles (65km) downstream. The Nawab then deployed his army near the village of Plassey, between the capital and Cutwa. Clive marched on Plassey and camped in a mango grove.

When dawn broke, Clive deployed his men in line in front of the grove (1), the sepoys on the flanks and his ten field-guns and howitzers in front. A party of fifty sailors supplied by Watson acted as artillerymen. An artillery duel began and Clive withdrew his men into the grove, where they sheltered behind the mudbanks and among the trees. The Indians made no real effort to attack the British positions, with the exception of a cavalry advance that was driven back by grapeshot. Midday rain did not stop the British gunners who kept their powder dry, but the Indians were less successful (2). As the Indian artillery retreated, Clive advanced to man the embankment surrounding the large village pond to the front of his position (3). An Indian infantry attack was repelled by Clive's artillery and infantry fire and, as the Indians retreated, Clive's men advanced rapidly, storming the Indian encampment. The Nawab had already fled (4).

Clive's force suffered about 60 casualties; his opponent's about 500 dead. The battle was followed by the defection of Mir Jaffir, who had failed to do so before the clash, as Clive had expected (5). Mir Jaffir's son had the Nawab killed and Mir Jaffir was installed as his successor. Clive received over £250,000 from Mir Jaffir, a sum that helped establish him as a politician, able to influence a number of parliamentary seats when he returned to England.

Clive at Plassey by W. Heath.

CONCLUSION: WORLD MILITARY POWER, 1792

EUROPEAN *weapons technology, seapower, and social organization were increasingly important in the eighteenth century. Industrial growth provided the basis for the production of large quantities of armaments, and buoyant metallurgical industries underlay both British and Russian military activity. Naval power was the most impressive feature of European military and industrial capability.*

THE OLD AND THE NEW IN 1792

If the old and new in military terms are generally seen in 1792 as the competing forces at Valmy in eastern France on 20 September – the Prussian invaders and the army of revolutionary France – it is possibly more appropriate to take a wider perspective. The world of mass politics and mobilization ushered in by the American and French Revolutions was to be of great importance, especially the latter because its more centralized nature and less individualistic political legacy permitted the greater mobilization of national resources. The newly created America was to become the first and foremost of the decolonized countries, best placed to take advantage of the potent combination of a European legacy, independence, and the new opportunities for expansion. Yet in terms of the projection of power and the shifting of global relationships, it was the terms imposed by the British on Tipu Sultan earlier that year that was the most significant development.

In some respects the British were just another non-Indian people winning Indian wealth and territory, but they were less willing than earlier conquerors to absorb Indian values, and the distance of their home country helped to preserve their distinct identity. It would be a mistake to think that British military reach, or that of other European powers, was effective all over the globe. Japan was still a closed world. In 1792, Cornwallis prudently ignored a Nepalese request for assistance against the Chinese invasion. The Russians had not attempted to reverse their expulsion from the Amur region by the Chinese. Much of Africa, Australasia, and the Pacific was as yet unaffected by Europeans.

But the areas outside European influence were shrinking: the eighteenth century was the great age of European exploration of the Pacific, much of it conducted by warships. In 1788, the British established a base in Australia. In the early 1790s they explored part of the coast of New Zealand, and claimed the Chatham Islands and Pitt Island.

RULING THE WAVES

Thus, as in 1492, it is naval power that is the most impressive feature of European military capability. Fleets of warships were complex, powerful military systems, sustained by mighty industrial and logistical resources. In the years between 1775 and 1790, formidable numbers of vessels were launched: the combined displacement of the British, French, and Spanish ships of the line rose from 550,000 to 729,000 tons (555,800–740,664 tonnes). This huge naval scale dwarfed that of non-European powers even more decisively than it had in the late fifteenth century.

But warfare is about far more than battles, and the Europeans, for all their advanced weaponry, were still unable to campaign with safety in much of the world: tropical diseases devastated their troops from Africa to the West Indies.

MAP 1

Chinese conquests in Mongolia and the Austrian gain of much of Hungary were the principal recent developments at the dawn of the eighteenth century.

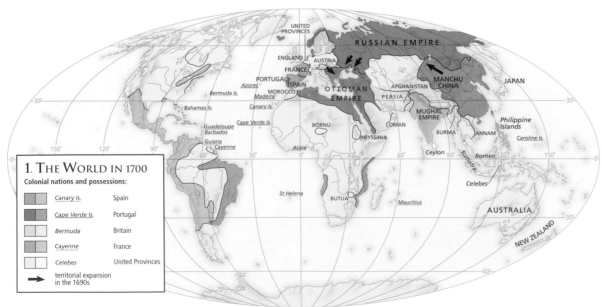

1. THE WORLD IN 1700

Colonial nations and possessions:

Canary Is.	Spain
Cape Verde Is.	Portugal
Bermuda	Britain
Cayenne	France
Celebes	United Provinces
→	territorial expansion in the 1690s

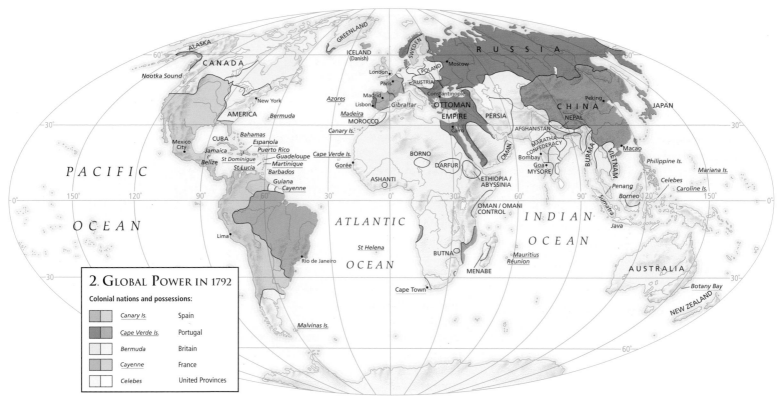

2. GLOBAL POWER IN 1792

Colonial nations and possessions:

	Canary Is.	Spain
	Cape Verde Is.	Portugal
	Bermuda	Britain
	Cayenne	France
	Celebes	United Provinces

MAP 2

As the French Revolutionary War began in Europe, the world was politically very different to 1700. This was less due to Chinese expansion than to the creation of an independent America, which was to be the most dynamic of the independent states in the western hemisphere.

Nevertheless, it was the Europeans' weaponry and technology that enabled them to transcend their position as a minority of the world's population (about 190 out of 900 millions in 1800) and to despatch armies all over the globe.

Systematic planning, like Cornwallis' in the Third Mysore War, was not exclusive to European societies, and Chinese military activity required much organization, but governmental and military organization combining such scale and sophistication was absent in Australasia, Africa, and the New World. In the early modern period, a number of different military systems co-existed; in the nineteenth century Europe's was to prevail.

A prospect of Havana, captured by the British from Spain in 1762. This was one of the great triumphs of British trans-oceanic amphibious operations. Havana was the major Spanish naval centre in the New World.

FURTHER READING

It is difficult to choose from among the wealth of fine studies on the period. For reasons of space, this list is very selective and concentrates on recent works in English and books as these are more accessible. Details of other relevant material can be found in the bibliographies of the works cited.

GENERAL

Anderson, M.S., *War and Society in Europe of the Old Regime 1618–1789* (London, 1988).

Black, J.M., *A Military Revolution? Military Change and European Society 1550–1800* (London, 1991).

Clark, G.N., *War and Society in the Seventeenth Century* (Cambridge, 1958).

Corvisier, A., *Armies and Societies in Europe, 1494–1789* (Bloomington, Indiana, 1979).

Duffy, M. (ed.), *The Military Revolution and the State* (Exeter, 1980).

Gooch, J., *Armies in Europe* (London, 1980).

Hill, J.M., *Celtic Warfare 1595–1763* (Edinburgh, 1986).

Howard, M., *War in European History* (London, 1976).

Jones, A., *The Art of War in the Western World* (Oxford, 1987).

Keegan, J., *A History of Warfare* (London, 1993).

McNeill, W.H., *The Pursuit of Power. Technology, Armed Force and Society since A.D. 1000* (Oxford, 1982).

Parker, G., *The Military Revolution. Military Innovation and the Rise of the West, 1500–1800* (Cambridge, 1988).

Strachan, H., *European Armies and the Conduct of War* (London, 1983).

Tallett, F., *War and Society in Early Modern Europe 1495–1715* (London, 1992).

Weigley, R.F., *The Age of Battles. The Quest for Decisive Warfare from Breitenfeld to Waterloo* (Bloomington, Indiana, 1991).

CONDUCT OF WAR

Chandler, D., *The Art of War in the Age of Marlborough* (London, 1976).

Creveld, M. van, *Supplying War. Logistics from Wallenstein to Patton* (Cambridge, 1977).

Creveld, M. van, *Technology and War from 2000 B.C. to the Present* (New York, 1989).

Duffy, C., *Siege Warfare. The Fortress in the Early Modern World 1494–1660* (London, 1979).

Duffy, C., *The Fortress in the Age of Vauban and Frederick the Great* (London, 1985).

Hughes, B.P., *Firepower. Weapons' Effectiveness on the Battlefield 1630–1850* (London, 1974).

Hughes, B.P., *Open Fire. Artillery Tactics from Marlborough to Wellington* (London, 1983).

Lynn, J.A. (ed.), *Feeding Mars. Logistics in Western Warfare from the Middle Ages to the Present* (Boulder, 1993).

Nosworthy, B., *The Anatomy of Victory. Battle Tactics 1689–1763* (New York, 1990).

Quimby, R., *The Background of Napoleonic Warfare* (New York, 1957).

Ross, S., *From Flintlock to Rifle. Infantry Tactics, 1740–1866* (Rutherford, New Jersey, 1979).

NAVAL WARFARE

Black, J.M. & Woodfine, P.L. (eds.), *The Royal Navy and the Use of Naval Power in the Eighteenth Century* (Leicester, 1988).

Bruijn, J.R., *The Dutch Navy of the Seventeenth and Eighteenth Centuries* (Columbia, South Carolina, 1993).

Capp, B., *Cromwell's Navy* (Oxford, 1992).

Glete, J., *Navies and Nations. Warships, Navies and State Building in Europe and America, 1500–1860* (Stockholm, 1993).

Harding, R., *The Evolution of the Sailing Navy, 1509–1815* (London, 1995).

Lavery, B., *The Ship of the Line, I. The Development of the Battlefleet, 1650–1850* (London, 1983).

Loades, D., *The Tudor Navy* (Aldershot, 1992).

Martin, C. & Parker, G., *The Spanish Armada* (London, 1988).

Pritchard, J., *Louis XV's Navy, 1748–1762* (Montreal, 1987).

Rodger, N.A.M., *The Wooden World. An Anatomy of the Georgian Navy* (London, 1986).

WARFARE OUTSIDE EUROPE

Cipolla, C.M., *Guns and Sails in the Early Phase of European Expansion 1400–1700* (London, 1965).

Lynn, J.A. (ed.), *Tools of War. Instruments, Ideas and Institutions of Warfare, 1445–1871* (Urbana, 1990).

McNeill, J.R., *Atlantic Empires of France and Spain. Louisbourg and Havanna, 1700–1763* (Chapel Hill, North Carolina, 1986).

Peckham, H.H., *The Colonial Wars, 1689–1972* (Chicago, 1964).

WARFARE IN AFRICA

Boxer, C.R. & Azevedo, C. de, *Fort Jesus and the Portuguese in Mombasa 1593–1792* (London, 1960).

Cook, W.F., *The Hundred Years' War for Morocco. Gunpowder and the Military Revolution in the Early Modern Muslim World* (Boulder, Colorado, 1994).

Hess, A.C., *The Forgotten Frontier. A History of the Sixteenth-Century Ibero-African Frontier* (Chicago, 1978).

Kea, R.A., *Settlements, Trade, and Politics in the Seventeenth-Century Gold Coast* (Baltimore, Maryland, 1982).

Smaldone, J.P., *Warfare in the Sokoto Caliphate* (Cambridge, 1977).

Smith, R.S., *Warfare and Diplomacy in pre-colonial West Africa* (London, 1976).

Thornton, J., *Africa and Africans in the Making of the Atlantic*

World, 1400–1680 (Cambridge, 1992).

Thornton, J., *Warfare in Atlantic Africa, 1500–1800* (London, forthcoming).

WARFARE IN THE AMERICAS

Black, J.M., *War for America. The Fight for Independence* (Stroud, 1991).

Edmunds, R.D. & Peyser, J.L., *The Fox Wars. The Mesquakie Challenge to New France* (Norman, Oklahoma, 1993).

Malone, P.M., *The Skulking Way of War. Technology and Tactics among the Indians of New England* (London, 1991).

Powell, P.W., *Soldiers, Indians and Silver. The northward advance of New Spain 1550–1600* (Berkeley, California, 1969).

Weber, D.J., *The Spanish Frontier on North America* (New Haven, Connecticut, 1992).

WARFARE IN ASIA

Arasaratnam, S., *Dutch Power in Ceylon, 1658–87* (Amsterdam, 1958).

Donnelly, A.S., *The Russian Conquest of Bashkiria, 1552–1740* (New Haven, Connecticut, 1968).

Forsyth, J., *A History of the Peoples of Siberia* (Cambridge, 1992).

Koenig, W.J., *The Burmese Polity, 1752–1819* (Ann Arbor, Michigan, 1990).

Perrin, N., *Giving up the Gun. Japan's Reversion to the Sword 1543–1879* (London, 1977).

Phul, R.K., *Armies of the great Mughals, 1526–1707* (New Delhi, 1978).

Richards, J.F., *The Mughal Empire* (Cambridge, 1993).

Ricklef, M.C., *War, Culture and Economy in Java, 1677–1726* (The Hague, 1990).

Sen, S.N., *The Military System of the Marathas* (Calcutta, 1970).

Struve, L.A., *The Southern Ming 1644–1662* (New Haven, Connecticut, 1984).

Yune-Hee, P., *Admiral Yi Sung-Shin and the Turtle-Boat Armada* (Seoul, 1978).

Wakeman, F., *The Great Enterprise. The Manchu Reconstruction of Imperial Order in Seventeenth-Century China* (Berkeley, 1985).

Wickwire, F. & M., *Cornwallis. The Imperial Years* (Chapel Hill, North Carolina, 1980).

WARFARE WITH THE TURKS

Allen, W.E.D., *Problems of Turkish Power in the Sixteenth Century* (London, 1963).

Barker, T.M., *Double Eagle and Crescent. Vienna's Second Turkish Siege* (Albany, New York, 1967).

Finkel, C., *The Administration of Warfare. The Ottoman Military Campaigns in Hungary, 1593–1606* (London, 1988).

Murphey, R., *Ottoman Warfare, 1500–1700* (London, forthcoming).

Olson, R.W., *The Siege of Mosul* (1975).

Stoye, J.M., *The Siege of Vienna* (London, 1964).

EUROPEAN WARFARE 1492–1648

Hale, J.R., *Renaissance War Studies* (London, 1983).

Hale, J.R., *War and Society in Renaissance Europe, 1450–1620* (London, 1985).

Hill, J.M., *War and the Rise of the Modern Nation-State, c.1500–1650* (London, forthcoming).

Lloyd, H.A., *The Rouen Campaign, 1590–1592. Politics, Warfare and the Early Modern State* (Oxford, 1973).

Mallet, M.E. & Hale, J.R., *The Military Organization of a Renaissance State. Venice c.1400–1617* (Cambridge, 1984).

Oakley, S.P., *War and Peace in the Baltic 1560–1790* (London, 1991).

Parker, G., *The Army of Flanders and the Spanish Road, 1567–1659. The Logistics of Spanish Victory and Defeat in the Low Countries* (Cambridge, 1972).

Parker, G., *The Thirty Years' War* (London, 1987).

Pepper, S. & Adams, N., *Firearms and Fortifications. Military Architecture and Siege Warfare in Sixteenth-Century Siena* (Chicago, 1986).

Roberts, M., *Gustavus Adolphus. A History of Sweden, 1611–1632* (2 vols., 1953–8).

Roberts, M., *Essays in Swedish History* (London, 1967).

Thompson, I.A.A., *War and Government in Habsburg Spain, 1560–1620* (London, 1976).

EUROPEAN WARFARE 1648–1792

Black, J.M., *Culloden and the '45* (Stroud, 1990).

Black, J.M., *European Warfare 1660–1815* (London, 1994).

Childs, J., *Armies and Warfare in Europe, 1648–1789* (Manchester, 1982).

Childs, J., *The Nine Years' War and the British Army 1688–97* (Manchester, 1991).

Duffy, C., *The Army of Frederick the Great* (London, 1974).

Duffy, C., *The Army of Maria Theresa* (London, 1977).

Duffy, C., *Russia's Military Way to the West. Origins and Nature of Russian Military Power 1700–1800* (London, 1981).

Duffy, C., *The Military Life of Frederick the Great* (London, 1985).

Ekberg, C.J., *The Failure of Louis XIV's Dutch War* (Chapel Hill, North Carolina, 1979).

Englund, P., *The Battle of Poltava* (London, 1992).

Francis, A.D., *The First Peninsular War, 1700–1713* (London, 1975).

Fuller, W.C., *Strategy and Power in Russia 1600–1914* (New York, 1992).

Jones, J.R., *Marlborough* (Cambridge, 1992).

Mackesy, P., *The Coward of Minden* (London, 1979).

McKay, D., *Prince Eugene of Savoy* (London, 1977).

Sturgill, C.C., *Marshal Villars and the War of the Spanish Succession* (Lexington, Kentucky, 1965).

Ultee, M. (ed.), *Adapting to Conditions. War and Society in the Eighteenth Century* (Tuscaloosa, 1986).

Wilson, P., *German Armies. War and German Society, 1648–1806* (London, forthcoming).

CHRONOLOGY

EUROPE	THE AMERICAS	REST OF THE WORLD
1485 Henry VII King of England		
1488 James IV King of Scotland		
	1492 Christopher Columbus discovers America	
	1494 Treaty of Tordesillas, pact between Spain and Portugal establishing a demarcation line for exclusive rights of exploration in South America	
1495 Charles VII of France invades Italy; driven out (1498) by Spanish		
1498 Louis XII King of France		
		1499 Turkish war with Venice
1500 France invades Italy; defeated at Battle of Cerignola		1500–05 Establishment of Portuguese trading posts on Indian west coast
	1508–18 Height of the Aztec Empire	
	1508–11 Spain conquers Puerto Rico	
1509 Henry VIII King of England		
		1510 Portuguese seize Goa
1511–14 English wars with France and Scotland	1511–15 Spain conquers Cuba	
1512 Battle of Ravenna, French victory over Spanish		1512 Selim I Sultan of Turkey
1513 Battle of Flodden, English victory over Scots		
		1514–16 Turkish war with Persia
		1515–26 Babur, King of Kabul, invades north India, conquers Punjab, occupies Delhi; Mughal empire established
1515 France invades Italy		1515 Battle of Chaldiran, Turkish army under Selim I routes Persians
1516 Treaty of Noyon between France and Spain		1516 Turkish forces occupy Syria
1517 Luther publishes his 95 Theses, beginning the Reformation		1517 Turks invade, conquer Egypt
	1518–19 Spanish expedition of Hernan Cortés	
1520 Field of the Cloth of Gold, alliance between England and France		1520 Suleiman I ('the Magnificent') Turkish sultan
1520–23 Successful revolt leads to Swedish independence		

EUROPE	THE AMERICAS	REST OF THE WORLD
		1521 Turks invade Hungary, capture Belgrade; Magellan claims Philippines for Spain
1522–23 Abortive English raids in France	1522–23 Spain conquers Nicaragua	1522 Turks take Rhodes
	1522–39 Spain conquers south Mexico and northern central America	
1524–25 The Peasants' War, Protestant uprising in Swabia and Franconia, cruelly suppressed		
		1526 Battle of Mohács, Turks destroy Hungarian army
1529 Turks besiege Vienna		
1530–34 Henry VIII breaks with Papacy, establishes independent Church of England		
	1531 Expedition of Francisco Pizarro	
1536 Turin captured by French		
	1540–61 Spanish conquer Chile	
1542 Solway Moss, English victory over Scots		
1542–50 English wars with France and Scotland; Henry VIII builds coastal fortifications, lays foundations of navy		
1543 Nice sacked by Franco-Turkish fleet		
1544 Mary Queen of Scots ascends throne; English capture Boulogne		
1547 Edward VI King of England; Battle of Pinkie, English defeat Scots		
1549 Peasants revolt in Norfolk, England, under Robert Kett		
1549–50 Renewed war between England and France		
		1551 Turks capture Tripoli from Knights of St John
1553 Protector Northumberland, on Edward VI's death, attempts to crown Lady Jane Grey, insurrection suppressed, Mary becomes Queen		
1554 Abortive insurrection in Kent, England, to prevent Queen Mary's marriage to Catholic Philip of Spain		
		1555 Treaty of Amasia ends war between Turkey and Persia
		1556 Akbar becomes Mughal sovereign
1556 Abdication of Charles V of Spain, Philip II becomes King		

EUROPE	THE AMERICAS	REST OF THE WORLD
1557–59 England, now Spain's ally, at war with France		1557 Portuguese establish base at Macao
1558 Calais, England's last possession in France, captured; Elizabeth I crowned Queen of England, which returns the country to Protestantism		
1560 Religious unrest in France becomes acute		1560 Reunification of Japan, a land of warring feudal nobles, begins
1562 Huguenot uprising; atrocities spread throughout France		
	1564 French establish colony in Florida; abandoned (1567) under Spanish pressure	
1566 Political, religious riots in the Netherlands		
1567 Mary Queen of Scots forced to abdicate; infant son, James VI, King; second Huguenot uprising		
		1568–84 Burmese invade and occupy Siam
1570–95 Sweden conquers Estonia, Livonia		
1571 Naval Battle of Lepanto, decisive Christian victory over Turks		
1572 Massacre of French Huguenots on St Bartholomew's Eve		
1577–80 Francis Drake circumnavigates the globe		
1577 English alliance with Netherlands		
1578 War of Succession in Iberian Peninsula; Portugal united to Spain		
1579 Union of Utrecht; the northern Netherlands provinces establish a confederation		
1584 Assassination of William of Orange		
1585 James VI of Scotland makes alliance with Elizabeth I, ending national wars	1585–86 Drake's English expedition sacks Santo Domingo, Cartagena, St Augustine	
1587 Drake's expedition to Cadiz; thirty-three Spanish vessels destroyed		
1588 Spanish Armada destroyed by English shps and violent storms		
1589 Religious wars rage throughout France		
		1592–98 Japanese invade Korea
1593 Henry IV of France unites nation by returning to Catholic faith		
1594– 1603 Tyrone rebellion in Ireland		

EUROPE	THE AMERICAS	REST OF THE WORLD
1598 Edict of Nantes; Henry IV ends Wars of Religion by granting religious freedom to Protestants		
1600–11 First Polish-Swedish war for Livonia		1600–15 Emergence of Manchu state in outer Mongolia
		1601 Arrival of Dutch in West Indies ends Portuguese trading monopoly
		1602 Portuguese establish base in Burma
		1602–12 Ottoman war with Persia
1604 Union of crowns of England and Scotland		1604 Russian expansion eastwards begins
		1605 Battle of Sis, Persians rout Turks; Treaty of Zsitva-Torok ends war between Turks and Austrians
	1607 British expedition settles at Jamestown	
		1608 English ships arrive at Surat, India, to gain trading rights
1609–18 Polish war with Russia	1609–27 French penetrate St Lawrence Valley	
1610 Louis XIII King of France		
1612 Matthias of Bohemia elected Emperor		
1613–17 Russo-Swedish war		
1614–21 Polish-Turkish war		
1617–29 Second Polish-Swedish war		
1618 Thirty Years' War begins		
1620 Imperial troops capture, sack Prague		
		1621–22 English ships capture Portuguese base at Ormuz
		1622–23 Mughal war with Persia, Kandahar captured
		1623–33 Inner Mongolia conquered by Manchus; renewed Ottoman-Persian war
1624 Cardinal Richelieu brings France into war against Habsburgs; Treaty of Compiègne, alliance of France and Holland, soon joined by England, Sweden, Denmark, Savoy, Venice against Habsburgs; Breda captured by Spanish		1624–25 Dutch establish posts on Taiwan
1625 Charles I King of England; Wallenstein appointed to command Imperial forces; Denmark invades Germany		

EUROPE	THE AMERICAS	REST OF THE WORLD
1626 Peace of Monzon; France withdraws from the war; Battle of Lutter, Danish forces routed by Imperialists		
1626–27 German harvest fails, country ravaged by famine, plague, violence		
1626–30 Anglo-French war		
1627–28 Siege of La Rochelle; Huguenot citadel falls to Richelieu's forces		
1628 Petition of Right, demands and grievances of English parliament		
	1629–60 Spain conducts punitive expedition against other colonial posts	
1630 Sweden's Gustavus Adolphus invades northern Europe		1630–41 Dutch capture Malacca
1631 City of Magdeburg sacked by Imperialists, only one-sixth of population survives; Battle of Breitenfeld, Swedes rout Imperialists		1631–32 Mughal war with Portuguese
1632 Battle of Lech; Swedish victory enables Gustavus to occupy Augsburg, Munich, southern Bavaria; Battle of Lützen; Swedes denied absolute victory by fog, Gustavus killed		
1632–34 Russo-Polish war		
1634 Battle of Nördlingen, Swedes routed by Imperialists; Richelieu assumes direction of Protestant cause		
1635 Imperial, Spanish forces invade north-east France; forced to withdraw by desertions, French resistance		
	1636 North American Colonists war with Pequots	1636 Ch'ing Dynasty established
		1638 Persian war with Mughals, Kandahar reconquered
1639 First Bishops' War, Scottish uprising against English religious policy		
1640–60 The Long Parliament		
1640 Second Bishops' War ended by Treaty of Ripon		
	1641–45 Algonquin War	
1642 The Grand Remonstrance, list of Parliamentary grievances against Charles I		
1642–46 First English civil war	1642–53 Iroquois War	

EUROPE	THE AMERICAS	REST OF THE WORLD
1643 Battle of Rocroi, French forces annihilate Spanish army; Louis XIV King of France		
1644 Battle of Marston Moor; Royalist defeat leaves north of England in Parliament's hands		
1645 New Model Army formed; Battle of Naseby leads to Royalist collapse		1645–80 Rise of the Marathas; intermittent war with Mughals
1649 Charles I beheaded, Commonwealth established under military control		1649–53 Persian war with Mughals over Kandahar
1649–50 Cromwell's reign of terror in Ireland to subdue Catholic Royalist strongholds [the most terrible atrocities in British history]		
1650 Battle of Dunbar, Cromwell defeats Scots		
1651 Battle of Worcester; Charles II's defeat by Cromwell ends civil wars		
1652 First Anglo-Dutch war, arising from maritime competition		1652 Dutch establish post at modern Cape Town
	1654 Jamaica taken by English	
1655–60 First Northern War		
1658 Battle of the Dunes, Anglo-French alliance defeats Spanish army		1658 Aurangzeb crowns himself Emperor at Delhi
1658–66 Russo-Polish war		
1660 Restoration of Charles II		
1665–67 Second Anglo-Dutch war		1664– Aurangzeb persecutes non-Muslims; constant turmoil ensues 1707
		1666 French establish post at Chandernagore on Ganges Delta
		1667 British establish a fort at Bombay
1668 Spain recognizes Portuguese independence		
1670 Secret Treaty of Dover between Charles II and Louis XIV		
1671–77 Polish-Turkish war		
1672–74 Third Anglo–Dutch war		
1683 Turks besiege Vienna		
	1684–89 Renewed Iroquois war	

EUROPE	THE AMERICAS	REST OF THE WORLD
1685 James II King of England; Battle of Sedgemoor, Monmouth's rebellion against James II crushed; Louis XIV revokes the Edict of Nantes		
1688 The 'Glorious Revolution', James II overthrown, William of Orange King		
1688–89 France devastates the Palatinate		
1688–97 War of the Grand Alliance; Louis XIV invades Germany		
1689 France declares war on Spain; Treaty of Vienna established; Grand Alliance against France	1689–97 European war of the League of Augsburg causes conflict between British and French in Hudson Bay, St Lawrence valley, Canada	
1690 Naval battle of Beachy Head, Anglo-Dutch fleet defeated by French; Turks recapture Belgrade; Battle of the Boyne, James II defeated in Ireland by William III		
1692 Decisive naval battle of La Hogue (Barfleur); France obliged to abandon plans to invade England		
1693 Battle of Neerwinden, French decisively defeat Allies		
1697 Treaty of Ryswjck, combatants agree to restore all territories taken since 1679		
1700–21 The Great Northern War, alliance of Russia, Poland, Denmark against Sweden		
1700 Battle of Narva, outnumbered Swedes under Charles XII annihilate Russian army		
1701–14 War of the Spanish Succession; Grand Alliance against France established		
1701 Kingdom of Prussia established		
1702 John Churchill (first Duke of Marlborough) appointed captain general of Anglo-Dutch forces		
1704 Marlborough, Eugene destroy Franco-Bavarian army at Blenheim		
1707 Union of England, Scotland; United Kingdom established		
1708 Marlborough, Eugene defeat French at Oudenarde; Allies besiege, take Lille		
1709 Costly Allied victory over French at Malplaquet; Battle of Poltava, Swedish army destroyed by Russians		

EUROPE	THE AMERICAS	REST OF THE WORLD
	1711–12 Tuscarora war, native uprising in the Carolinas	
		1712–20 Spread of Maratha power into Hindustan
1713 Treaty of Utrecht; Pragmatic Sanction, Emperor Charles VI's will regarding succession		
1714–18 Turkish war with Venice, Austria		
1715 Jacobite uprising in Scotland	1715–23 Yamasee war against Carolinian colonists	
		1717 Siamese invade Cambodia
1718–20 War of the Quadruple Alliance, England, France, Holland, Austria oppose Spanish ambitions		
	1720–22 Spanish occupy Texas	1720 Manchu conquest of Tibet
	1720–38 British, French build forts on Great Lakes	
1721 Treaty of Nystad ends Great Northern War; Russia supplants Sweden as dominant Baltic power	1721–25 Paraguyan revolt against Buenos Aires dominance	
	1726 Montevideo established	
1730–35 Ottoman war with Persia		
1733–38 War of the Polish Succession	1735–37 Spanish-Portuguese war following friction in River Plate area	
1736–39 Unco-ordinated Austro-Russian war with Turkey		
1740–48 War of the Austrian Succession		
1740 Frederick II ('the Great') of Prussia invades Silesia		
		1741 Dupleix appointed French Governor-General in India
1743 Battle of Dettingen, Anglo-Hanoverian victory over French		1743–47 Ottoman war with Persia
1744 Prussia invades Bohemia		1744–48 First Carnatic War
1745 Battle of Fontenoy; Allies invade Prussia; Jacobite uprising in Scotland; Jacobites defeat English at Prestonpans	1745 British besiege and take heavily fortified Louisbourg	1745 Madras captured by French
1745 Battle of Culloden crushes Jacobite uprising		
		1749–54 Second Carnatic War
		1751 Arcot captured by Robert Clive; China invades, occupies Tibet after revolt
	1754–63 French and Indian wars	
	1755 Montcalm appointed Commander of French forces in Canada	
1756–63 Seven Years' War		1756 Calcutta captured by Nawab Siraj-ad-Daula of Bengal, Europeans thrown into 'Black Hole'
1756 Frederick II of Prussia invades Saxony		

EUROPE	THE AMERICAS	REST OF THE WORLD
1757 Frederick defeats Austrians at Prague; Allies launch four invasions of Prussia; outnumbered Frederick defeats Allies at Rossbach; decisively defeats Austrians at Leuthen	1757 Montcalm's Indians treacherously kill many of surrendered garrison at Fort William Henry	1757 British recapture Calcutta; Clive destroys Nawab Siraj-ad-Daula's army Plassey
1758 Frederick ends Russian threat at Battle of Zorndorf		
1759 Prussians, British defeat French at Minden; Frederick defeated at Kunersdorf by Austro-Russian Army; British naval victory off Quiberon Bay ends French naval power for rest of war	1759 Battle of the Plains of Abraham; Wolfe captures Québec, secures British dominance in Canada	
		1760 Clive's troops capture Pondicherry; Boers cross Orange River
1761–2 Spanish invade Portugal; repulsed		
1762 Death of Elizabeth of Russia; Tsar Peter III begins peace negotiations; Frederick drives French across Rhine	1762 British conquer Martinique	
1763 Treaty of Hubertusburg ends Seven Years' War		
		1765–69 China invades Burma; forced to withdraw
		1766–69 First Mysore War in India
1768–74 Catherine the Great's first war with Turkey		1769 Egypt declares independence from Turkey
	1771 North Carolina settlers defy royal rule; suppressed	
1772 Royal coup d'etat in Sweden; first Partition of Poland		
	1773 'Boston Tea Party'	1773– Civil war in Vietnam 1801
	1775 First shots of American Revolution fired at Lexington; George Washington appointed to command Continental forces; Battle of Bunker Hill, tactical British victory; Montréal taken by Continentals	
	1775–76 Siege of Boston	
	1776 British abandon Boston; France, Spain give support to Continentals; Declaration of Independence; Continentals abandon New York; Battle of Trenton	

EUROPE	THE AMERICAS	REST OF THE WORLD
1777–79 War of Bavarian Succession	1777 Battle of Princeton; British capture Fort Ticonderoga; Battle of Saratoga, Continental victory, turning point in war; British occupy Philadelphia	
	1778 War between England, France; British evacuate Philadelphia; Battle of Monmouth	
	1779 Siege of Savannah; Siege of Gibraltar	
1780–84 Anglo–Dutch war	1780 Siege of Charleston	1780–83 Second Mysore War
	1781 Continentals besiege Yorktown; Cornwallis surrenders	
	1782 Britain sues for peace; Treaty of Paris recognises independence of USA	
1785–87 Netherlands civil war; Prussian troops restore order under Stadtholder		
1787–91 Austro-Turkish war		1787 Sierre Leone acquired by Britain
1787–92 Catherine the Great's second war with Turkey		
1788–90 Swedish war with Russia, Denmark		
		1795–96 British expedition to Ceylon; becomes a colony (1798)

INDEX

Picture acknowledgements

Every effort has been made to obtain permission to use the copyright material listed below; the publishers apologise for any errors or omissions and would welcome these being brought to their attention.

The following abbreviations have been used:
AA&A: Ancient Art & Architecture Collection, London
AKG Lon: Archiv für Kunst und Geschichte, London
BL: British Library, London
BM: British Museum, London
Bridgeman: Bridgeman Art Library, London
ETA: E. T. Archive, London
Peter Newark: Peter Newark, Bath
Royal Armouries: The Board of Trustees of the Royal Armouries, London
Royal Collection: Royal Collection Enterprises © Her Majesty the Queen
V&A: by Courtesy of the Trustees of the V&A Museum, London
Wallace: The Trustees of the Wallace Collection, London (a national museum, admission free)

Half-title page Wallace; **title page** Wallace; **8–9** ETA; **10** Bridgeman; **12** ETA; **15** ETA; **16** ETA; **19** AA&A/G Tortoli; **20** ETA; **23** Bridgeman; **24** Sonia Halliday Photographs; **28** AKG Lon/Topkapi Serail-Museum, Istanbul; **29** AKG Lon/Palace of the Doge, Venice; **30** Sonia Halliday Photographs; **33** top ETA; **33** bottom BL; **36** BM; **37** Tower Armouries; **40** ETA; **43** ETA; **44** ETA; **46–47** Bridgeman; **50** AKG Lon/Erich Lessing; **52** AKG Lon/Gall. Naz. di Capodimonte, Neapel; **54** BM; **59** ETA; **61** ETA; **63** top National Maritime Museum, London; **63** bottom AKG Lon/Landesmus. Tirol; **64–65** AKG Lon/Heeresgeschichtliches Museum, Vienna; **66** AKG Lon/Theatrum Europaeum; **72** BL; **77** Anne S. K. Brown Military Collection, Brown University Library; **83** ETA; **86** ETA; **91** Musée de L'armee, Paris; **92–93** Hubert Josse; **94** ETA; **95** ETA; **96** ETA; **101** ETA; **107** Hubert Josse; **114** ETA; **116–17** ETA; **121** top Kunsthistorisches Museum, Burgring, Vienna; **121** bottom ETA; **126** AKG Lon/Zorndorf, Munich; **127** Royal Collection; **128** ETA; **131** AKG Lon; **133** AKG Lon; **135** Anne S. K. Brown Military Collection, Brown University Library; **136–37** Peter Newark; **139** right & left BL; **141** top HM Tower Armouries; **141** bottom Royal Armouries; **142** V&A; **143** Hutchison Library; **144** Werner Forman Archive; **147** ETA; **148** top & bottom Peter Newark; **151** ETA; **152** Anne S. K. Brown Military Collection, Brown University Library; **155** Peter Newark; **158** Peter Newark; **159** ETA; **163** National Army Museum, London; **165** National Army Museum.